The Long Walk
to Equality

The Long Walk to Equality

Perspectives on Racial Inequality, Injustice and the Law

Edited by
Avis Whyte, Patricia Tuitt
and Judith Bourne

University of Westminster Press
www.uwestminsterpress.co.uk

Published by
University of Westminster Press
115 New Cavendish Street
London W1W 6UW
https://www.uwestminsterpress.co.uk

Cover design: Nicky Borowiec at www.nickyborowiec.com

Print and digital versions typeset by Siliconchips Services Ltd.

ISBN (Paperback): 978-1-914386-40-4
ISBN (PDF): 978-1-914386-41-1
ISBN (EPUB): 978-1-914386-42-8
ISBN (Mobi): 978-1-914386-43-5

DOI: https://doi.org/10.16997/book63

The full text of this book has been peer-reviewed to ensure
high academic standards. For full review policies, see:
https://www.uwestminsterpress.co.uk/site/publish

Suggested citation: Whyte, A., Tuitt, P. and Bourne, J. (eds.) 2024. *The Long
Walk to Equality: Perspectives on Racial Inequality, Injustice and the Law*.
London: University of Westminster Press.
DOI: https://doi.org/10.16997/book63. License: CC-BY-NC-ND 4.0

To read the free, open access version of this book online, visit
https://doi.org/10.16997/book63 or scan this QR code with your
mobile device: Insert QR code here.

Contents

List of Figures and Tables

Figure

Tables

CHAPTER 1

Introduction

Avis Whyte, Patricia Tuitt and Judith Bourne

One of the most pressing and seemingly intractable questions of the contemporary age is how to accommodate difference. In global terms, this question has centred most prominently on differences constructed from so-called 'innate' or 'immutable' human characteristics, such as sex and race. From these contemplations have emerged a wealth of legal concepts that, in various ways and degrees, attempt to circumscribe the impulse to attach negative or positive qualities to markers of difference and to withhold from or confer on individuals public goods according to whether they possess 'desirable' or 'undesirable' differences. Thus, as a result of a proliferation of international, regional and domestic rules governing equality and non-discrimination, which began from the second half of the 20th century, the question of how to treat difference has become, fundamentally, a question of law. Such laws that exist, in form and in application, must be viewed as the outward signs of contesting stances on how differences are produced and how they should be valued.

At one end of the spectrum, formal equality perspectives pertaining to the legal regulation of discriminatory practices demand that the law views differences as elements that can be abstracted from an individual, enabling a distribution of goods between persons of, for example different races or religions equally, because—successfully dispossessed of those differences—they become 'neutral' subjects before the law, pursuing the same outcomes. At the other end, substantive equality perspectives view the task of the law as being

How to cite this book chapter:
Whyte, A., Tuitt, P. and Bourne, J. 2024. Introduction. In: Whyte, A., Tuitt, P. and Bourne, J. (eds.) *The Long Walk to Equality: Perspectives on Racial Inequality, Injustice and the Law*. Pp. 1–12. London: University of Westminster Press. DOI: https://doi.org/10.16997/book63.a. License: CC-BY-NC-ND 4.0

to acknowledge and preserve difference, eradicating instead the processes that lead to the stigmatisation and stereotyping of differences. Against an evolving list of identifying features that typically prompt unequal treatment, such as— in addition to race and sex—age, disability, gender reassignment and marital status,[1] substantive equality perspectives also orient toward dismantling those social structures that present barriers to individuals who, precisely because of the differences between them, may legitimately pursue very different outcomes.

It is not the purpose of this introduction (or of the volume in general) to chart the fluctuating influences of these two perspectives on the development of the various legal frameworks governing equality and non-discrimination; nor do we intend, by naming formal and substantive equality, to deny the exist- ence of more nuanced positions along the spectrum on how the law should address discriminatory practices. Instead, we begin our intervention from the standpoint that the present phase in equality and non-discrimination law is one that is more aligned to substantive equality visions. In terms of the treat- ment of difference, the prevailing wisdom is that, to quote Sandra Fredman, 'the problem is not the diversity of characteristics, but the detrimental treat- ment attached to them. Thus the aim should not be to eliminate difference, but to prohibit the detriment attached to such difference, preferably by adjusting existing norms to accommodate difference' (2016: 70).

Spanning a range of public and private institutions, including universities (Bourne & Tuitt), so-called 'magic circle' law firms (Chronopoulou & Whyte), the police (Kandelia), financial services (Vasileiadou) and immigration ser- vices (Smith), the various contributions to this volume enter and extend the extant debate from the vantage point of law's engagement with racial difference.

The re-theorising of foundational concepts like race and difference and emerging concepts like diversity and inclusion which this collection undertakes rightly entails revisiting older theories: theories that can be read anew or incor- porated in different contexts. Thus, it will be seen that the chapters are inspired by some well-established theories, notably, the theory of intersectionality first articulated by Kimberlé Crenshaw (1989). Our understanding of difference as a concept that has been significantly shaped by the law brings the theory of intersectionality back to the specific site of equality legislation, as Crenshaw originally intended. Additionally, underlying several chapters is the persistence in which different property values have been ascribed to whiteness in contrast to blackness. As many chapters demonstrate, this racial schema is evident even in ostensibly progressive diversity and inclusion initiatives. Although pub- lished long before the language of diversity and inclusion began to dominate discourses on equality and non-discrimination, Cheryl Harris's (1993) article 'Whiteness as property' remains an indispensable intellectual resource.

---

[1] These features are sometimes referred to as 'protected characteristics'. See, for exam- ple, section 4 of the UK Equality Act 2010.

Although critical of the law and informed by a number of interdisciplinary critiques of existing laws and legal institutions, this volume sees the law—as it is typically manifested in legislation, case law and the intervention in various legal arena of legal practitioners (broadly conceived to include academics and activists, for example)—has still a leading role to play in tackling racial discrimination, harm and violence. Moreover, as the opening lines to this introduction indicate, the volume lays emphasis on the fact that questions pertaining to how the law negotiates the differences that we highlight are, to a greater or lesser degree, of global import. In Keane's words 'discrimination is international between states, as well as national within states' (Chapter 2, pp28–29). Thus, whilst more than half of the chapters draw evidence from institutions located in the UK and the US, the volume opens with two chapters which explore how racial equality legislation is conceived and implemented at an international level.

The Particularity of Race Discrimination

The number and range of human and social features that are recognised as prompting discriminatory and violent acts from both private citizens and organs of government are growing. In the contemporary world, for example, disability, age and transgender discrimination are as prominent in the work of the courts and in public and policy discourses as is discrimination based on racial difference. Within a context of multiple and interlocking sites of discrimination, a decision to focus attention on one axis requires explanation. This volume is primarily concerned to probe how differences are mediated in law, and, in this light, it was important for the various contributors to highlight, first and foremost, that the question of racial difference has been at the heart of the earliest articulations of the concepts of equality and non-discrimination. Here, we are reminded of Derrida's provocation to scholars to carefully trace and document the ways in which 'interval, distance, *spacing* occur ... actively, dynamically and with a certain perseverance in repetition' (1982: 5). Thus, the focus of the volume is, in large measure, a response to the very evident 'perseverance' in which lines are drawn between individuals and their life opportunities on the grounds of their belonging to 'undesirable' communities of colour. However, also uppermost in the minds of the contributors was the understanding that alongside the long and troubled history of racial violence and discrimination have been active forms of resistance, which have been partially captured in various academic and activist texts. This has enabled the contributors to incorporate insights from a rich archive of analysis on the various ways in which 'interval, distance ... among ... different elements' (Derrida 1982: 260) are constructed when markers of difference are considered undesirable. Whilst the archive which the collection draws on is undoubtedly propelled by a history of the social construction of racial difference, the chapters bring insights from the archive that exceed the particular instance of racial difference and discrimination, and thereby offer accounts and interrogations which will also shed light on the mechanisms by which difference is conceived and operationalised in other equality spheres.

The substantive part of the volume opens with a chapter by Keane which provides an account of the contribution to continuing efforts to promote and instantiate an ethic of 'global racial equality' (Chapter 2, pp13–32) of one of the earliest legal instruments, the International Convention on the Elimination of All Forms of Racial Discrimination (ICERD). Keane's analysis reveals that, in spite of the Treaty's near-universal acceptance, and the 'immense symbolic and legal significance' (ibid., p28) it has acquired since its adoption in 1965, discrimination and violence directed toward racial and ethnic minorities persists. Often this emerges in the context of a clash of fundamental rights, which the chapter that follows, by Vasileiadou, highlights. Vasileiadou demonstrates that one contemporary context in which this 'clash' is evident is the global legal services market. Participation rates in the financial services markets by actual and potential entrepreneurs of Muslim origin have been compromised by regulatory measures imposed on financial services providers with the ostensible aim of combatting terrorism. Vasileiadou shows how measures designed to secure peace and security by, in part, imposing financial penalties on financial services providers for failures in monitoring the uses to which funds they hold on behalf of clients are used, has led to breaches of the equally fundamental right of non-discrimination. This is because 'major banks prefer to exclude customers than face liability, as money laundering or terrorist financing accusations can harm their reputation' (Chapter 3, p42).

Both chapters critically reflect upon how the law operates and how it can be strengthened and improved. For Keane, the absence of binding judgements and enforcement mechanisms from the Treaty's infrastructure is to be regretted. This weakness notwithstanding, Keane's chapter demonstrates how ICERD has used its power to make recommendations, issue concluding observations and activate early warning systems and measures to 'give support and strength to … international NGOs and civil society … [and to] … [provide] a voice … at the UN and communicate directly to the State signalling … the voices of those most affected by racial discrimination' (Chapter 2, p28). Vasileiadou highlights the impact that exclusion from financial markets has on an individual's access to legal institutions and therefore their access to justice, finance being 'the main and sometimes only means to exercise several fundamental rights … [a] person with no bank account cannot find an "official" job and "officially" be paid, cannot rent a house or ask for medical care. We could say that a person with no bank account does not "officially exist"' (Chapter 3, p42). Vasileiadou suggests that, in the absence of the law, the task of exposing the racially discriminatory acts and decisions of financial services providers across the globe has been left to the media.

Other chapters in the volume highlight the still pervasive nature of racial violence and discrimination from the point of view of national laws. For example,

Kandelia's exploration of UK police 'stop and search' policies and practices reminds readers of an area of state activity which has consistently made communities of colour 'hyper-visible' from the moment that they arrived in countries of settlement. Kandelia's chapter examines how UK police attitudes to racial minorities have been expressed in the operationalisation of stop and search policies from the so-called 'sus' laws emanating from the Vagrancy Act 1894 to the present-day provisions under the Police, Crime, Sentencing and Courts Act 2022. A key focus of the chapter is how—in pursuance of racial equality—the law attempts to regulate these interactions between police and minority communities. Kandelia concludes that 'every year, the statistics tell the same story: people from ethnic minority groups are overrepresented in the figures' (Chapter 8, p171) on police stop and search. In common with other contributors to the volume, Kandelia assesses the effectiveness of the law *per se* in achieving racial justice in the context of how black and brown communities are policed, noting—in similar terms to Vasileiadou—that media outlets often prove to be a better regulator of the use of stop and search than the law.

Keane, whose chapter we discussed earlier in this introduction, also addresses the question of police violence. Writing of the unlawful killing of George Floyd, Keane notes that the ICERD 'has long signalled its deep concern with the issues raised by "Black Lives Matter" in the United States' (Chapter 2, p27). Continuing the theme of how international legal instruments can be part of the beginnings of a global ethic of racial justice, Keane argues that the ICERD's interventions undoubtedly influenced the terms of what emerged as a global debate about race and racism which extended beyond the theme of police brutality to encompass the question of how communities of colour are represented in institutional settings. Kandelia documents police practices toward racial minorities—especially young black men—which have resulted in their huge over-representation in prisons. Together, these chapters highlight the fact that racial discrimination and violence has persisted throughout virtually every phase of equality legislation.

Immigration is another context in which racial difference has become a fundamental feature of its institutional ordering in Western democracies, and this is highlighted in Smith's chapter. It centres on the controversial immigration policies of the Trump administration in the US, and the 'hostile environment' policies in the UK (especially associated with the former UK Prime Minister, Theresa May's time—both in that office and before as the UK Home Secretary). Both sets of policies, to a greater or lesser extent, received the endorsement of the highest domestic courts, in spite of their racially discriminatory impacts. As Smith notes, 'the US Supreme Court's … legal interpretation … departed from both academic and popular opinion on the fundamental question of what constitutes discrimination' (Chapter 9, p180). As to the 'hostile environment' policies, they were condemned by the UN Special Rapporteur on Contemporary Forms of Racism, Racial Discrimination, Xenophobia and Related Intolerance for their tendency to capture and punish racial and ethnic minorities with clear legal entitlements to be in the UK, with the right to work and seek recourse to health and housing services which accompanies such entitlements. These basic rights were found to have been wrongly withheld in defiance of the laws governing race discrimination. Referring also to the Windrush scandal, in which Caribbean migrants arriving in the UK between 1948 and 1973 as Commonwealth citizens with full rights to settle, live and work in the UK without restriction were denied these rights due to the lack of paperwork explicitly recognising these entitlements, Smith argues that both the US and UK policies are 'popularist' in that they form part of a 'political transaction with subjective individual voters [that seeks to] maximise their partial, self-interested concerns in return for their committed political support' (ibid., p195).

Being Different and Making a Difference: An Interrogation of Diversity and Inclusion Practices

In the contemporary landscape, the commitment to substantive equality requires more than that differences—whether ostensible, such as race, or non-ostensible, such as with certain forms of disability—are acknowledged as valuable personal and social attributes. It also requires that social institutions take steps to ensure that they are inhabited, in numbers proportionate to their numbers in society, by the presence of individuals who hitherto have been under-represented in those institutions precisely because of their perceived negative differences (diversity). Further, institutions are required to take steps to ensure that once in the institution, those 'marginalised' individuals are made to feel a full part of the institution—able to shape its future direction (inclusion). Thus, 'diversity' and 'inclusion' are terms that have become synonymous with equality and have been the subject of much academic analysis and criticism. Its premise is aptly and succinctly expressed by Verna Myers in a 2016 address to the Cleveland Bar Association: 'Diversity is being invited to the party; inclusion is being asked to dance.'

One way in which this volume departs from other works that address diversity and inclusion initiatives and practices is in its suggestion that whilst greater focus on inclusion initiatives would go some way to improving the institutional experiences of persons of colour, the position of these individuals is compromised and will remain so for as long as diversity is wedded to the idea that the presence of individuals of colour in institutions will lead to positive change in the racial ideologies and structures that underlie those institutions. To put it another way, it is generally and largely uncritically assumed that difference should make a difference, and it is the normative relation between *being different and making a difference* that the chapters in this part of the collection encourage us to explore. As stated earlier, whilst the collection's focus is on the treatment of racial difference, the idea that difference should make a difference to exclusionary ideologies and structures is a philosophy that extends to other marginalised groups. In addition, then, to interrogating an assumption that, we argue, has not been sufficiently attended to in the extant literature on diversity and inclusion, the collection also offers a framework of analysis that could be utilised by those writing about non-racial markers of difference, including those markers that have not yet assumed the status of 'protected characteristics', such as class, and, to a large extent, nationality.

When we speak of 'difference making a difference', we speak of a widespread and largely accepted idea that a key justification for diversity and inclusion initiatives is that those once excluded from institutions can *and should* bring about positive institutional change. The way that this change may come about is variously articulated: their experiences of exclusion can be drawn upon by the institutions to dismantle exclusionary structures, or their presence may improve the ratio between the members of institutions with diverse characters and those individuals or groups that the institution is intended to serve. However articulated, the expectation is that those marked as different and therefore hitherto undesirable and unwanted members of an institution cannot expect to join such institutions with the ambition of simply improving their economic and professional standing and job satisfaction. Rather, they are assigned a task that arguably eclipses the personal desires that animate other organisational members who are not marked out as different because they appear to conform to the dominant norm. The additional task assigned is intimately connected to an idea that difference should impel or animate difference. We see this idea performed in action whenever black or Asian government ministers concerned with matters of immigration are publicly criticised whenever they implement, or are otherwise seen to support, racially exclusionary immigration policies. Implicit and sometimes explicit in these criticisms is that, unlike non-racialised immigration officials, black and Asian officials should not have the option to capitulate to policies they might not sympathise with because to do so would further their careers. Perhaps even more problematically, the criticism fails to recognise that the pervasive nature of racial ideas and practices—their deep embeddedness in all institutions—will inevitably result in individuals of colour struggling in equal measures with their white counterparts to disentangle their own ideas and practices from the exclusionary frameworks that may have become all too familiar, and thus may find it easier to immediately navigate than would be more desirable, inclusive frameworks.

In *Demography, Discrimination and Diversity: A New Dawn for the British Legal Profession* Donald Nicholson revealed that statistics show that 'in England and Wales the number of ethnic minorities now substantially exceeds their general social presence not just in terms of admissions but also total numbers' (2016: 207). In addition to supporting the prevalent 'inclusion lagging behind diversity' explanation for the fact that, despite their representative numbers, black, Asian and other racial minority 'trainees feel far less comfortable than whites in their work environments' (ibid.: 208), not least because many face the double discrimination of race and class, Nicholson offers a mild but still welcome challenge to the idea that individual differences should result in positive institutional change, arguing that, 'there is no guarantee that lawyers from disadvantaged communities will accept that they owe special duties to members of their original communities' (ibid.: 219). He goes on to highlight the inequity that emerges when 'the burdens of remedying social injustice [are placed] on those who have had to struggle to overcome such injustice in order to become lawyers, leaving white, middle-class lawyers to pursue their careers and private lives unhampered by such duties' (ibid.).

In light of the many complexities explored above, the volume's authors offer different theories of race – ones that attempt to account for both the potential positive and negative outcomes of racial diversity and inclusion initiatives. Overall, they combine to create theories of difference that can interrupt what Derrida speaks of as the repetitive cycle in which distance is produced between various 'differents' (1982: 5). We do not claim to have produced such an over-arching theory in this collection, but by interrupting, *whilst not absolutely repudiating*, the link between *being different* and *making a difference* we hope to begin an important conversation.

Thus, many of the chapters begin from the premise that diversity and inclusion are dominant concepts driving contemporary equality and racial justice measures. They examine how diversity initiatives have increased the presence of communities of colour in public and private institutions, including by offering empirical (Whyte, Chapter 5) or partially empirical (Bourne, Chapter 6; Chronopoulou, Chapter 4) accounts of diversity initiatives operating in various prominent public and private institutions. However, the key question underlying all chapters is that of the relation—theoretically and empirically—between diversity and inclusion and equality and justice. What the chapters highlight is that this relation is contingent and inherently problematic, and if the complexities of the relation are not well understood by those driving racial diversity and inclusion initiatives, such initiatives could/will reproduce and heighten old/existing forms of racial exclusion. In this vein, several of the chapters offer a reading of the current diversity and inclusion orientation of the general substantive equality doctrine as one that continues the racial disadvantage of communities of colour either because they remain 'invisible' in various key institutions (Bourne, Chapter 6; Chronopoulou, Chapter 4; Vasileiadou, Chapter 2) or because, conversely, they are 'hypervisible' (Kandelia, Chapter 8; Tuitt, Chapter 7).

Chronopoulou's chapter (Chapter 4) begins a series of interrogations into the way in which diversity and inclusion policies are conceived and implemented. Drawing on a sample of recruitment material from the 'upper echelons' of UK solicitors firms and barristers' chambers, Chronopoulou shows how these firms construct an image of the 'diverse' aspiring lawyer as being one who participates in certain forms of consumption: one who embraces or is willing to embrace a certain lifestyle—such as gym attendance, theatre going and fine dining. Whilst this advertising material 'creates the appealing impression of an all-inclusive workplace and culture' (ibid., p68), this seeming cultural diversity is in practice expressive of the 'consumptions … of a … lifestyle associated with a privileged, predominantly white elite' (ibid., p61). Here, diversity and inclusion are attained through 'the portrayal of predominantly "white" aspects of lifestyles … [and] the tactful avoidance of reference to different lifestyles which would eventually challenge that "whiteness"' (Chapter 4, p69). In Chronopoulou's view, inclusion and diversity in the UK's elite law practices entails just the minimum that the law demands. Chronopoulou urges scholars concerned with the question of racial diversity in the legal profession to give more attention to how racialised persons are excluded by the emphasis, during the socialisation process, of specific 'practices of consumption'. Ultimately, Chronopoulou argues that the current conception of diversity in the legal services arena has led to a position in which race constitutes 'just another commodity in the legal services market' (ibid., p67), one in which racial difference is sometimes negatively and sometimes positively deployed.

As previously stated, the volume interrogates, but does not completely reject, the idea that being different and making a difference are constitutively linked. This is demonstrated especially in Bourne's chapter, which argues—in common with many other scholars and higher education policy specialists— that the potential for diversity initiatives to become another means through which racial discrimination is perpetrated is essentially because 'inclusion' initiatives currently lag behind 'diversity' initiatives—because, in other words, institutions recruit individuals of colour into institutions with structures that lead to their internal marginalisation, including through the implementation of directly or indirectly discriminatory policies. Writing in the context of the UK university, Bourne argues that in terms of the share of academics of colour currently employed in universities and the statistics on the progress of students of colour toward an academic career, diversity is happening, but inclusion remains a distant aspiration. Outlining the many obstacles in the way of inclusion—such as the failure of universities to take responsibility for disparities in degree outcomes of university students of colour in comparison with their white counterparts—Bourne explains why, in her view, true 'ethnic diversity is good, and worth striving for' (Chapter 6, p114). The chapter examines the role of the law in ensuring that diversity policies are matched with inclusion policies. In this regard, Bourne criticises what she sees to be the progressive weakening of the Public Sector Equality Duty (PSED) under section 149 of the Equality Act, which, if strengthened would place the onus on academic institutions to undertake the work needed to achieve inclusion—which is currently reliant on academics of colour pursuing individual complaints. However, Bourne also cautions against over-reliance on the law to resolve the problems of deep-seated discrimination that is prevalent in UK society (ibid., p130).

The chapter which precedes it, by Whyte, questions the extent to which large UK solicitors firms, especially those with a commercial clientele, can evidence a link between particular diversity and inclusion initiatives and a more racially inclusive organisational culture. Focusing on one initiative that has attracted considerable attention, the Freshfields Stephen Lawrence Scholarship (FSLS), Whyte's scrutiny of the available data draws attention to some of the ways in which diversity initiatives can reinforce exclusionary practices. For example, the eligibility criteria for the FSLS is that the male, black (African, African-Caribbean), or mixed race candidates are 'exceptionally talented' (Chapter 5, p86), recalling to mind the oft-cited claim that black (and Asian) individuals must be twice as talented as their white counterparts to gain access to the most financially lucrative opportunities in the legal services market. Whilst the FSLS and others like it have undoubtedly improved the rates of entry of those they target into the commercial law sector, progress to senior positions and partnerships remains 'quite stagnant' (ibid., p104). To ensure that diversity talk and action is matched with similar levels of energy at the inclusion level, Whyte argues that 'firms must … publicly *evidence* how their initiatives, practices and policies work on the ground and fundamentally whether their workplace culture actually supports, promotes and sustains ethnic diversity' (ibid., p105).

Concluding this theme, Tuitt's chapter is concerned with the data collection exercises that invariably accompany diversity and inclusion initiatives. Like Bourne's chapter, Tuitt's is located within the UK university setting. Drawing on a number of government-supported investigations into the experiences and academic achievements of students of colour, the chapter draws comparisons between contemporary data collection exercises and the ways and means by which a distorted 'knowledge' of racial minorities had been acquired and disseminated in earlier colonial settings. The main purpose of Tuitt's chapter is to demonstrate how these official reports paint a negative picture of students of colour as being inherently resistant to higher learning and that these portrayals are entirely compatible with institutional discourses and strategies ostensibly aimed at encouraging and supporting racial diversity.

The Limits of Racial Justice

In light of the discussion of diversity above, it is noteworthy that three of the chapters in the volume (Kandelia, Chapter 8; Smith, Chapter 9; Vasileiadou, Chapter 2) provide accounts of the *presence* of individuals and communities in which change, especially in the immigration process (Smith), has led to greater, not lesser, exclusion of black and brown communities—and greater levels of violence directed toward them—in spite of an increased representation of black, Asian and other racial minority police, immigration officials and participants in the financial services market. The question which these chapters prompt is whether concepts like equality and justice—and relatedly the positive force that diversity and inclusion initiatives might offer—reach their limits when they encounter the non-citizen (migrant) or the compromised citizen (criminal/terrorist). Communities of colour and individuals are disproportionately exposed to being constructed according to the categories of migrant, criminal or terrorist, whether or not they inhabit them in fact.

The ease with which visible racial minorities can be constructed as unlawful immigrants was recently demonstrated by the UK Windrush scandal in which the descendants of individuals who had arrived in the UK from the Caribbean in the 1950s and 1960s, and who since had acquired indefinite leave to remain in the UK, were, following the enactment of the UK Immigration Act 2014, effectively reclassified as illegal immigrants by the UK Home Office with the consequence that they were dispossessed of jobs, homes and, in several cases, deported from the UK to countries they had not resided in since early childhood. In short, all three chapters demonstrate how far away the law is from managing differences that are seen to threaten the boundaries of the nation.

It is on the question of the limits of racial justice that the volume ends. Its concluding chapter, by Smith, prompts readers to consider whether the 'global ethic of racial justice' that was invoked in the opening chapter, by Keane, reaches its limit at the boundaries of the citizen/non-citizen distinction. In examining this question, Smith explores what philosophers such as Kant, Rawls, Dworkin and Nagel have contributed to contemplations on whether it is 'justifiable, or merely morally permissible perhaps, for nation States to grossly restrict … entitlements in pursuit of their own national self-interest before the moral duties we owe to others from outside our own political community' (Chapter 9, pp181–182). Drawing on these philosophical accounts, Smith concludes that highly restrictive immigration policies of the kind exemplified in the US and by the UK's hostile environment measures fail the test of legitimacy unless the explanations behind them—the justifications for their existence—are understood and accepted by those whose rights are to be curtailed or erased by them.

References

Crenshaw, K. (1989). Demarginalizing the intersection of race and sex: A black feminist critique of anti-discrimination doctrine, feminist theory and anti-racist politics. *University of Chicago Legal Forum*, 1: 138–167.

Derrida, J. (1982). 'Différance', translated by Alan Bass, *Margins of Philosophy*. Chicago: University of Chicago Press, pp. 3–27.

Fredman, S. (2016). Substantive equality revisited. *International Journal of Constitutional Law*, 14(3): 712–738.

Harris, C. (1993). Whiteness as property. *Harvard Law Review*, 16(8): 1707–1791.

Myers, V. (2016). Diversity is being invited to the party; inclusion is being asked to dance. Cleveland.com, 25 May. https://www.cleveland.com/business/2016/05/diversity_is_being_invited_to.html

Nicholson, D. (2005). Demography, discrimination and diversity: A new dawn for the British legal profession. *International Journal of the Legal Profession*, 12(2): 201–228.

CHAPTER 2

Assessing the Contribution of the International Convention on the Elimination of All Forms of Racial Discrimination to Global Racial Equality

David Keane

Introduction

The International Convention on the Elimination of All Forms of Racial Discrimination (ICERD), adopted on 21 December 1965, is the first of the nine core United Nations (UN) human rights treaties. Its Preamble expresses a resolve 'to build an international community free from all forms of racial segregation and racial discrimination'. In that light, it reaffirms that:

> ... [D]iscrimination between human beings on the grounds of race, colour or ethnic origin is an obstacle to friendly and peaceful relations among nations and is capable of disturbing peace and security among peoples and the harmony of persons living side by side even within one and the same State.

How to cite this book chapter:
Keane, D. 2024. Assessing the Contribution of the International Convention on the Elimination of All Forms of Racial Discrimination to Global Racial Equality. In: Whyte, A., Tuitt, P. and Bourne, J. (eds.) *The Long Walk to Equality: Perspectives on Racial Inequality, Injustice and the Law*. Pp. 13–32. London: University of Westminster Press. DOI: https://doi.org/10.16997/book63.b. License: CC-BY-NC-ND 4.0

The Preamble thus captures the inter-State character of the treaty 'among nations', as well as its intra-State character 'within one and the same State'. The principles of the Convention are widely accepted as representing conduct prohibited by customary international law. In order to achieve its principles, the treaty would establish the first UN treaty body, the Committee on the Elimination of Racial Discrimination (CERD), which began its work in January 1970 once the treaty had entered into force.

This chapter assesses the contribution of ICERD to global racial equality. The treaty has 182 States Parties, and a truly global picture cannot be provided in a single chapter. Instead, some of the treaty's achievements are emphasised, while also identifying certain weaknesses and gaps. Section one examines the significance of ICERD's emergence as the first of the core UN human rights treaties. It underlines its status as a pioneering treaty, opening the door to the realisation of a UN human rights treaty system, while also discussing how this has had a continuing impact on certain of ICERD's monitoring provisions. Section two reflects on the treaty's status as a global, but not universal, treaty. All of those States that are *not* a party to the treaty are identified, and prospects for universal ratification considered. Section three looks at a major weakness in the operation of the treaty since its adoption: the failure of the majority of States Parties to make the Article 14 declaration allowing for individual communications. To what extent States Parties may be encouraged to allow for this important mechanism is considered. Section four offers a brief thematic study, outlining the contribution and response of the treaty in light of the recent 'Black Lives Matter' movement. The international nature of the movement emphasises the importance of ICERD as a global legal standard on the elimination of racial discrimination. In conclusion, the chapter reflects on ICERD's critical mandate amid growing awareness of the essential nature of its object and purpose.

1. The First UN Human Rights Treaty

The study of human 'races' dates to antiquity (Cavalli-Sforza et al. 2012: 16). However, the beginning of African colonisation and the 'discovery' of America and the sea route to India by Europeans caused a 'considerable increase in race and colour prejudice' (Comas 1958: 9). Race prejudice developed into a regular doctrinal system during the eighteenth and nineteenth centuries. In the twentieth century, when the UN was built 'on the ashes of the most destructive war in history', it focused its attention on racial discrimination, with the understanding that ideas of racial superiority had been in some way responsible for the Holocaust and other atrocities (Schabas 2017: 181). As Schabas highlights, 'the root of the problem was more visceral and it could not be blamed on the Nazis alone', with manifestations including 'the scourge of slavery and the slave trade, by then abolished but of recent and enduring memory, and colonialism very much a reality as the UN addressed the corrupted mandate system it had been bequeathed by the League of Nations' (Schabas 2017: 181). Thornberry adds that early UN action on racial discrimination was also motivated by 'the affront to humanity represented by apartheid' built on 'centuries of racial theorising' (Thornberry 2017: 1).

The UN combined statements of principle with practical methodologies to express a new ethic of global racial equality. The elimination of racial discrimination is a founding principle of the UN, with Article 1(3) of the UN Charter 1945 describing one of the four purposes of the organisation as: 'respect for human rights and for fundamental freedoms for all without distinction as to race, sex, language, or religion'. The UN General Assembly (UNGA) would express concern about racial discrimination from its earliest sessions, declaring in a 1946 resolution on Persecution and Discrimination that it is 'in the higher interests of humanity to put an immediate end to … racial persecution and discrimination' (UNGA, 1946). Article 2 of the Universal Declaration of Human Rights 1948 (UDHR) affirmed that, 'everyone is entitled to all the rights and freedoms set forth in this Declaration, without distinction of any kind, such as race, colour, sex, language, religion.' The 1950s–60s was a period of rapid change for the UN, that saw its membership grow significantly with decolonisation and the emergence of newly independent nations in Africa and Asia. The first non-Western European UN Secretary-General, U Thant of what was then Burma, was appointed in 1961, symbolising the growing presence of these nations in the organisation. In his memoirs, Thant highlighted: 'the outstanding difference that distinguished me from all other Secretaries General of the League of Nations or of the United Nations lay in the fact that I was the first non-European to occupy that post' (Thant 1978: 36).

This period also saw a key evolution in international human rights law, with the shift from non-binding, declaratory rights listed in the UDHR, to a legally binding system of international human rights treaties and their monitoring bodies. The intention had been firstly to create an 'International Bill of Rights' composed of a declaration, a convention and measures of implementation, that applied to civil, political, economic, social and cultural rights. Following on from the adoption of a 'declaration' in the UDHR 1948, differences arising from the Cold War saw a split in the proposed 'convention' so that in 1954, the Commission on Human Rights set out a draft Covenant on Civil and Political Rights and a draft Covenant on Economic, Social and Cultural Rights (UN Economic and Social Council 1954). It included as 'measures of implementation' the first proposed UN treaty body, the Human Rights Committee, but applied only to civil and political rights (Schwelb 1968: 838–9). The realisation of these instruments would continue to take time due to differences between the Eastern and Western blocs, with substantial revisions to the proposed drafts in the Third Committee from 1954 to 1966 (Schabas 2019: LXIII). The International Covenant on Civil and Political Rights (ICCPR) and International Covenant on Economic, Social and Cultural Rights (ICESCR) were adopted on 16 December 1966.

By contrast, the movement towards an international treaty on racial discrimination began much later than the 'International Bill of Rights', originating in
the winter of 1959–60 as a series of UN resolutions in response to a global out-
break of antisemitic propaganda known as the 'Swastika epidemic' (Keane 2007:
371). It developed much more quickly with the support of the newly emergent
African and Asian nations for whom the elimination of racial discrimination
was a priority; their focus was colonialism and apartheid. It followed the same
pattern of declaration, convention and measures of implementation. In 1963,
the UN Declaration on the Elimination of Racial Discrimination was pro-
claimed. On 21 December 1965, ICERD was adopted as a convention, with
built-in measures of implementation via the first UN treaty body, CERD. It fell
to Secretary General U Thant to usher in ICERD and a new age of UN human
rights treaties and their monitoring bodies. He stated to the General Assembly:

> In the Charter, the peoples of the United Nations proclaimed their deter-
> mination to reaffirm faith in human rights and in the dignity and worth
> of the human person. The Convention which the General Assembly has
> just adopted represents a significant step towards the achievement of
> that goal. Not only does it call for an end to racial discrimination in all
> its forms; it goes on to the next, and very necessary, step of establish-
> ing the international machinery which is essential to achieve that aim.
> (UNGA 1965 PV.1406, para. 138)

As Thant highlighted above, it is the 'international machinery' that distinguished ICERD from what the UN had achieved up to that date in the realm of
human rights. CERD monitors the treaty through State reports (Article 9); inter-
State communications (Articles 11–13); individual communications (optional,
Article 14); and a compromissory clause allowing for dispute resolution before
the International Court of Justice (ICJ) (Article 22). CERD would evolve its
practice in relation to issuing concluding observations, general recommendations, early warning measures and urgent procedures, all based around the
reporting procedure in Article 9. ICERD as the first UN human rights treaty
had no exact precedent for its measures of implementation, but it did draw
on related instruments and documents, including the European Convention on
Human Rights (ECHR) 1950, the draft of the Covenants 1954 and treaties
on discrimination of the International Labour Organisation and the United
Nations Educational, Scientific and Cultural Organisation. It would in turn
provide a precedent and template for all of the future 'core' UN human rights
treaties, of which there are nine in total today. It ensured also that final obstacles in relation to realising the ICCPR and the ICESCR would be overcome.

While all the UN human rights treaties have certain common features,
each remains distinctive. For example, ICESCR was drafted without a treaty
body. The Convention on the Elimination of Discrimination Against Women
(CEDAW) and the Convention on the Rights of the Child (CRC) were drafted

without an individual and inter-State communications provision. The ICCPR and ICESCR were drafted without a compromissory clause allowing for dispute resolution before the ICJ. These differences have been elided over time through optional protocols and more streamlined drafting of later treaties, so that today the UN treaty bodies broadly utilise the same supervisory mechanisms. They all have a treaty body. They all receive State reports, and issue concluding observations and general recommendations or comments. They all have an optional individual communications provision, which States Parties must opt in to in order to allow individuals to petition the committees. Most have an optional inter-State communications provision to the relevant treaty body (CEDAW still does not). Some have a compromissory clause allowing for dispute resolution before the ICJ, although no treaty has added such a clause via an optional protocol.

ICERD retains distinctive features within the UN human rights treaty system. To a certain extent, it benefitted from its early status as a pioneering treaty and was drafted with the full range of supervisory mechanisms in its Parts II and III, meaning there was never a need for an optional protocol. In fact, the text has remained unchanged since 1965. Importantly, it has a unique feature in that its inter-State communications mechanism under Articles 11–13 is compulsory. This is a legacy of the 1954 draft of the Covenants from which ICERD drew, which provided for compulsory inter-State communications as well as a compromissory clause allowing for referral to the ICJ. For the ICCPR, the revision process in the Third Committee changed the inter-State communications mechanism from compulsory to optional, and removed the compromissory clause allowing for referral to the ICJ. No such revision occurred in the Third Committee for ICERD. This was deliberate, in that a broad grouping of States felt justified in affording to CERD stronger powers than what would be granted to the Human Rights Committee under the ICCPR. As a result, under Article 11, any State Party to ICERD can bring an inter-State communication against another State Party. In all other UN treaties where inter-State communications provisions are found, they are optional, meaning States Parties must make an extra declaration recognising the competence of the committee to receive such communications. The result of this in practice is that to date, CERD is the only treaty body that has received inter-State communications, three in total: *Qatar v Kingdom of Saudi Arabia* (2018), *Qatar v United Arab Emirates* (2018) and *Palestine v Israel* (2018). In *Palestine v Israel*, CERD stressed the 'collective enforcement' character of the inter-State communications mechanism as it relates to all States Parties, and not only to the individual disputants (Eiken & Keane 2022).

The distinctiveness of its provisions should, however, not be overstated, and today CERD broadly engages in the same work as all the UN treaty bodies. This means that it suffers from the same common weaknesses, including that its recommendations—whether issued through concluding observations, general recommendations, early warning measures and urgent procedures, inter-State communications or individual communications—are not *stricto sensu* legally binding. In this way, the UN treaty bodies differ from regional human rights courts in particular, which issue legally binding judgments. As a result, individual decisions, interpretations or recommendations of CERD are open to challenge by States Parties, which may not implement a decision, or apply an interpretation or recommendation. Nevertheless, the treaty has proven effective at ensuring its provisions are implemented through its network of non-binding recommendations. In addition, such recommendations may often refer to international standards that have a customary status. As Thornberry summarises: '[t]he complex of mechanisms has … been pivotal in the development of an expansive network of standards that contributes to the formation of customary law even if specific decision-making procedures do not possess a legally "binding" quality' (Thornberry 2016: 65).

Beyond the narrow and not always helpful dialectic of binding and non-binding, CERD sees the treaty as a living instrument that responds to victims of racial discrimination. CERD builds a 'dialogue' with States Parties over periodic reports, in which it also integrates information from NGOs and civil society, as the optimal means of ensuring compliance over time. This can involve recognition of new categories of rights-holders and innovation in monitoring, reflective of increased NGO and civil society participation in the Committee's work (IMADR 2011). CERD has, in turn, served to provide a 'legal cutting edge to defend their rights' (IMADR 2011: Preface (by Thornberry 2016)). This may be seen in particular in its range of general recommendations (GRs) which may identify groups that require a specific focus under the treaty, such as indigenous peoples (GR 23), the Roma (GR 27), caste groups (GR 29) or people of African descent (GR 34), or engage with themes that impact all States Parties, such as special measures (GR 32) or combatting racist hate speech (GR 35). CERD will reference its general recommendations in the State reporting process and guide States Parties towards legal responses and other remedies in relation to Convention groups and themes, in line with their Article 2 ICERD obligation 'to pursue by all appropriate means and without delay a policy of eliminating racial discrimination'.

2. From a Global to a Universal Treaty

ICERD is subject to signature, ratification and accession under Articles 17–18. To date it has 182 States Parties and, in terms of ratifications, is nearing universal acceptance. There are just 15 States that have not ratified the treaty. Three of these have signed but not ratified ('Signatories') and twelve of have neither signed nor ratified ('No Action'). These are:

- Bhutan, Nauru and Palau ('Signatories')
- Brunei, Democratic People's Republic of Korea (DPRK, or North Korea), Malaysia, Myanmar, South Sudan, and the Pacific Island nations of the

Cook Islands, Kiribati, Micronesia, Niue, Samoa, Tuvalu and Vanuatu ('No Action').

In 2019, Angola (which had been a signatory), and Dominica and the Marshall Islands ratified the treaty. Dominica's ratification meant that ICERD covers the entire Caribbean region. Of the remaining States outside the treaty, we may assume that the three signatories will ratify, although it should be noted this is not an obligation (Bradley 2012: 208). Similarly, the remaining Pacific Island nations will in all likelihood ratify the treaty at some point. In general, objections among Pacific Island nations to ratifying human rights treaties are based on capacity, in that their small size and remoteness means that such nations cannot easily meet the costs of ratification, including reporting obligations. Olowu among others has criticised this position, arguing that the 'fiscal constraints justification misses the essence of the UN human rights treaty system' (Olowu 2006: 165). A recent initiative by the Committee on the Rights of the Child, which in March 2020 conducted an extraordinary 84th session in Samoa, sends a signal that the UN treaty bodies are willing to assist the Pacific nations in meeting their reporting obligations (OHCHR 2020). This may encourage ratifications of remaining treaties, including ICERD, by Pacific Island nations.

DPRK or North Korea has signed and ratified several human rights treaties, including the CRC, CEDAW, CRPD, ICCPR and ICESCR. Overall, the human rights situation in DPRK is extremely concerning. A recent report of the UN Special Rapporteur on the situation of human rights in DPRK found 'no sign of improvement in the human rights situation, nor progress in advancing accountability and justice for human rights violations' (HRC 2020: 3). The Special Rapporteur has encouraged the Government of DPRK to engage with the international human rights mechanisms. ICERD is not specified, but its ratification ought to form part of this process of engagement.

South Sudan became independent from Sudan on 9 July 2011. Prior to the referendum on independence, the territory had formed part of the Republic of Sudan, which ratified ICERD in 1977. Thus, the peoples of South Sudan had the protection of the Convention from 1977 to 2011. In that period, CERD offered Concluding Observations in 1987, 1994, 1995 and 2001. In 1987, for example, CERD commended the Sudanese report which described how the country was 'overcoming the after-effects of a repressive regime and embarking on the reinstatement of human rights' (CERD 1987: para. 487). CERD also understood that 'the most important problem facing the Government was the crisis between the north and the south, which was jeopardizing the full application of the Convention' (CERD 1987: para. 492). Thus, CERD recognised from an early point that the peoples of South Sudan required a particular focus under the Convention. It would appear essential that the newly independent nation would ratify the treaty and affirm the provisions that applied for 35 years prior to independence.

The Pacific Island nations, DPRK and South Sudan have not expressed any formal opposition to ICERD or its provisions. The situation changes in

Southeast Asia, where such opposition has been voiced. In Malaysia, there were widespread demonstrations following an announcement before the UNGA that the government would 'ratify all remaining core UN instruments related to the protection of human rights', including ICERD (Tew 2020: 218). The announcement was made in September 2018, then retracted in November 2018, but the demonstrations went ahead as a 'celebration' of the retraction in December 2018. This remains the only global example of a specific anti-ICERD demonstration. The opposition centred on Articles 1(4) and 2(2), the provisions governing special measures or affirmative action (Sendut 2018). While ICERD allows for such measures under Article 1(4), the provision reads also that these cannot lead to 'the maintenance of separate rights for different racial groups and … shall not be continued after the objectives for which they were taken have been achieved'. Opponents of ICERD ratification in Malaysia argue that this clause is incompatible with Article 153 of the Federal Constitution of Malaysia 1957, which enshrines the 'special position of the Malays and natives of any of the states of Sabah and Sarawak'. The perception was that Malaysia's ratification of ICERD would warrant either the immediate repeal of Article 153, or set an expiry date on the special position of these groups. However, this position is not accurate. Article 153 appears to be compatible with Articles 1(4) and 2(2) ICERD, which allows for special measures for certain groups (Sendut 2018). A CERD member visiting Malaysia at the time described the controversy as a 'misunderstanding' (Pillai 2018).

In June 2021, a comprehensive report was published by Professor Datuk Dr Denison Jayasooria with the assistance of the UN in Malaysia, on the question of understanding ICERD in the context of the Federal Constitution, human rights and Malaysian society (Jayasooria 2021). Importantly, the report noted the examples of the United States, India and South Africa, all of which have ratified ICERD while implementing affirmative action policies of varying forms for Convention groups. The South African example was considered particularly salient since, like Malaysia, it involved such measures in favour of an historically disadvantaged majority, rather than a minority. The report affirmed that '[t]he South African Government and CERD do not see the South African special measures for the majority of the Black community as discriminatory, and CERD is not pressuring South Africa to repeal these special measures' (Jayasooria 2021: 60). The report concluded that it is necessary for the national political leadership to review ICERD ratification, consult all parties concerned and explore the evidence in an open and objective way (Jayasooria 2021: 61).

Myanmar, like Malaysia, participated in the drafting process for ICERD. In 1965, in the Third Committee, U Myat Thun (Burma) stated: 'Burma, with its centuries-old tradition of religious, cultural and social tolerance, was opposed to all forms of racial discrimination anywhere' (UNGA 1963: para. 38). Burma voted on many other provisions of the draft treaty, but it clearly did not consider it to be of relevance to its own domestic minority groups. On 15 December 1965, when the Third Committee unanimously adopted the text of the draft ICERD, U Vum Ko Hau (Burma) stated: 'his delegation wished, on the occasion of the unanimous adoption of the draft Convention, to reaffirm that racial prejudice and national and religious intolerance were, by tradition, non-existent in Burma' (UNGA 1965 SR.1374: para. 46). This was not an unusual position, with many other States seeing the draft treaty in a similar light— as an internationalist statement that did not have internal relevance. As Lady Gaitskell (United Kingdom) commented at the same meeting: 'to judge from the [Third] Committee's discussions, the world suffered greatly from racial discrimination, but no particular country seemed to have it' (UNGA 1965 SR.1374: para. 61). On 21 December 1965, when ICERD was adopted by the General Assembly sitting in plenary by 106 votes to none, Burma was among the States voting in favour (UNGA 1965 PV.1406: para. 60).

Today's Myanmar is a state 'where multi-National races collectively reside', according to Article 3 of its 2008 Constitution. The military regime has constructed eight major ethnic groups, broken down further into 135 'national races'. Although widely cited, the latter number has never been formally announced or explained (Cheesman 2017: 8). What is apparent is that the number is arbitrary and does not correspond to 135 identified national races, but is considered instead to be the number that naturally exist, some of which are yet to be recognised. Importantly, 'national race' membership has become the key criterion for membership in the country's political community (Cheesman 2017: 1). It defines those who 'belong' in Myanmar; all others, including the Rohingya, regardless of how many generations they have lived in Myanmar, are considered outsiders or immigrants. In September 2018, the Human Rights Council published the report of its Independent International Fact-Finding Mission on Myanmar (IIFFMM 2018), accusing Myanmar of 'the gravest crimes under international law', and recommending that named senior generals of the Myanmar military be investigated and prosecuted in an international criminal tribunal for genocide, crimes against humanity and war crimes (IIFFMM 2018: para. 100). The lack of 'national race' status of the Rohingya dramatically increased their vulnerability, which contributed to the extreme scale and intensity of the violence that has resulted against them (IIFFMM 2018: para. 81).

The Fact-Finding Mission proposes an accountability process that is transformative, victim-centred, comprehensive and inclusive. The process is aimed at contributing to three fundamental shifts: breaking the climate of impunity; ensuring that all State institutions, including the security forces, are answerable to the people; and promoting a concept of the State and the nation of Myanmar that is inclusive, based on equality and respect for the human rights of all (IIFFMM 2018: para. 99). The first two 'fundamental shifts' are to some extent in motion. Three weeks after the Mission report, the Prosecutor of the International Criminal Court (ICC) launched preliminary investigations into the alleged deportation of 70,000 Rohingya Muslims from Myanmar to Bangladesh as a possible crime against humanity (ICC Pre-Trial Chamber I, 2018). In 2019, The Gambia instituted proceedings before the ICJ alleging violations of the Convention on the Prevention and Punishment of the Crime of Genocide (the 'Genocide Convention') through 'acts adopted, taken and condoned by the Government of Myanmar against members of the Rohingya group' (*The Gambia v. Myanmar*, 2019), which has progressed to the merits phase. It is difficult to gauge at this point whether these mechanisms will be successful, but their initiation is a step towards combatting impunity.

The third is a longer-term fundamental shift aimed at addressing the 'root causes' of Myanmar's recurrent problems. It recognises that gross human rights violations and abuses committed in Kachin, Rakhine and Shan states 'stem from deep fractures in society and structural problems that have been apparent and unaddressed for decades … reflective of the situation in Myanmar as a whole' (IIFFMM 2018: para. 100). Pederson argues that while mechanisms of international justice play an important role, 'little attention is paid to the causes of the crimes or identifying sustainable solutions' (Pedersen 2019: 13). The best long-term hope lies 'within a reformed state committed to democratic values and a broader, more tolerant and inclusive sense of ethnicity' (ibid.: 12). It is noteworthy that the two international human rights treaties that would support such a longer-term reform, ICERD in terms of ethnic, minority and indigenous peoples' rights, and the ICCPR in terms of civil and political rights, have not been ratified by Myanmar.

3. Individual Communications

The individual communications system under ICERD is optional, as it is under all of the UN human rights treaties. Under Article 14(1):

> A State Party may at any time declare that it recognizes the competence of the Committee to receive and consider communications from individuals or groups of individuals within its jurisdiction claiming to be victims of a violation by that State Party of any of the rights set forth in this Convention.

The emergence of an individual communications system was an innovation in ICERD as the first UN human rights treaty. ICERD would draw on the ECHR as a template for its provision on individual communications. The right of individual petition under ex-Article 25 ECHR was optional at the time, so that Schwelb would comment in a 1966 piece that 'the optional character is a common feature of the two instruments' (Schwelb 1966: 1042). The differences between the instruments was also recognised at the drafting stage. Lowrey (Australia) pointed out that the ECHR was a regional instrument relating to a group of relatively homogenous countries, while the draft ICERD was universal with a much wider field of application, meaning the Third Committee 'was entering a field where it must walk warily' (UNGA 1965 SR.1357: para. 3).

Capotorti (Italy) by contrast emphasised the cautious nature of the ICERD provision in its use of the word 'communication', and that it was 'in no way comparable' to the ECHR which could refer a case to the European Court of Human Rights (UNGA 1965 SR.1357: para. 30). Nevertheless, as Combal (France) summarised, the right of individual petition 'was a familiar concept, but it had never been recognised in a universally applicable international text' (UNGA 1965 SR.1357: para. 22).

There remains a gap between the regional and international human rights systems in terms of the compulsory character of individual communications. The Inter-American Commission on Human Rights has an automatic right to hear individual petitions under the American Convention on Human Rights 1969 (Shelton 2015). The African Commission on Human Rights has an automatic right of individual petition under the African Charter on Human and Peoples Rights (Gumedze 2003). Access to the regional human rights courts under the Inter-American and African systems is, however, more restricted (Vargas 1983–4; de Silva 2019). Protocol No 11 (1998) of the ECHR grants compulsory jurisdiction of the European Court of Human Rights over individual applications or cases. Hence, all three regional human rights systems provide a means of automatic access for individuals to a regional human rights body.

At the international level, while all the UN human rights treaties have an individual communications system, it remains optional, and not all States Parties to the treaties have ratified the relevant optional article or protocol. Smith points out the important fact that 'the world's most populous countries, China, India, Indonesia and the United States of America generally do not accept individual communication mechanisms for treaties to which they are party' (Smith 2015: 184). The failure of States Parties to opt in to the individual communications system is particularly pronounced under ICERD. To date, 59 States Parties have made the requisite declaration under Article 14, a notably low number given the treaty dates from 1965 and has always had the procedure (Thornberry 2016: 69). The absence of the world's most populous countries means an international individual remedy for racial discrimination is not available to the majority of the world's population. Unlike ICERD itself, Article 14 cannot be considered properly global in effect, although there is potential for it to become so. Thornberry writes of 'heart-searching' on the part of the Committee as to why more States Parties have not opted in, believing that '[p]art of the answer may lie in the unpalatability of a finding of racial discrimination' (Thornberry 2016: 69). Recommendations from the Committee to States Parties to accept the procedure appear to have had limited effect (ibid.: 56). Thornberry also points out that of the 59 States Parties that have made the declaration, communications have emanated from fewer than a quarter of these. The total of CERD individual communications remains about 60.

There are clearly wider issues with the individual communications system under the UN human rights treaties. Only the Human Rights Committee under the ICCPR has a substantive jurisprudence, receiving thousands of individual complaints (Gerber & Gory 2014: 405). The figures then drop significantly for the other UN treaty bodies. This is partly explained for some treaties by the delay in having such a procedure in the first place, for instance, ICESCR, CEDAW and the CRC were drafted without an individual communications procedure, and adopted a relevant protocol decades later. But this does not explain the low take-up under ICERD and other treaties. It is apparent that individual communications 'are not especially popular with States, or even individual complainants' (Smith 2015: 178). A 2018 *Universal Rights Group* (URG) report found that 34% of States that have accepted one or more communications procedure have *never* been the subject of an individual complaint, with the majority of these from Africa and Asia. The report found in its year of review that 19% of all treaty body petition cases concluded were from just one state: Denmark (URG 2018: 22). UN treaty bodies may also lack capacity to deal with large numbers of individual communications, should these arise—to a certain extent they rely on an under-used system. These weaknesses are well known, with a number of initiatives proposed for strengthening the UN treaty body system. A 2006 concept paper from then High Commissioner Louise Arbour setting out a 'unified standing treaty body' proved divisive, and is no longer being pursued (UN High Commissioner 2006; O'Flaherty and O'Brien 2007). While treaty body strengthening will continue, we may assume that this will not involve dissolving the treaty bodies into a single body or any other reform that would require amendment of treaty provisions. In that sense, an optional individual communications system under each UN human rights treaty will remain.

There are therefore a number of weaknesses to be addressed that apply to CERD, as well as the other UN treaty bodies, including: (i) the low rate of acceptance by States Parties; (ii) the low rate of take-up of the mechanism by individuals (and groups) in States which have made the requisite declaration or ratification; (iii) State Party compliance with recommendations in individual communications; and (iv) greater treaty body capacity to examine individual communications. For CERD, the starting point must be the low number of States Parties to the Article 14 declaration. It could launch a 'thematic discussion' to explore the reasons behind States Parties' reluctance to recognise the competence of the Committee to receive individual communications. However, the Committee may be hesitant to do this. As one CERD member put it in the context of the ratification controversy in Malaysia, '[i]t would be difficult to promote ICERD to a non-signatory state … It would backfire, and seem as though the UN is imposing something (forcefully)' (Pillai 2018). The same considerations may be seen to apply *mutatis mutandis* to States Parties and Article 14. Hence, CERD may wish to restrict itself to encouraging States to opt in under Article 14 in the reporting process, but may not wish to take further steps in that regard.

The Committee could also consider a general recommendation on Article 14 that encourages each State Party to make the declaration under Article 14 in its preamble, stressing the importance of the individual remedy to the object and purpose of the treaty. It could then set out how States Parties that have made the declaration may ensure individuals and groups are aware of, and have access to, the remedy. It could reflect on the status of its recommendations in individual communications, and their effective implementation. There is a model for such an initiative in the Human Rights Committee's General Comment 33 (2008) on the obligations of States Parties under the Optional Protocol to the ICCPR (CCPR 2008). The General Comment notes in the context of the ICCPR that a majority of States Parties have become a party to the Protocol, which is 'organically related to the Covenant' (CCPR 2008: para. 2). It continues:

> while the function of the Human Rights Committee in considering individual communications is not, as such, that of a judicial body, the views issued by the Committee under the Optional Protocol exhibit some important characteristics of a judicial decision. They are arrived at in a judicial spirit, including the impartiality and independence of Committee members, the considered interpretation of the language of the Covenant, and the determinative character of the decisions. (CCPR 2008: para. 11)

At present, Article 14 individual communications have not been a relative success under ICERD, and heart-searching on the part of the Committee is perhaps not enough given the essential role individual communications can play in the elimination of racial discrimination. The absence of a clear majority of ICERD States Parties from Article 14, including all of its most populous States, is undermining the global ethic of the treaty.

4. A Thematic Exploration of CERD Mechanisms: 'Black Lives Matter'

The issuance of concluding observations in response to State reports is arguably the 'single most important activity of human rights treaty bodies' (O'Flaherty 2006: 29). In that light, CERD's examination of State reports under Article 9 'remains the centrepiece of its work' (Thornberry 2016: 45). General recommendations, of which there are currently 36, are directed at all States Parties and are often issued as a response to themes or patterns that arise in the State reporting procedure. From 1993, CERD has also adopted early warning measures and urgent procedures as part of its regular agenda (CERD 1993 and 2007). These are not optional and may be issued in relation to any State Party. In addition, these are not tied to the reporting cycle and can be issued at any time. They are aimed at preventing existing situations escalating into conflicts, and to respond to problems requiring immediate attention to prevent or limit the scale or number of serious violations of the Convention.

In 2020, 'Black Lives Matter' further underlined the significance of the treaty's object and purpose and the importance of CERD's mandate. In June 2020, an 'urgent debate' in the Human Rights Council discussed 'racially inspired human rights violations, systemic racism, police brutality and violence against peaceful protests' (OHCHR 2020). We may consider the extent to which CERD has understood and responded to information and patterns of police brutality in the United States. The United States signed ICERD in 1966 but did not ratify until 21 October 1994. It submitted its first report in 2001, when CERD also adopted its first concluding observations. These read in an early passage: 'The Committee notes with concern the incidents of police violence and brutality, including cases of deaths as a result of excessive use of force by law enforcement officials, which particularly affect minority groups' (CERD 2001b: para. 394). At the next reporting cycle in 2008, CERD found:

> While recognising the efforts made by the State Party to combat the pervasive phenomenon of police brutality, the Committee remains concerned about allegations of brutality and use of excessive or deadly force by law enforcement officials against persons belonging to racial, ethnic or national minorities, in particular Latino and African American persons and undocumented migrants crossing the US-Mexico border. (CERD 2008: para. 25)

It recommended that 'the State Party increase significantly its efforts to eliminate police brutality and excessive use of force against persons belonging to racial, ethnic or national minorities' (ibid.). In its most recent concluding observations, issued in 2014, the Committee again 'reiterates its previous concern at the brutality and excessive use of force by law enforcement officials against members of racial and ethnic minorities' (CERD 2014: para. 17).

Importantly, CERD has intervened twice in relation to the United States under its early warning measures and urgent procedures. In 2017, it issued a Decision 'recalling the horrific events in Charlottesville of 11–12 August 2017 leading to the death of Ms. Heather Heyer', as well as expressing alarm at 'racist demonstrations, with overtly racist slogans, chants and salutes by individuals belonging to groups of white nationalists, neo-Nazis, and the Ku Klux Klan, promoting white supremacy and inciting racial discrimination and hatred' (CERD 2017). The Decision recalled its previous concluding observations and called on the United States to fully respect its international obligations arising from ICERD. In June 2020, it issued a Statement in which it expressed alarm at 'the horrific killing of George Floyd in Minneapolis on 25 May 2020', as well as 'the recurrence of killings of unarmed African Americans by police officers and individuals over the years' (CERD 2020a). In the Statement, CERD remains 'convinced that systemic and structural discrimination permeates State institutions and disproportionately promotes racial disparities against African Americans', as well as 'noting the announcement of police reforms by the local authorities in Minneapolis, as well as similar announcements by other local governments to redirect policing budget to social services' (CERD 2020a). The Statement again calls on the United States to fully respect its international obligations arising from ICERD. It urges the Government of the United States 'to publicly recognize the existence of structural racial discrimination in the society, as well as to unequivocally and unconditionally reject and condemn racially motivated killings of African Americans and other minorities' (CERD 2020a).

In 2001, CERD issued General Recommendation 31 on the prevention of racial discrimination in the administration and functioning of the criminal justice system, applicable to all States Parties. It read:

> States Parties should pay the greatest attention to the following possible indicators of racial discrimination: The number and percentage of persons belonging to the groups referred to in the last paragraph of the preamble who are victims of aggression or other offences, especially when they are committed by police officers. (CERD 2001a: para. 1(a))

In November 2020, CERD issued its most recent GR 36 on preventing and combatting racial profiling by law enforcement officials (CERD 2020b). The initial draft of GR 36, circulated for comments by States Parties, civil society and others, referred only to preventing and combating racial profiling, to which 'by law enforcement officials' was subsequently added (Keane 2020). GR 36 refers to CERD's 'extensive practice in combatting racial profiling by law enforcement officials', noting how racial profiling 'has been a historic feature of policing in countries such as the US and Brazil' (CERD 2020: para. 4). It is the first general recommendation or comment to put law enforcement officials in its title, marking a specific focus by a human rights body on the police. In the initial draft of GR 36, Section D was called 'Dialogue with Communities'. In their observations on the draft, the Group of Independent Eminent Experts on the Implementation of the Durban Declaration and Programme of Action suggested renaming it to 'Community Policing'. This is a subtle change, but one that captures the idea that policing should not be a two-way interaction but rather controlled by the people that are policed (Keane 2020).

In sum, CERD has long signalled its deep concern with the issues raised by 'Black Lives Matter' in the United States. All three of its concluding observations to the United States from 2001 onwards express condemnation of police killings in relation to racial and ethnic minorities in the strongest terms, referring also in all three to 'police brutality'. In addition, it has deployed its early warning measures and urgent action procedures twice against the United States, following events in Charlottesville in 2017 and then Minneapolis in 2020. These operate outside the reporting schedule and signal the Committee's deep concern. As noted, the United States has not made the relevant declaration under Article 14, and no individual communication may be taken against the United States in relation to police killings. An inter-State communication under Articles 11–13 is possible, and one United States commentator has suggested just such an action (Ukabiala 2020). However, the difficulty lies in finding a State Party willing to do this. The absence of a contentious jurisdiction for individuals and groups under ICERD in most States Parties remains the treaty's biggest accountability gap.

CERD's recommendations relevant to the issues touched on by 'Black Lives Matter' are prescient and significant. They also highlight the weaknesses of the UN treaty body system—despite repeated expressions of concern, there is little indication of specific action on the part of the United States in response to CERD's recommendations. Concluding observations give support and strength to domestic and international NGOs and civil society that may battle the injustices of police brutality and killings. CERD provides a voice for this struggle at the UN and communicates directly to the State Party that such practices are a violation of international human rights standards and its obligations under the treaty. CERD's recommendations in this and related areas deserve closer attention and implementation by States Parties, signalling as they do the voices of those most affected by racial discrimination.

Conclusion

ICERD is the only global treaty in the area of racial discrimination, and is of immense symbolic and legal significance. It has a strong range of mechanisms by UN standards, benefitting from its status as the first, pioneering human rights treaty. These are best considered as interlocking and mutually supportive, involving State reports, concluding observations, inter-State communications and disputes, individual communications, early warning measures and urgent action procedures. No State should be outside the protections afforded by the treaty, given that its provisions largely have a customary status. It is important that it moves from a global treaty with 182 States Parties, to a universal treaty, which may require a greater focus on the small number of States that have yet to ratify. For example, Myanmar's absence from the treaty means a gap in international knowledge of patterns of racial discrimination that may contribute to the gross violations of group rights that have occurred there. Similarly, the low number of States Parties that accept an individual's right to communicate to CERD under Article 14 is out of sync with a contemporary world that increasingly understands the urgency felt by individuals and groups to eliminate racial discrimination. Individual communications provide examples of how a failure to implement treaty provisions is lived by individuals and groups. The majority of States Parties in their absence from the Article 14 procedure are undermining the global ethic of the elimination of racial discrimination.

In recent years, ICERD has gained in prominence. Inter-State cases have underlined that racial discrimination is international, between States, as well as national, within States. The national and international reaction to George Floyd's killing has emphasised the importance of ICERD's object and purpose. It is apparent that CERD has a mandate for radical change within the parameters of the treaty. Its recommendations are not always immediately effective and lack the character of a court judgment. But they also drive legislative change, ensuring an administrative focus on Convention groups as well as effective redress for violations. This is a continuous process of dialogue, decisions and recommendations, rooted in the binding provisions of the treaty. The growing voices for change from Convention groups will become increasingly difficult for States Parties to ignore. ICERD assures those voices that their calls are rooted in international legal standards, while CERD's mandate is to translate those standards into meaningful recommendations that advance towards global racial equality.

References

Bradley, C. A. (2012). Treaty Signature. In: Hollis, Duncan, B. (ed.) *The Oxford Guide to Treaties*. Oxford: Oxford University Press, pp. 208–219.

Cavalli-Sforza, L. L., Menozzi, P. and Piazza, A. (1994). *The history and geography of human genes*. New Jersey: Princeton University Press.

Cheesman, N. (2017). How in Myanmar 'national races' came to surpass citizenship and exclude Rohingya. *Journal of Contemporary Asia*, 47(3): 461–483. https://doi.org/10.1080/00472336.2017.1297476

Comas, J. (1958). *Racial myths*. Paris: UNESCO.

De Silva, N. (2019). Individual and NGO access to the African Court on Human and Peoples' Rights: The latest blow from Tanzania. *Ejil: Talk!*, 16 December. https://www.ejiltalk.org/individual-and-ngo-access-to-the -african-court-on-human-and-peoples-rights-the-latest-blow-from-tanzania/

Eiken, J. and Keane, D. (2022). Towards an amicable solution: The inter-state communications procedure under ICERD. *The Law and Practice of International Courts and Tribunals*, 21(2): 302–341.

Gerber, P. and Gory, J. (2014). The UN Human Rights Committee and LGBT rights: What is it doing? What could it be doing? *Human Rights Law Review*, 14(3): 403–439. https://doi.org/10.1093/hrlr/ngu019

Gumedze, S. (2003). Bringing Communications before the African Commission on Human and Peoples' Rights. *African Human Rights Law Journal* 3: 118–148.

International Movement Against All Forms of Discrimination and Racism (IMADR) (2011). *ICERD and CERD: A guide for civil society actors*. Geneva: IMADR.

Jayasooria, D. (2021). *Understanding ICERD in the wider context of the federal constitution, human rights and Malaysian society*. Putrajaya: United Nations in Malaysia, Singapore and Brunei Darussalam.

Keane, D. (2007). Addressing the aggravated meeting points of race and religion. *Maryland Law Journal of Race, Religion, Gender and Class*, 6: 353–391. https://digitalcommons.law.umaryland.edu/rrgc/vol6/iss2/8

Keane, D. (2020). Guidance at a critical moment – CERD general recommendation 36 on racial profiling by law enforcement officials. *Völkerrechtsblog*. https://voelkerrechtsblog.org/guidance-at-a-critical-moment-thoughts -on-the-cerds-general-recommendation-on-racial-profiling/

O'Flaherty, M. (2006). The concluding observations of United Nations Treaty Bodies. *Human Rights Law Review*, 6(1): 27–52. https://doi.org/10.1093 /hrlr/ngi037

O'Flaherty, M. and O'Brien, C. (2007). Reform of UN Human Rights Treaty monitoring bodies: A critique of the concept paper on the High Commissioner's Proposal for a Unified Standing Treaty Body. *Human Rights Law Review*, 7(1): 141–172. https://doi.org/10.1093/hrlr/ngl035

Olowu, D. (2006). The United Nations Human Rights Treaty System and the challenges of commitment and compliance in the South Pacific. *Melbourne Journal of International Law*, 7: 155–184.

Pedersen, M. B. (2019). The ICC, the Rohingya and the limitations of retributive justice. *Australian Journal of International Affairs*, 73(1): 9–15. https:// doi.org/10.1080/10357718.2018.1548562

Pillai, V. (2018). UN man dumbfounded by Malaysia's resistance to ICERD. *Free Malaysia Today*, 26 December. https://www.freemalaysiatoday.com/category /nation/2018/12/26/un-man-dumbfounded-by-malaysias-resistance-to-icerd/

Schabas, W. (2017). Genocide and the ICERD. In: Keane, D. and Waughray, A. (eds.) *Fifty Years of the International Convention on the Elimination of All Forms of Racial Discrimination: A Living Instrument*. Manchester: Manchester University Press.

Schabas, W. (2019). *U.N. International Covenant on Civil and Political Rights: Nowak's CCPR commentary*. Kehl: N. P. Engle.

Schwelb, E. (1966). The International Convention on the Elimination of All Forms of Racial Discrimination. *International and Comparative Law Quarterly*, 15: 996–1068.

Schwelb, E. (1968). Civil and political rights: The international measures of implementation. *American Journal of International Law*, 62: 827–868.

Sendut, J. H. (2018). Malaysia and the ICERD: Closer to home than you'd think. *Medium*, 11 November. https://medium.com/@jhs_/malaysia-and-the-icerd -closer-to-home-than-youd-think-6afd97ab68cc

Shelton, D. (2015). The rules and the reality of petition procedures in the Inter-American Human Rights System. *Notre Dame Journal of International and Comparative Law*, 5(1): 1–28. https://scholarship.law.nd.edu/ndjicl/vol5/iss1/2

Smith, R. (2015). The Third Optional Protocol to the UN Convention on the Rights of the Child? – Challenges arising transforming the rhetoric into reality. In: Freeman, M. (ed.) *The future of children's rights*. Leiden: Brill.

Tew, Y. (2020). *Constitutional statecraft in Asian courts*. Oxford: Oxford University Press.

Thant, U. (1978). *View from the UN*. New York: Doubleday.

Thornberry, P. (2016). *The International Convention on the Elimination of All Forms of Racial Discrimination: A commentary*. Oxford: Oxford University Press.

Thornberry, P. (2017) Preface. In: Keane, D. and Waughray, A. (eds.) *Fifty years of the International Convention on the Elimination of All Forms of Racial Discrimination: A living instrument*. Manchester: Manchester University Press, pp. xiv–xix.

Ukabiala, N. (2020). *How inter-state procedures in human rights treaties can support the Black Lives Matter movement*. New York: Just Security.

Universal Rights Group (URG) (2018). *Reform of the UN Petitions System: An assessment of the UN Human Rights communications procedures and proposals for a single integrated system*. Geneva: URG.

Vargas, M. D. (1983-4). Individual access to the Inter-American Court of Human Rights. *New York University Journal of International Law and Politics*, 16: 601–617.

UN/Legal Documents

Application of the Convention on the Prevention and Punishment of the Crime of Genocide (*The Gambia v. Myanmar*). (2019).

Charter of the United Nations (1945). 1 UNTS XVI.

Committee on the Elimination of Racial Discrimination (CERD) (1987). *Report of the Committee of the Elimination of Racial Discrimination (CERD) A/42/18*.

Committee on the Elimination of Racial Discrimination (CERD) (1993). *Prevention of racial discrimination, including early warning and urgent procedures: Working paper adopted by the Committee on the Elimination of Racial Discrimination. A/48/18*.

Committee on the Elimination of Racial Discrimination (CERD) (2001a). *General recommendation 31 on the prevention of racial discrimination in the administration and functioning of the criminal justice system. A/60/18*.

Committee on the Elimination of Racial Discrimination (CERD) (2001b). *Concluding observations – United States of America. A/56/18*.

Committee on the Elimination of Racial Discrimination (CERD) (2007). *Guidelines for the early warning and urgent action procedure. A/62/18*.

Committee on the Elimination of Racial Discrimination (CERD) (2008). *Concluding observations – United States of America. CERD/C/USA/CO/6*.

Committee on the Elimination of Racial Discrimination (CERD) (2014). *Concluding observations – United States of America. CERD/C/USA/CO/7-9*.

Committee on the Elimination of Racial Discrimination (CERD) (2017). *Decision 1 (93) United States of America*.

Committee on the Elimination of Racial Discrimination (CERD) (2020a). *Statement 1 United States of America*.

Committee on the Elimination of Racial Discrimination (CERD) (2020b). *General recommendation 36 on racial profiling by law enforcement officials.* CERD/C/GC/36.

Constitution of the Republic of the Union of Myanmar (2008). Nay Pyi Taw: Ministry of Information.

Human Rights Committee (CCPR) (2008). *General comment 33 on the obligations of states parties under the optional protocol to the ICCPR. CCPR/C/GC/33.*

International Criminal Court (ICC) Pre-Trial Chamber I (2018). *Decision on the Prosecution's request for a ruling on jurisdiction under Article 19(3) of the statute. ICC-RoC46(3)-01/18-37.*

UN Economic and Social Council (1954). *Draft international covenants on human rights. E/2573 Annex I.*

UN General Assembly (UNGA) (1946). *Persecution and discrimination. GA res. 103 (I).*

UN General Assembly (UNGA) (1948). *Universal Declaration of Human Rights. GA res. 217 A (III).*

UN General Assembly (UNGA) (1963). *Summary records of the Third Committee of the General Assembly. A/C.3/SR.1217.*

UN General Assembly (UNGA) (1965). *Summary records of the Third Committee of the General Assembly. A/C.3/SR.1357.*

UN General Assembly (UNGA) (1965). *Summary records of the Third Committee of the General Assembly. A/C.3/SR.1374.*

UN General Assembly (UNGA) (1965). *Verbatim records of the United Nations General Assembly. UN Doc. A/PV.1406.*

UN General Assembly (UNGA) (1966). *International Convention on the Elimination of All Forms of Racial Discrimination. 660 UNTS 195.*

UN High Commissioner for Human Rights (2006). *Concept paper on the High Commissioner's proposal for a unified standing treaty body. HRI/MC/2006/2.*

UN Human Rights Council (HRC) (2018). *Report of the Independent International Fact-finding Mission on Myanmar (IIFFMM) and Report of the detailed findings of the IIFFMM. A/HRC/39/64 and A/HRC/39/CRP.2.*

UN Human Rights Council (HRC) (2020). *Report of the Special Rapporteur on the situation of human rights in the Democratic People's Republic of Korea. A/HRC/43/58.*

UN Office of the High Commissioner for Human Rights (OHCHR) (n.d.). *Treaty body strengthening.* Geneva: OHCHR. https://www.ohchr.org/en/treaty-bodies /treaty-body-strengthening

UN Office of the High Commissioner for Human Rights (OHCHR) (2020). *Child rights in the Pacific: UN body concludes historic session in Samoa.* Geneva: OHCHR.

UN Office of the High Commissioner for Human Rights (OHCHR) (2020). *Human Rights Council holds an urgent debate on current racially inspired human rights violations.*

CHAPTER 3

Averting Terror Funds: New Grounds for Racial Discrimination?

Georgia Vasileiadou

Introduction: Penalising the Financing of Terrorism

As defined by the International Convention for the Suppression of the Financing of Terrorism (1999), terrorist financing constitutes an offence committed by a person who:

> ... by any means, directly or indirectly, unlawfully and wilfully, provides or collects funds with the intention that they should be used or in the knowledge that they are to be used, in full or in part, in order to carry out an act [of terrorism] (Article 2, para. 1)

Enforcers and investigators of terrorist incidents, such as J. Roth et al. (n.d.), have found that contemporary terrorist attacks require relatively insignificant sums of money. This has changed the concept of terrorism as a phenomenon, and during the last two decades legislation has been focused on everyday financial transactions which has been found to predominantly fund terrorism.

The whole idea of criminalising the financing of terrorism is based on the widespread idea of preventing all economic crimes that could endanger the integrity of financial markets, national security and social development.

How to cite this book chapter:
Vasileiadou, G. 2024. Averting Terror Funds: New Grounds for Racial Discrimination? In: Whyte, A., Tuitt, P. and Bourne, J. (eds.) *The Long Walk to Equality: Perspectives on Racial Inequality, Injustice and the Law*. Pp. 33–54. London: University of Westminster Press. DOI: https://doi.org/10.16997/book63.c. License: CC-BY-NC-ND 4.0

Effective prevention depends on financial intelligence (McCulloch & Carlton 2006: 403), thus classical financial principles, such as data confidentiality and the fiduciary duty, are no longer applied to this fight. Furthermore, measures taken to fight terrorist financing branch off into obligations imposed by the General Data Protection Regulation (GDPR) 2016/679. It is generally accepted that finances could be misused for terrorist purposes, if there is no control, or no adequate control, of the customers of financial institutions and their transactions.

The fight against terrorist financing establishes a duty to secure national safety and state sovereignty. This duty, although traditionally executed by the State and its official bodies, has been transferred to the private sector and especially to financial services providers, despite the fact that the aim of ensuring national security seems incompatible with the lucrative purposes of the latter. As highlighted by scholars such as Mugarura (2015), financial institutions are transforming into a kind of economic police force (ibid.: 352) which controls customers, rejects those who seem 'suspicious' and blocks transactions which could put an institution's reputation[1] and economic status[2] at stake. The whole structure of the system set to prevent terrorist financing turns out to be extremely vulnerable to discriminatory practices (McCulloch & Carlton 2006: 405). In this sense, the classic rhetoric on how terrorism threatens peace, security and the Rule of Law meets the other side of the coin: how counterterrorism becomes the vehicle of legalising restrictions to fundamental human rights recognised and protected in most developed countries.

With special focus on the UK, this chapter seeks to investigate the implicit impact of the European counterterrorist policy on human rights, based on the structure and philosophy of the preventive system applied in the private sector. Firstly, it is argued that financial institutions have been assigned a duty to monitor closely and effectively the money transferred through their channels, with the support and supervision of competent national authorities. Secondly, several cases are analysed to demonstrate how the policy on countering the financing of terrorism may in practice give rise to discrimination against specific ethnicities or religions. Finally, the chapter concludes with recommendations for achieving a better balance between these two essential purposes: the prevention of terrorist financing and most importantly for this volume, the elimination of discrimination in the financial sector.

---

[1] Often, supervisory authorities publish their decisions on an institution's failure to comply with CFT obligations. See e.g., Financial Conduct Authority. (2017). Final Notice on Deutsche Bank AG, point 7.5.

[2] The most common penalty for not complying with CFT obligations is the payment of heavy fines. See, e.g., Canara Bank and Sonali Bank (UK) Ltd were fined £896,100 by the FCA in June 2018 for breaching Principle 3 of the FCA's Principles for Businesses (taking reasonable steps to organise its affairs responsibly and effectively, with adequate risk management systems).

Legal and Ethical Duties on Financial Institutions

National, international (FATF[3] 2012–2022) and European (Directive 2015/849 as amended) regulations illustrate in general the obligations of financial institutions concerning the prevention of terrorist financing. So, each institution must put into force the most appropriate measures in regard to the nature of its services, the size of its business, the extent of its activities and any other specific characteristics. All these measures and internal policies adopted by each operator are regularly examined in situ and surveyed by the relevant national authorities[4] through obligatory reports submitted by every responsible entity as identified by the applicable national law. Competent national authorities can either make recommendations for possible ameliorations of the terrorist-tracking system in place or impose high fines and administrative penalties in order to sanction the business for failing to conform to its legal obligations. In the author's opinion, this system constitutes a particular form of Corporate Social Responsibility (hereinafter CSR), given that the nature and number of measures and policies to fight possible financing of terrorism (i.e., internal conduct codes) are chosen freely by each obliged entity (Joint Committee 2017: 24) and are usually coordinated by their CSR managers. Traditionally, CSR is linked to voluntary initiatives taken with the discretionary power of commercial enterprises, in order to contribute to the welfare of the society in which they conduct their business. However, in principle there are no mechanisms of judicial oversight to control the respect of these obligations and their effective application. By contrast, in the case of measures and policies to counter the financing of terrorism (hereinafter CFT), it is the law that dictates their general adoption and demands that these measures and policies prove able to fulfil their ultimate purpose. It follows that financial institutions have to fight terrorism in any way they deem to be effective and appropriate. If this legal obligation is not thoroughly respected, it can lead to sanction of the institution in question. In the case of CSR initiatives, however, the liability of a company for not respecting its own engagements can only be sanctioned indirectly and through complicated court cases, if it is first proven that the company's failure to provide appropriate measures resulted in consumers being hurt.

In Europe, member States are supposed to '*monitor effectively*' the compliance of financial institutions in their legal duty of preventing terrorist financing (EU Directive 2015/849, article 48(1)). This control covers the whole process of adopting CFT measures until their effective application in practice. Neither the EU Directive 2015/849 nor UK law determines the regularity of the evoked

---

[3] The Financial Action Task Force (FATF) is an intergovernmental policy-making organisation which issues non-binding recommendations on money laundering and terrorist financing, conducts research and monitors the level of security in all countries.

[4] In the UK, this duty is upon the Financial Conduct Authority (FCA).

control. However, the phrase '*monitor effectively*' implies regularity of examination that will permit national bodies to have an actualised knowledge of the CFT policies used by each institution under their authority. As discussed below, in case of insufficient or inadequate measures applied by the obliged entities, national authorities are competent to order immediately financial and non-financial penalties with serious consequences for the implicated institutions.

Menace of Severe Penalties for Insufficient CFT Measures

National legislation provides for a varied number and type of sanction. In the UK and USA, for example, financial institutions can be found liable for civil and penal[5] infractions for failing to comply with their CFT obligations. For instance, the Financial Conduct Agency (FCA), which is the competent authority in the UK, has ordered several substantive financial penalties, such as a fine of £896,100 imposed on Canara Bank for having failed to establish and design adequate internal systems and controls of risk assessment (2015). Moreover, the FCA temporarily prohibited the Bank of Beirut from offering any services aimed at acquiring new customers who 'were residents or incorporated in "high risk jurisdictions"' (Artingstall et al. 2016: 17).

The problem of establishing efficient and up to date CFT systems is even more complicated for European financial institutions with branches or affiliates in the USA, and since Brexit, in the UK as well.[6] They face a greater risk of being punished twice, i.e., once in each country or once only in the USA. In the USA, sanctions include even higher fines or bans from executing dollar transactions, thus bans from the international market, given that the dollar is the common currency in international trade (McCulloch & Carlton 2006: 405; Wolosky & Heifetz 2002: 2). Such was the case of the British bank, Barclays Bank Plc which, in 2016, was found liable under US law and ordered to pay a fine of $2,485,890 (approximately £1,976,618) to the American Office of Foreign Assets Control (OFAC 2016). Another British bank, HSBC, faced a similar situation in 2012: after a settlement with the US authority and the US Department of Justice, it agreed to pay a fine of $1.9 billion (approximately £7,286,767,841.08)[7] and since then stopped paying out remittances at its Mexican branches (Corkery 2014). It is obvious that these penalties harmed the bank's fortune and endangered its global reputation as 'the world's local bank' (Slater & Scuffham 2013; Durner & Shetret 2015: 11). Consequently, HSBC's long-term profitability could be put at risk. In the harsh world of business,

---

[5] In most European countries, sanctions against moral persons can only be administrative or civil.

[6] After Brexit, the UK is free to impose its own sanctions and freeze assets at a lower threshold than that of the EU.

[7] The penalty was equal to 11% of the bank's profit the previous year (Tangel 2012).

reputation plays an important role in a business's development and affects its principal aim of profitability. As will be demonstrated below, this factor appears to make financial institutions extremely cautious when dealing with certain groups of people and their transactions.

The Abstract Concept of the Risk-Based Approach in Implementing Counterterrorist Policies

The measures that financial institutions must adopt are summarised by two main obligations: customer due diligence (or the 'know your customer' obligation) and the reporting of 'suspicious' transactions. The first obligation means that financial institutions should regularly verify the identity, home and professional addresses, employment details, as well as the family and legal status of all their existing and future customers to ensure that the latter have no connections to blocked countries or entities[8] in order to establish their overall profile, which must be kept current (FATF 2012–2022: 72). This profiling method serves to effectively monitor customers, allowing the punctual ascertainment of transactions that do not seem to fit the customer's financial behaviour and economic status, thus raising suspicions of criminal activity (FATF 2002). The second requirement follows on from the due diligence obligation. Consequently, once a transaction is found to be suspicious by the obliged entity, it must refrain from executing it and must immediately disclose that transaction to the competent authority[9] for further examination and permission regarding whether or not to proceed with the transaction.[10] In practice, this means that a transaction characterised as 'suspicious', founded on the risk-based approach elaborated by each financial operator and on a de-risking method, could be suspended for a very long time or for an indefinite period.[11] The risk-based approach is the method of assessing the potential terrorist financing risk of each operation before its execution.[12] However, the de-risking strategy,

---

[8] These lists include the names of individuals, companies and associations sentenced by national jurisdictions or with connections to countries excluded from the EU market or for whom there is a number of indications for their exclusion from the financial market.

[9] This obligation is known as 'Suspicious Activity Report' (SAR).

[10] In the UK this authority is the Serious Organised Crime Agency (SOCA).

[11] See case: *Shah and another v HSBC Private Bank (UK) Ltd* [2012] EWHC 1283 (QB), in which HSBC was found not liable for the economic damage suffered by its customer due to a SAR she executed delaying the execution of the transaction demanded by the claimant. The Court considered that the bank acted according to the legal framework of its anti-money laundering (AML) and CFT obligations.

[12] This assessment is being made mostly in an automated way through special software. Based on the customers' personal, professional and financial information collected by financial institutions, this software has the ability to categorise each transaction

which is adopted by most financial institutions, constitutes an internal process of minimising the risks of criminal activity by de-banking certain groups of people or legal entities categorised as high risk clients (Durner & Shetret 2015: 1).

The Financial Action Task Force (hereinafter FATF), national authorities and individual states have suggested several criteria and guidelines for the assessment of risks and the categorisation of clients and transactions as at low, medium, high or very high risk of terrorism.[13] Although risk management is considered a well-developed economic practice in the financial sector, financial crime risk, as yet, cannot be calculated as accurately as credit risk. The parameters of criminal risks are not purely economic, but involve various other social, typical and atypical elements, such as a person's geographical origin, which cannot be assessed a priori as a good or bad factor.

The fluidity of notions such as 'suspicious transactions', adopted by the law, undeniably contribute to the proliferation of racial and religious discrimination. Competent authorities receive thousands of Suspicious Transactions Reports (STRs) every day.[14] This is because financial institutions are not willing to take responsibility and decide whether a transaction which may seem suspicious does indeed conceal criminal intentions. They prefer to freeze the transaction and refer the case directly to the competent authority[15] (see, for example, *R v Da Silva* [2006], *Shah v HSBC Private Bank (UK) Ltd* [2012] and *Iraj Parvizi v Barclays Bank* [2014]). What makes this situation worse is that the general criteria suggested by the national authorities and/or international institutions (such as FATF) for reporting a transaction are dangerously vague and ambiguous.[16] As a result, competent authorities cannot act promptly, despite the importance of the transaction in question to the client. This issue has been highlighted at the latest review of the UK's Anti-Money Laundering (AML)/CFT Regulations conducted by the HM Treasury (2022: 36).

Moreover, financial institutions have gained the power to determine if a person has the right to access the financial system or not on the grounds of executing their duty to protect national security and the integrity of the market. Consequently, it tends to have been accepted by market operators that the exclusion of *certain people* is necessary for achieving a high level of protection.

---

as regular or suspicious. Blocked countries, individuals and other entities are regularly added to this system as an indication of risks of criminal activity (see: FATF 2014a).

[13] See e.g., FATF 2013.

[14] The number of transactions being reported is increasing across Europe and especially in the UK. See further: Vedrennem 2019.

[15] It is worth noting that in this case UK law (subsection 4A into s. 338 of the Proceeds of Crime Act UK 2002) protects financial institutions from civil liability for breaching confidentiality duty, provided that the disclosure has been made in good faith.

[16] These criteria usually comprise a certain threshold amount above which all transactions must be reported to the competent authority and the subjective judgement of each entity based on the information it has collected. See further: Ping 2005.

According to a survey conducted by John Howell & Co. Ltd at the request of the FCA (Artingstall et al. 2016), it was found that high compliance costs oblige banks to refrain from providing services to customers who they consider able to abuse their services for terrorist purposes or for who they think they cannot apply the necessary and highly expensive monitoring controls. So, financial exclusion tends to be justified and completely lawful under anti-money laundering/combatting the financing of terrorism (AML/CFT) regulation. FATF has raised awareness about this extremely perilous situation (2014) and suggested actions to mitigate the negative repercussions of overly stringent prevention mechanisms (2017). These issues will be further analysed in the following section.

Discrimination in the Financial Sector – The Legal Framework Against Discrimination

The prohibition of discrimination constitutes the core of human rights protection law and cannot be permitted under any circumstances. The notion of discrimination appears in both international and European law. According to article 1 of the International Convention on the Elimination of All Forms of Racial Discrimination (ICERD 1999; see further Keane, Chapter 1), discrimination is defined as:

> any distinction, exclusion, restriction or preference based on race, colour, descent, or national or ethnic origin which has the purpose or effect of nullifying or impairing the recognition, enjoyment or exercise, on an equal footing, of human rights and fundamental freedoms in the political, economic, social, cultural or any other field of public life.

The fight against racial discrimination is coordinated internationally by the Committee on the Elimination of Racial Discrimination. In this context, the UN adopted a project to fight xenophobia and racial discrimination (Durban Declaration and Programme of Action 2002), as well as another more specific project aiming to fight, in particular, ethnic, religious and ideological discrimination (Rabat Plan of Action 2013).

The conflict of laws concerning anti-terrorism strategies and the protection of human rights was acknowledged by the General Assembly of the UN through its resolution 60/288 (The UN Global Counter-Terrorism Strategy 2006). In this text, the General Assembly explicitly held that anti-terrorist actions must be compatible with international law and especially with human rights law, refugee law and international humanitarian law.

At a regional level, the EU is very sensitive to matters of discrimination of any type. It has established a rigorous system of common rules for all member states relating to non-discrimination (see for example articles 18 and 45 of the TFEU, Employment Equality Directive 2000/78/EC, Racial Equality Directive

2000/43/EC, Gender Equality Directive 2006/54/EC) complemented by the powers of the European Court of Justice and the European Court of Human Rights to prevent discrimination and to punish States or individuals engaging in discriminatory acts. This system is applied in a great number of countries, each with different legal systems so is consequently considered, worldwide, as the most important system. The European Court of Human Rights plays a determinative role in the respect and the evolution of these rules. Indeed, abolishment of discrimination can be found in:

- Directive 2000/43/EC against discrimination on grounds of race and ethnic origin;
- Article 14 of the European Convention for the Protection of Human Rights and Fundamental Freedoms;
- Article 2 of the 14th Protocol attached to the Convention, in recommendation no. 8 ('Combating Racism while Fighting Terrorism') of the general policy of the Commission against Racism and Intolerance; and
- Article 21 of the Charter of Fundamental Human Rights of the European Union.

It is worth mentioning that the EU Network of Independent Experts on Fundamental Rights has raised the issue of profiling using contested criteria, such as birthplace, nationality and religion, which reproduces discriminatory beliefs (2006, 13–15, 40). Also, the European Commission against Racism and Intolerance (hereinafter ECRI)[17] recommends that Member States should ensure that national legislation and national enforcement policies secure the right to equal and non-discriminative treatment (2004: 4–5).

Background Reasons of Discrimination when Applying CFT Regulation

The Western world traditionally connects terrorism with Arabic and Muslim organisations (Corbin 2017), as it is usually considered to be religiously motivated.[18] However, religiously motivated terrorism constitutes only a small percentage of all terrorist attacks that occur worldwide. In Europe, in 2018, there were only seven completed jihadist attacks as opposed to 83 ethno-nationalist and separatist terrorist attacks (Europol Report 2019). A recent report of the UN Human Rights Council entitled 'Report of the Special

---

[17] For details on the role and the activities of this body visit: https://rm.coe.int/leaflet -ecri-2019/168094b101.

[18] Nevertheless, according to the most recent report of the Institute for Economics and Peace: 'political terrorism has now overtaken religious terrorism in the West, with religiously motivated attacks declining 82 per cent in 2021. There were 40 politically motivated attacks, compared with just three religiously motivated attacks' (Global Terrorism Index 2022: 4).

Rapporteur on contemporary forms of racism, racial discrimination, xenophobia and related intolerance' (2017) emphasised the fact that the overall fight against terrorism feeds xenophobia and inequality based on the ethnic origin and religious beliefs of certain people or groups of people (2017: 11). According to this report, there is a proliferation of anti-Muslim rhetoric that creates a hostile environment for refugees and immigrants from Muslim countries (2017: 4–5). These people suffer the inherent suspicion of terrorism because of their nationality and/or religion and the destination country of their financial transactions, e.g., when they send money to their families or pay taxes in their country of origin (Bantekas 2003: 321). They also often lack a number of identification documents due to the different bureaucracies in the countries they move to and their country of origin, and of course, in the case of refugees, because of the traumatic circumstances in which they may have left their homes (The White Collar Crime Centre 2018: 16).

The UK, because of its role as 'a major global financial centre and the world's largest centre for cross-border banking' (FATF 2018: 18) engaged early in the fight against terrorist financing. Since the 1990s, when the UK enacted several anti-money laundering legislative acts, based on the 'know your customer' idea, banks have been obliged to seek information regarding the true identity of their clientele. Moreover, the UK was one of the first Member States to apply the EU's anti-money laundering and counterterrorist financing legislation. Post-Brexit, its legislation remains harmonised at the level of the 5th EU AML Directive. In particular, the Money Laundering, Terrorist Financing and Transfer of Funds (Information on the Payer) Regulations 2017,[19] as amended by the Money Laundering and Terrorist Financing (Amendment) Regulations 2019,[20] require all regulated bodies (including banks, and other financial institutions, such as insurance and real estate companies) to obtain information on the identity, origin, home and work addresses, employment details and the family status of every customer, in order to prevent accounts being used for terrorist aims (either by financing an attack or by financing a terrorist group or a combat organisation). All this information is stored in one or more electronic databases of the obliged entity, and it is checked through adequate algorithms. This is the case for international markets as well. As this technique is applied worldwide, the initial financial exclusion of certain people is usually due to their inability to provide the correct documents deemed by law as 'necessary' for opening an account, for applying for credit or for securing health insurance. Usually, those

---

[19] These Regulations implemented the 4th EU AML Directive (EU) 2015/849 and transposed all new standards suggested by the FATF to the national legislation.

[20] These Regulations implemented the 5th EU AML Directive (EU) 2018/843 which came into force on 10 January 2020 while the 6th EU AML Directive 2018/1673 which harmonises the definition of predicate offences against money laundering across the EU was not transposed to British legislation because of its withdrawal from the EU.

who have no proof of residence or no employment contract are not accepted as customers. Several scholars have identified the opposing nature of each party's needs: one to prevent money laundering on the basis of de-risking practices and the other to have access to the financial system (de Koker 2006: 27; Durner & Shetret 2015; McKendry 2014). They all agree that law enforcement requires regulatory authorities to find the right balance between these needs, although it may be difficult to satisfy both.

Practically, major banks prefer to exclude customers rather than face liability, as money laundering or terrorist financing accusations can harm their reputation and cause further economic problems (Nakajima 2017: 132). This issue was noticed and publicly addressed by the FCA in February 2016 following the financial exclusion of certain legal entities by some English banks. The FCA acknowledged the discretionary authority of a financial institution to deny an entity as its customer but suggested that this authority should only be used as a last resort, if no other viable solution could be found between the contracting parties. Recently, the European Banking Authority (EBA) published an opinion regarding this emerging situation and called on national authorities and EU institutions to provide financial operators with clearer instructions on how to abstain from 'unwarranted de-risking' (2022: 4–5).

Access to finance may not be an official fundamental right, although it is undeniably the main and sometimes only means by which to exercise several fundamental rights (such as the right to property, the right to social life or the right to health) in contemporary societies (Hudon 2009; Kumar 2014: 3–4). In other words, a person with no bank account cannot find an 'official' job and 'officially' be paid, cannot rent a house or ask for medical care. We could say that a person with no bank account does not 'officially exist'.

Research conducted by economists (Stefan et al. 2018: 3) has also pointed out this inherent subconscious discriminatory behaviour of the private financial sector (Sciurba 2019: 161). Bankers, in the context of CFT obligations, take discriminatory decisions that lead individuals to financial and social exclusion and therefore to criminality (de Koker 2006: 27). Moreover, employees, who can also be found liable for not effectively applying CFT controls, when making decisions take into account a number of inappropriate factors, such as their own personal experiences and social prejudices (McCulloch & Carlton 2006: 404; Rondel 2017). In other words, analysis of the risk of terrorism linked to an individual or a transaction is not absolutely objective but rather the result of the interaction between an employee's subjective opinion and an indication from the compliance software. Further, this software is driven by algorithms, programmed by 'subjective' humans, that raise the alarm when one or more criteria, selected by designers of the software, are fulfilled. It is therefore possible that such software, like any other AI tool, enhances discrimination.[21] This

---

[21]   In fact, in recent years, and especially after the Covid-19 crisis, a wide range of AI systems have been integrated in several sectors of public life (i.e., health, administration,

implies that a risk-based approach is not unbiased and objective and cannot fully preserve the integrity of financial markets. The British Joint Money Laundering Steering Group explicitly suggests in its Guidance that 'firms have to make their own determination as to the risk weights. Parameters set by law or regulation may limit a firm's discretion' (2018: 50). However, in practice the law gives financial institutions great latitude.

This situation is also encouraged by international bodies, which, in the context of protecting global peace and security, declare specific countries to be at a high risk of terrorism, although in reality such declarations indirectly serve their economic and political interests (Sullivan & Hayes 2010). In 2010, based on UN resolution 1373, which encouraged member states to set up their own blacklists, more than 200 were adopted worldwide, each containing different countries, individuals and legal entities (de Goede 2012: 178). The large number of countries on these blacklists created numerous problems and uncertainty for financial institutions who were supposed to follow these resolutions and immediately integrate them into their warning systems as long as they were engaged in executing international transactions. In addition, it must be kept in mind that these lists are extremely controversial because the process followed for their establishment raises serious concerns regarding transparency, equality and respect of the internationally recognised right to property (Office of the UN High Commissioner for Human Rights, Terrorism and Counter-terrorism 2008: 20). Both the UN and USA have the power, and often use this power, to impose sanctions against countries whose regimes they disagree with. These sanctions, no matter how well-meaning, can in turn create prejudice against citizens of those sanctioned countries, even when its social status indicates no, or an extremely low, risk of terrorist financing. Considering that people suffering from financial exclusion usually have limited or no access to the justice system, few cases of discrimination have been brought to court (Durner & Shetret 2015: 21). Nonetheless, several cases can be found in the media, as discussed further below.

Indicative Discrimination Cases Connected to CFT Measures

According to the Financial Ombudsman's statistics, bank customers all across the UK have been subject to the closure of their accounts (Artingstall et al. 2016: 13) as a result of discrimination (Sciurba 2019: 160). As mentioned in a report conducted by the Global Center on Cooperative Security (Durner & Shetret 2015: 23), no financial institution has admitted or will ever admit that their de-risking methods are driven mainly by religious or cultural indications.

---

justice) and a debate has begun worldwide as to whether these systems may or may not discriminate against certain people based on their race, their gender, their age etc. See e.g., Equality and Human Rights Commission 2022.

The following indicative examples of cases involving racial or religious discrimination has been confirmed by the FCA (Artingstall et al. 2016).[22]

In the past, such behaviour rarely reached the courts or other dispute resolution bodies. However, in the last few years the media has shone some light on this phenomenon and encouraged individuals to claim their legal rights. One example concerns an Irish bank which was found liable by the Workplace Relation Commission (WRC) for demonstrating discriminatory behaviour based on race in relation to an Iranian couple (Deegan 2018). The couple in question had functioning accounts with the bank for over five years, worked legally in Ireland as doctors, and the wife possessed Irish citizenship. Despite this, the bank unilaterally decided that, due to their ethnicity, the couple presented a high risk of terrorist financing. As a result, it imposed, without prior warning, restrictions to the functional conditions of their business relationship. The couple were deprived of their right to make any transactions involving Iran, regardless of the amount of the transaction or the reasons for the transfer. The bank was finally ordered to pay damages of €12,000 to the wife and €8,000 to the husband as moral damages, i.e., damages for the psychological and reputational harm caused.

Similarly, Allied Irish Bank was ordered to pay €4,000 to a dentist after refusing to open an account in his name on the grounds that he was a refugee from Syria, a country which is blacklisted by the UN (Deegan 2019). The WRC found that, under the Equal Status Acts 2000–2015, Allied's action was direct discrimination based on race (WRC ADJ-00013897 2018).

Further, in 2012, HSBC, following the fine imposed by the American authorities for lax controls in its anti-money laundering/counter-terrorist systems (as discussed above), shut down several accounts belonging to Muslim customers, with the justification that their religion and/or nationality presented risks incompatible with the bank's updated risk assessment policy (Laurie 2014). Customers were not given prior warning of the closure of their accounts and were only subsequently sent short letters, in which the bank implied that the decision was not driven by Islamophobia but by its proper interests: to mitigate the risk of being sanctioned again for failing to prevent illegal money transfers (Laurie 2014). It is worth noting, however, that despite these decisions, HSBC was sentenced, in 2021, by the FCA to pay a civil penalty of £63.9 million due to deficiencies in its transaction monitoring systems during the period 2010–2018 (FCA 2021).

Barclays Bank, while trying to comply with the UK's AML/CFT rules, decided unilaterally and without warning, to terminate several client relationships that it considered to be 'suspicious' (*The Guardian* as cited by Tins 2017),

---

[22] In this report entitled 'Drivers & Impacts of Derisking' it is claimed that some clients were cut off by their banks with no specific justification and without having the chance to demand further information, prove their case or seek remediation (Artingstall et al. 2016: 43–44).

and similar cases concerning accusations against financial institutions are regularly published by the media internationally (Jones 2018). Even though these disputes are usually not resolved by independent bodies, national authorities or by national courts as the individuals involved usually do not have the necessary financial resources to claim their rights, these cases still raise questions about the existence of racist incentives behind a private actor's internal policies.

In another case, the Finnish National Discrimination Tribunal identified that a bank's policy led to ethnic discrimination, given that only individuals with Finnish identity cards could be accepted as customers (Ministry of the Interior 2014). The Tribunal considered that neither national legislation nor international and EU standards concerning the fight against terrorist financing, prevented the bank from accepting customers of a different nationality. Consequently, the Tribunal imposed a fine of €5,000 to the Finnish bank for denying its services to someone who had provided an Estonian passport as proof of identity (Ministry of the Interior 2014).

In this context, one of the most important discrimination cases of international interest is the case of Ahmed Ali Yusuf, brought before the European Tribunal of First Instance (T-306/01). Yusuf was a Swedish citizen of Somalian origin and an entrepreneur whose bank accounts were frozen by a decision of the UN Security Council for a period of five years due to a suspicion that the accounts were facilitating international organised crime. This suspicion was based on the fact that Yusuf worked for Al Barakaat, a network of independent money remitters. This organisation was established in Sweden and was considered a terrorist shell company, used to move money to Somalian combatants. Yusuf's name remained on the UN blacklist, although other members' names were de-listed and no other evidence or judicial decisions had been produced. As a result, this caused Yusuf problems in his social and family life, and though the European Tribunal ordered the bank to unfreeze his assets, the damage caused to Yusuf's professional reputation was irreparable (Guild 2008: 182–183).

Another illustrative EU case concerned Kadi, a Saudi entrepreneur whose property remained frozen for eight years under authority of EU Council Regulation No. 881/2002.[23] As a consequence, certain specific restrictive measures were imposed and directed against certain persons and entities associated with Osama bin Laden, the Al-Qaida network and the Taliban. Only after Kadi addressed the Court of Justice of the European Communities (cases C-402/05 P and C-415/05 P) did he regain his assets. The Court held that Kadi had not been informed of the grounds for his inclusion on the list of individuals and entities subject to the sanctions adopted by the UN, nor had he been given any opportunity to challenge this decision (CJEC C- 402/05 P and 415/05, para. 343–352, 368–370). As a result, his fundamental human

---

[23] This regulation transposed Resolution No 1390 (2002) of the Security Council.

rights to respect for property, to be heard and to effective judicial review were unlawfully violated.

In contrast, the Court of Justice of the European Union (CJEU), in case C-668/15, considered that a provision in a bank's policy demanding additional identification documents for those having been born in a country other than Denmark was not based on ethnic origin and therefore did not constitute direct or indirect discrimination under article 2 para. 2 of Directive 2000/43/EC. Rather it was merely a lawful practice applied by the bank in its effort to comply with the provisions of the anti-money laundering Directive in force at the time of the dispute. The CJEU explained that the contested policy did not put potential customers of a certain ('specific') origin in a less favourable situation as it was a very general and abstract provision, thus no grounds for discrimination could be established (CJEU C-668/15, para. 33–37).

In terms of legal argument, the CJEU's justification is in line with the aforementioned Directive. However, the request for additional documentation in place only for certain clients clearly indicates the protectionist attitude of financial operators. In other words, such disputes arise when financial institutions, instead of taking responsibility and verifying a low risk of terrorism, prefer to apply stringent criteria regarding access to financial services unless they are given official guidance by state authorities. It may be argued that, in case C-668/15, the CJEU should not have limited its judgment on whether the criterion of place of birth is related to ethnic origin within the meaning of article 2, but instead should have assessed more thoroughly whether such a policy could eventually result in discrimination against people of a certain ethnic or racial origin. The CJEU's reasoning could be used in the future as a lawful basis for establishing other conservative banking practices which, although neutral in principle, may camouflage racism and indirectly jeopardise the rule of law. In the author's opinion, if a similar case was to be heard in the European Court of Human Rights (ECHR) instead of the CJEU, a broader approach of the discrimination risks surrounding the application of the AML/CFT rules and the respect of human rights, as defined in the European Convention of Human Rights, would probably have been followed. This is because, firstly, the ECHR solely addresses issues of human rights violation. Secondly, a less strict approach in terms of proving 'indirect discrimination' based on origin has already been adopted in the landmark case Biao v Denmark (no 38590/10, para. 110–114).

Conclusion: Potential Solutions

Undeniably, anticipation and prevention of terrorist attacks is an absolute necessity for the protection of national and regional security. However, if financial exclusion is used as a means of combatting terrorist financing and thus terrorism, it can lead to the increased use of shadow banking methods (de Koker 2014: 27; Durner & Shetret 2015: 19), including 'hawala' offices[24] and cryptocurrencies as alternative, less visible means of funding terrorism. Exclusion from official financial markets does not therefore lead to the elimination of terrorism.

Experts have repeatedly argued that as long as financial institutions intensify controls over the funds they manage, terrorists will keep trying to find new ways to finance their activities. This is why the EU adopted a new regulation system for virtual currencies (Directive 2018/843). In the author's opinion, even though regulation is important, it cannot be the answer to every problem. There is no doubt that people involved in criminal economic activity will keep finding new ways to bypass the official system. For that reason, it is important to have as many people as possible under surveillance, meaning more people should be accepted into the official financial system to ensure scrutiny of their movements and therefore prevent a terror attack or even discover a terrorist organisation (Gordon 2014: 280). Additionally, national authorities should assist financial institutions in finding the right balance between financial inclusion and the prevention of terrorism by expanding the resources available. Given that national security is at stake, some of the national budget should be invested for these purposes, especially for smaller companies who face difficulties in covering the costs of prevention. Currently, risk assessment is left to the discretion of financial officers and is thus interconnected with their ethics, beliefs and values. A possible measure to reduce the likelihood of such indirect discrimination could be continuous training of staff. For example, regular seminars could be organised internally and in collaboration with the State or academic institutions to train staff to be able to make the distinction between possible terrorists and innocent people of a certain origin. According to experts, that was the case with the 2015 Paris terror attacks. Those involved in the attacks lived in France legally and there was no obvious evidence linked them to jihad or the Islamic State (ICSR 2016: 44). Further, several other terrorist attacks were partially or completely financed via the receipt of cash funds (Oftedal 2015: 22). This demonstrates that the fight against terrorist financing, as long as it remains focused on the official financial sector, tends to be unable to achieve its main objective of preventing the circulation of terror funds as terror groups use shadow banking systems and therefore avoid the traditional financial sector (Centre on Law and Globalization 2014: 51).

In the author's opinion, in order to control terror funds, states must 'follow the money', i.e., let money circulate in a system equipped with all the necessary tools to prevent terror funds from arriving at their ultimate destination. Moreover, this approach can facilitate enforcement authorities in identifying

---

[24] Hawala is the self-regulated Islamic bank system that permits Muslims to transfer remittances through 'hawala' offices established all over the world. Because of its nature, it is considered to be one of the main methods of 'shadow banking' which enables economic crime.

and imprisoning terrorists before they commit a terrorist attack. In other words, terror fighters are the 'soldiers' of the terrorist 'army' that could possibly lead police authorities to the upper commanders, that is to the heart of terrorist organisations. Further, states, the EU and the international community should re-examine the effectiveness of CFT measures in light of their impact upon society and the international economy because, as the ECRI clearly states, 'the fight against terrorism should not become a pretext under which racism, racial discrimination and intolerance are allowed to flourish' (2004: 3).

References

Books

de Goede, M. (2012). *Speculative security: The politics of pursuing terrorist monies*. Minneapolis: University of Minnesota Press.

Nakajima, C. (2017). The international pressures on banks to disclose information. In: Booysen, S. and Neo, D. (eds.) *Can banks still keep a secret? Bank secrecy in financial centres around the world*. Cambridge: Cambridge University Press, pp. 114–133.

Sciurba, M. (2019). *The incompatibility of global anti-money laundering regimes with human and civil rights: Reform needed?* Baden-Baden: Nomos Verlag.

Articles

Bantekas, I. (2003). The international law of terrorist financing. *The American Journal of International Law*, 97(2): 315–333.

Corbin, C. M. (2017). Terrorists are always Muslim but never white: At the intersection of critical race theory and propaganda. *Fordham Law Review*, 86: 455.

Corkery, M. (2014). Immigrants From Latin America and Africa squeezed as banks curtail international money transfers. *The New York Times*, 9 July. https://dealbook.nytimes.com/2014/07/06/immigrants-from-latin-america -and-africa-squeezed-as-banks-curtail-international-money-transfers/

de Koker, L. (2006). Money laundering control and suppression of financing of terrorism. *Journal of Financial Crime*, 13(1): 27.

Deegan, G. (2018). Bank fined €20k for discriminating against Iranian couple. *The Irish Times*, 7 June. https://www.irishtimes.com/business/work/bank -fined-20k-for-discriminating-against-iranian-couple-1.3522868

Deegan, G. (2019). AIB ordered to pay €4,000 over refusal to open account for Syrian dentist: WRC found AIB discriminated against man on grounds of race. *The Irish Times*, 9 April. https://www.irishtimes.com/business/financial -services/aib-ordered-to-pay-4-000-over-refusal-to-open-account-for -syrian-dentist-1.3854740

Durner, T. and Shetret, L. (2015). Understanding bank de-risking and its effects on financial inclusion: An exploratory study. *Washington: Global Center on Cooperative Security*. https://www.globalcenter.org/wp-content/uploads/2015/11/rr-bank-de-risking-181115-en.pdf

Equality and Human Rights Commission. (2022). *Equality watchdog takes action to address discrimination in use of artificial intelligence*, 1 September. https://www.equalityhumanrights.com/en/our-work/news/equality-watchdog-takes-action-address-discrimination-use-artificial-intelligence#:~:text=There%20is%20emerging%20evidence%20that,its%20new%20three%2Dyear%20strategy

FATF. (2014). The danger of driving both illicit markets and financial exclusion, 8 October. http://www.fatf-gafi.org/publications/fatfgeneral/documents/danger-illicit-markets-financial-exclusion.html

Gordon, R. (2014). A tale of two studies: The real story of terrorism finance. *University of Pennsylvania Law Review Online*, 162(1): 269–281.

Guild, E. (2008). The uses and abuses of counter-terrorism policies in Europe: The case of the 'Terrorist Lists'. *JCMS: Journal of Common Market Studies*, 46(1): 173–193.

Hudon, M. (2009). Should access to credit be a right? *Journal of Business Ethics*, 84(1): 17–28.

Jones, R. (2018). NatWest closed my account with no explanation. *The Guardian*, 3 February. https://www.theguardian.com/money/2018/feb/03/natwest-closed-my-account-with-no-explanation

Kumar, P. (2014). Access to Finance and Human Rights, University Library of Munich. https://mpra.ub.uni-muenchen.de/80336/1/MPRA_paper_80336.pdf

Laurie, D. (2014). HSBC closes some Muslim groups' accounts. *BBC*, 30 July. https://www.bbc.com/news/business-28553921

McCulloch, J. and Carlton, B. (2006). Pre-empting justice: Suppression of financing of terrorism and the 'war on terror'. *Current Issues in Criminal Justice*, 17(3): 397–412.

McKendry I. (2014). Banks face no-win scenario on AML de-risking. *American Banker*, 17 November. https://www.americanbanker.com/news/banks-face-no-win-scenario-on-aml-de-risking

Mugarura, N. (2015). The jeopardy of the bank in enforcement of normative anti-money laundering and countering financing of terrorism regimes. *Journal of Money Laundering Control*, 18(3): 352.

Ping, H. (2005). The suspicious transactions reporting system. *Journal of Money Laundering Control*, 8(3): 252–259. https://doi.org/10.1108/13685200510620948

Rondel, A. (2017). Discriminations des clients des banque: C'est toute l'organisation du travail qui pousse à ces pratiques. *LCI*, 21 September. https://www.lci.fr/societe/c-est-toute-l-organisation-du-travail-qui

-pousse-a-la-discrimination-dans-les-banques-client-sexisme-racisme
-villeurbanne-2065102.html

Slater, S. and Scuffham, M. (2013). HSBC to raise dividends in show of capital strength. *Reuters*, 4 March. https://www.reuters.com/article/us-hsbc -earnings-idUSBRE92300320130304

Stefan, M., Holzmeister, F., Mullauer, A. and Kirchle, M. (2018). Ethnical discrimination in Europe: Field evidence from the finance industry. *PLoS ONE*, 13(1). https://doi.org/10.1371/journal.pone.0191959

Sullivan G. and Hayes B. (2010). Blacklisted: Targeted sanctions, pre-emptive security and fundamental rights. *European Center for Constitutional and Human Rights*. https://www.ecchr.eu/fileadmin/Publikationen/Blacklisted .pdf

Tangel, A. (2012). HSBC to pay $1.9 billion to settle U.S. money-laundering case. *Los Angeles Times*, 11 December. https://www.latimes.com/business /la-xpm-2012-dec-11-la-fi-hsbc-fine-20121212-story.html).

Tins, A. (2017). Barclays took my £440,000 and put me through hell. *The Guardian*, 22 January. https://www.theguardian.com/money/2017/jan/22 /barclays-took-my-440000-customers-caught-up-banks-de-risking -money-laundering-laws

Vedrennem, G. (2019). Suspicious activity reporting varies significantly across Europe, *ACAMS*, 28 August.

Wolosky, L. and Heifetz, S. (2002). Regulating terrorism. *Law & Policy in International Business*, 34(1).

Legal texts

Council Directive (EU) 2000/78/EC of 27 November 2000 establishing a general framework for equal treatment in employment and occupation, OJ L 303, 2.12.2000, p. 16–22.

Directive (EU) 2015/849 of the European Parliament and of the Council of 20 May 2015, on the prevention of the use of the financial system for the purposes of money laundering or terrorist financing, amending Regulation (EU) No 648/2012 of the European Parliament and of the Council, and repealing Directive 2005/60/EC of the European Parliament and of the Council and Commission Directive 2006/70/EC, OJ L 141, 06.06.2015, p. 71–116.

Directive 2000/43/EC of 29 June 2000 implementing the principle of equal treatment between persons irrespective of racial or ethnic origin, OJ L 180, 19.7.2000, p. 22–26.

Directive 2005/60/EC of the European Parliament and of the Council of 26 October 2005 on the prevention of the use of the financial system for the purpose of money laundering and terrorist financing (Text with EEA relevance), OJ L 309, 25.11.2005, p. 15–36.

Directive 2006/54/EC of the European Parliament and of the Council of 5 July 2006 on the implementation of the principle of equal opportunities and equal treatment of men and women in matters of employment and occupation (recast) OJ L 204, 26.7.2006, p. 23–36.

Directive (EU) 2015/849 of the European Parliament and of the Council of 20 May 2015 on the prevention of the use of the financial system for the purposes of money laundering or terrorist financing, amending Regulation (EU) No 648/2012 of the European Parliament and of the Council, and repealing Directive 2005/60/EC of the European Parliament and of the Council and Commission Directive 2006/70/EC (Text with EEA relevance), OJ L 141, 5.6.2015, p. 73–117.

Directive (EU) 2018/843 of the European Parliament and of the Council of 30 May 2018 amending Directive (EU) 2015/849 on the prevention of the use of the financial system for the purposes of money laundering or terrorist financing, and amending Directives 2009/138/EC and 2013/36/EU (Text with EEA relevance) PE/72/2017/REV/1, OJ L 156, 19.6.2018, p. 43–74.

Directorate general for internal policies (Policy department C) (2016) Evaluation of EU measures to combat terrorist financing: in depth analysis for the LIBE committee. April 2014. https://www.europarl.europa.eu/RegData/etudes/note/join/2014/509978/IPOL-LIBE_NT(2014)509978_EN.pdf

Financial Conduct Authority. (2017). Final Notice on Deutsche Bank AG. 30 January. https://www.fca.org.uk/publication/final-notices/deutsche-bank-2017.pdf

Financial Conduct Authority. (2018). Final Notice. 6 June. https://www.fca.org.uk/publication/final-notices/canara-bank-2018.pdf

Financial Conduct Authority. (2021). Decision Notice. 14 December. https://www.fca.org.uk/publication/decision-notices/hsbc-bank-plc.pdf

International Convention on the Elimination of all Forms of Racial Discrimination (ICERD) (1999).

International Covenant on Civil and Political Rights (adopted 16 December 1966, entered into force 23 March 1976) 999 UNTS 171 (ICCPR), art. 4 (1).

Office of the High Commissioner for Human Rights. (2002). Durban Declaration and Programme of Action. https://www.ohchr.org/sites/default/files/Documents/Publications/Durban_text_en.pdf

Office of the High Commissioner for Human Rights. (2013). The Rabat Plan of Action. https://www.ohchr.org/en/documents/outcome-documents/rabat-plan-action

Proceeds of Crime Act. (2002). https://www.legislation.gov.uk/ukpga/2002/29/contents

Regulation (EU) 2016/679 of the European Parliament and of the Council of 27 April 2016 on the protection of natural persons with regard to the processing of personal data and on the free movement of such data, and repealing Directive 95/46/EC (General Data Protection Regulation), OJ L 119, 4.5.2016, p. 1–88, art. 45.

The Money Laundering, Terrorist Financing and Transfer of Funds (Information on the Payer) Regulations 2017, Statutory Instruments 2017, No. 692,
part 6, chapter 1, section 46.

United Nations. (1999). International Convention for the Suppression of the
Financing of Terrorism. Treaty Series. 2178. New York: United Nations.
https://www.un-ilibrary.org/content/books/9789210552134s002-c022_

UN General Assembly. (2006). The United Nations Global Counter-Terrorism
Strategy: resolution/adopted by the General Assembly, 20 September 2006,
A/RES/60/288.

UN Security Council. (2001). Security Council resolution 1373 on threats to
international peace and security caused by terrorist acts, 28 September
2001, S/RES/1373.

UN Security Council resolution 1390 (2002) on continuation of measures
against the Taliban and Al-Qaida, S/RES/1390(2002) (16 January 2002).
https://digitallibrary.un.org/record/456589?ln=en

Reports

Artingstall, D., Dove, N., Howell, J. and Levi, M. (2016). *Drivers & impacts of
derisking.* Shamley Green: John Howell & Co. Ltd. https://www.fca.org.uk
/publication/research/drivers-impacts-of-derisking.pdf

Center on Law and Globalization. (2014). *Global surveillance of dirty money.
Assessing assessments of regimes to control money-laundering and combat the
financing of terrorism.* http://www.americanbarfoundation.org/news/475

European Bank Authority. (2022). *Opinion of the European Banking Authority 'de-risking' EBA/Op/2022/01.* https://www.eba.europa.eu/sites/default
/documents/files/document_library/Publications/Opinions/2022/Opinion
%20on%20RTS%20on%20OF%20and%20EL%20%28EBA-Op-2022
-04%28/1029944/EBA%20Opinion%20on%20amendments%20to%20the
%20RTS%20on%20OF%20and%20ELs.pdf

European Commission against Racism and Intolerance. (2004). *General policy
recommendation no. 8: Combating racism while fighting terrorism.* http://
hudoc.ecri.coe.int/eng?i=REC-08-2004-026-ENG

EU Network of Independent Experts on Fundamental Rights. (2006). *Ethnic profiling.* http://lesaf.org/wp-content/uploads/2012/12/11_eu_experts_droits
_ethnic_profiling.pdf

Europol. (2019). *Terrorism situation and trend report (TE-SAT).* 27 June. https://
www.europol.europa.eu/activities-services/main-reports/terrorism-situation
-and-trend-report-2019-te-sat

FATF. (2002). *Guidance for financial institutions in detecting terrorist financing,*
24 April. https://www.fatf-gafi.org/media/fatf/documents/Guidance%20
for%20financial%20institutions%20in%20detecting%20terrorist%20
financing.pdf

FATF. (2012). *International standards on combating money laundering and the financing of terrorism & proliferation*. 16 February. https://www.fatf-gafi .org/en/publications/Fatfrecommendations/Fatf-recommendations.html

FATF. (2013). *National money laundering and terrorist financing risk assessment*. https://www.fatf-gafi.org/media/fatf/content/images/National_ML_TF _Risk_Assessment.pdf

FATF. (2014a). *Guidance for a risk-based approach: The banking sector*. https:// www.fatf-gafi.org/media/fatf/documents/reports/Risk-Based-Approach -Banking-Sector.pdf

FATF. (2017). *Guidance. Anti-money laundering and terrorist financing meas- ures and financial inclusion*. http://www.fatf-gafi.org/media/fatf/content /images/Updated-2017-FATF-2013-Guidance.pdf

FATF. (2018). *Anti-money laundering and counter-terrorist financing meas- ures – United Kingdom, fourth round mutual evaluation report*. http://www .fatf-gafi.org/publications/mutualevaluations/documents/mer-united -kingdom2018.html

Financial Conduct Authority. (2016). *De-risking: managing money-laundering risk*. https://www.fca.org.uk/firms/money-laundering/derisking-managing -risk

Financial Conduct Authority. (2021). *Decision Notice*. 14 December. https:// www.fca.org.uk/publication/decision-notices/hsbc-bank-plc.pdf

Global Terrorism Index. (2022). https://reliefweb.int/attachments/a62d4dc4 -c69b-49ee-8ef5-50d98205e70d/GTI-2022-web_110522-1.pdf

HM Treasury. (2022). *Review of the UK's AML/CFT regulations*. https://assets .publishing.service.gov.uk/government/uploads/system/uploads/attachment _data/file/1085407/MLRs_Review_Report_-_2.5_for_publication.pdf

ICSR Report. (2016). *Criminal pasts terrorist future: Jihadists and the new crime terror nexus*. https://icsr.info/2016/10/11/new-icsr-report-criminal-pasts -terrorist-futures-european-jihadists-new-crime-terror-nexus/

Joint Committee. (2017). *Guidelines to prevent transfers of funds can be abused for ML and TF (JC/GL/2017/16)*. https://eba.europa.eu/regulation-and -policy/anti-money-laundering-and-e-money/guidelines-to-prevent -transfers-of-funds-can-be-abused-for-ml-and-tf

Ministry of the Interior. (2014). *National discrimination tribunal prohibited ethnic discrimination in the provision of banking services*. https://kestavakehitys.fi/en /current-issues/article/-/asset_publisher/1410869/national-discrimination -tribunal-prohibited-ethnic-discrimination-in-the-provision-of-banking -services

National Commission on Terrorist Attacks upon the United States. (2004). *Monograph on terrorist financing*. http://www.9-11commission.gov/staff _statements

Office of Foreign Assets Control. (2016). *Enforcement information for February 8, 2016*. https://home.treasury.gov/system/files/126/20160208_barclays.pdf

Office of the United Nations High Commissioner for Human Rights. (2008). *Human rights, terrorism and counter-terrorism. 2008 – Fact sheet no. 32.* http://www.ohchr.org/Documents/Publications/Factsheet32EN.pdf

Oftedal, E. (2015). *The financing of jihadi terrorist cells in Europe – Report by the Norwegian Defence Research Establishment (FFI), No. 2014/02234.* Kjeller: FFI. https://www.ffi.no/no/Rapporter/14-02234.pdf (Accessed: 30 July 2023).

Roth, J., Greenburg, D. and Wille, S. (n.d.). *National Commission on terrorist attacks upon the United States: Monograph on terrorist financing.* https://govinfo.library.unt.edu/911/staff_statements/911_TerrFin_Monograph.pdf

The Joint Money Laundering Steering Group. (2017). *Guidance for the UK financial sector.* https://secureservercdn.net/160.153.138.163/a3a.8f7.myftpupload.com/wp-content/uploads/2019/09/Board_approved_final_Guidance_Part_I_December_17_CLEAN.pdf

The White Collar Crime Centre. (2018). *Submission in response to the Treasury Committee's economic crime inquiry (ECR0026).* http://data.parliament.uk/writtenevidence/committeeevidence.svc/evidencedocument/treasury-committee/economic-crime/written/82429.html

UN Human Rights Council. (2017). *Report of the Special Rapporteur on contemporary forms of racism, racial discrimination, xenophobia and related intolerance submitted pursuant to General Assembly resolution 71/179,* 26 April, A/HRC/35/42. https://www.refworld.org/docid/5939412e4.html

Case Law

Case of Biao v. Denmark App no. 38590/10 (ECHR, 24 May 2016).

Case C-402/05 P and 415/05 *Kadi and Al Barakaat International Foundation v Council and Commission* [2008] ECR II-364.

Case C-668/15 *Jyske Finans* [2017].

Case T-306/01 *Yusuf and Al Barakaat International Foundation v Council and Commission* [2005] ECR II–3533.

Financial Conduct Authority. (2015). Final Notice. 4 March. http://www.fca.org.uk/your-fca/documents/final-notices/2015/bank-of-beirut-uk-ltd

Iraj Parvizi v Barclays Bank [2014] EWHC B2 (QB).

R v Da Silva [2006] EWCA Crim 1654.

Shah and another v HSBC Private Bank (UK) Ltd [2012] EWHC 1283 (QB).

Workplace Relations Commission. (2018). *A Syrian Refugee v A bank,* ADJ-00013897. 6 April. https://www.workplacerelations.ie/en/cases/2019/march/adj-00013897.html

CHAPTER 4

Neo-tribal Sociality in the Upper Echelons of the Legal Profession: Issues of Race

Anna Chronopoulou

Introduction

Exclusionary practices have constituted one of the main subjects of study in relation to the social composition of the legal profession in England and Wales. Mainly, this body of literature examines how exclusionary practices impact on issues of gender, class and more recently race. Despite attempts to conceptualise race and the way it is negotiated in the legal profession, the commodification of race has remained underexplored in the organisational context of the legal profession. This chapter examines the commodification of race as a recruitment strategy seemingly adopted by the upper echelons of the legal profession (for the purposes of this chapter, these are large commercial solicitors' law firms and commercial barristers' Chambers). It further investigates the impact of the commodification of race on legal professional identity. This chapter suggests that the commodification of race, featuring largely in the advertising material of these firms and Chambers, reproduces the creation of a predominantly white image through either referring to cultural practices

---

How to cite this book chapter:
Chronopoulou, A. 2024. Neo-tribal Sociality in the Upper Echelons of the Legal Profession: Issues of Race. In: Whyte, A., Tuitt, P. and Bourne, J. (eds.) *The Long Walk to Equality: Perspectives on Racial Inequality, Injustice and the Law*. Pp. 55–75. London: University of Westminster Press. DOI: https://doi.org/10.16997/book63.d. License: CC-BY-NC-ND 4.0

of consumptions or merely silencing these practices. This might function as an exclusionary practice impacting on the creation of subtle racial inequalities in the organisational context of large commercial law firms and Chambers. In exposing alternative forms of exclusionary practices, this chapter deploys the theoretical framework of neo-tribal sociality, associated with the French philosopher Michel Maffesoli. Methodologically, the main objective of the chapter is qualitatively sought through an analysis of a small sample of older and more recent advertising material and websites of large commercial law firms and Chambers.

This chapter is divided into four parts. The first part introduces the theory of neo-tribal sociality and explains the reasons for its deployment in the chapter. The second part examines exclusionary practices in the legal profession and links the notion of neo-tribal sociality to the commodification of race. The third part explores how self-presentation of large commercial law firms and Chambers is now promoted and produced by reference to consumption. It explores this further by concentrating on issues of profiling through a series of identifications that seemingly extend beyond leisure activities commonly associated with lawyers, informing the presence and the absence of race. The final part provides a critique of the way the advertising material deals with race issues and exposes the juxtapositions the advertising material raises.

Neo-tribal Sociality and its Application in the Upper Echelons of the Legal Profession

The notion of neo-tribal sociality constitutes the theoretical basis of this chapter. Maffesoli's theory of neo-tribal sociality translates into voluntary movement and mobility from one consumer tribe to the next (Maffesoli 1996). According to Maffesoli, tribes are expressed through participation in cultural practices of consumptions (ibid.). Examples of postmodern tribes can be found in youth culture and in professional cultures. The notion of neo-tribal sociality is based on a sense of free mobility from one tribe to another and a sense of mobility from tribes towards and from the masses. The Maffesolian theory of neo-tribal sociality perceives the movement of professional and youth tribes to and from the masses as free-floating and as being part of the logic of identifications. The logic of identity disappears in the process only to be reinstated and reinforced through consumer-based identifications.

There are two main reasons why the notion of neo-tribal sociality is being deployed here. First, it addresses issues of the consumer-based nature of the upper echelons of the legal profession and the way race is renegotiated through practices of consumption. Secondly, neo-tribal sociality considers forms of cultural practices of consumption evident in the advertising material of large commercial law firms and Chambers that demonstrate the commodification of race. From this perspective, it could offer alternative insights into the way the upper echelons of the legal profession deal with issues of diversity, while exploring alternative theorisations of race. Crucially, this alternative perspective creates different interpretations and meanings which expose different aspects of the organisational context of the legal profession. The Maffesolian theory of neo-tribal sociality does not come without criticisms regarding its application in employment contexts[1] and more specifically the context of the legal profession,[2] as it tends to disregard the limitations professional cultures impose. These limitations will be discussed in the context of the commodification of race at the upper end of the legal profession. The thrust of the argument will be that although large commercial law firms and Chambers seem to embrace diversity and inclusion initiatives, what they do amounts to the commodification and demarginalisation of race (Crenshaw 1989), and it is exactly through this commodification that exclusion happens on issues of race. This argument will be discussed and explored throughout this chapter.

Exclusionary Practices of the Upper Echelons of the Legal Profession: Neo-tribal Sociality and Retheorisations of Race

Exclusionary practices constitute a mechanism commonly found amongst professions and organisations to perpetuate themselves in their own image (Nicholson 2005). The legal profession is obsessed with status and elitism,[3] and its social composition has been solidified using exclusionary practices and mechanisms reaffirming the reproduction of a predominantly white image (Crenshaw 1989; Harris 1993). One of these strategies is recruitment which reinforces distinctions within the hierarchy of the profession. Many commentators suggest that the upper echelons of the profession, namely the Bar and large commercial law firms, remain predominantly male, middle-class and white,

---

[1] One of the main criticisms that has been expressed by critics of Maffesoli's work is that the theory of neo–tribal sociality cannot apply to professional cultures. My suggestion is that it has not even been tested against professional cultures. See for example, Evans, D. (1997). Michel Maffesoli's Sociology of Modernity and Postmodernity: An Introduction and Critical Assessment. *The Sociological Review* 45(2): 221–43.

[2] On the application of neo-tribal sociality in the legal profession for the first time, see Chronopoulou, A. (2014). Neo-tribal Socialities in the Legal Profession: The Role of Consumption in Forming Legal Professional Identities (unpublished PhD thesis), Birkbeck College, University of London. See also Chronopoulou, A. (2015). From a professional tribe to a business no-tribe: Towards a theory of consumer-based lifestyles in the legal profession. *Athens Journal of Law* 1(1): 64–84.

[3] A number of accounts refer to exclusionary practices in the context of the legal profession and organisational literature in general. See by way of illustration: Thornton (1996); Francis and Sommerlad (2009); Sommerlad, Duff & Webley (2010); Webley et al. (2016).

whereas other areas of practice and the lower ranks of the profession are more varied in terms of these social characteristics (Zimdars 2010). Boon et al. argue that segmentation starts at the early stages of candidates' selection and recruitment (Boon et al. 2001), depicting law firms' and Chambers' preferences. In analyses of the profession, it is widely demonstrated that large firms, both City and provincial, and the Bar, prefer a certain type of candidate (Rolfe & Anderson 2003). Preference is shown to candidates suggestive of privileged white background, rather than to candidates who are of lower-class or other ethnic backgrounds (Baker 2003). The former may be seen as the 'best' candidates, and to recruit the best, large City firms sometimes offer to finance them through their studies (Vignaendra 2001). The focus on the transition from legal education to the legal profession and therefore a legal career is permeated with issues of race. Cohort studies (Shiner 2000; Vignaendra 2001; Webley 2016) concentrate on gaining access to the profession and the difficulties that young students face in relation to components of self-identity, such as race (Boon & Whyte 2015, 2018). Despite difficulties in the demanding entry requirements and increased competition (Rolfe & Anderson 2003), a few qualitative accounts reveal that these are suggestive of discrimination. For instance, Boon et al. (2001, 2005) suggest that differentiation and subordination that occur within the profession reflect the law firms' and Chambers' preferences as opposed to the individual young lawyer's aspirations in entering legal practice.

Socialisation into the upper echelons of the legal profession includes exclusionary practices as played out through social practices, which in turn expose issues of race and the legitimisation of whiteness (Crenshaw 1989; Harris 1993). For example, preference for the 'best' candidates means those who have been socialised in Russell Group Universities[4] – themselves majority white institutions – which is again suggestive of a certain background. Thornton (1996) notes that homosociability, the process of socialising among groups possessing similar social characteristics, including race, is promoted and reinforced in the legal profession. More importantly personal contacts, in turn according to Harris (1993), allude to reconfirmation of race as a group and self-identity, as these are created through homosociality, in this context the creation of networks and social bonding, and homosociability. They are important in either getting a training contact or even getting access to relevant information on the profession, by either having an insider in the firm or family members in the profession (Webley & Duff 2007; Webley 2016). This means that those with

---

[4] These universities have huge social, economic and cultural impacts locally, across the UK and globally. And they are responsible for over two thirds (68%) of the world's leading research produced in UK universities (see https://russellgroup .ac.uk/about/). The group constitutes 24 universities, the top five being Oxford, Cambridge, Imperial College London, University College London and the University of Edinburgh.

greater access to the right networks, which are usually produced through exclusionary practices, are in an advantageous position when compared to those
who do not possess the necessary contacts.

Socialisation through collective associations involving cultural practices of
consumption may articulate and negotiate aspects of *habitus* (Bourdieu 1990)
in the upper echelons of the legal profession informing race. Reinforcing Harris's (1993) point on the valorisation of race through social networks, Skeggs
(2004a, 2024b) also suggests that the conversion of race from a cultural trait
and factor to an economic value occurs more effectively for those with access
to social networks. Similarly, professional identity formation has been related to
consumption and has been associated with professional groups. From this
perspective, cultural practices of consumption associated with the upper
echelons of the legal profession are capable of reinforcing status through renegotiations of race as the bearer of symbolic, cultural and economic value. For
example, the study by Savage et al. (1992) draws on the notion of Bourdieu's
habitus. It concentrates on the consumption habits of occupational groups,
examining methods of identity formation within professional groups through
patterns of consumption. Their research suggests that consumer-based aspects
associated with high culture are permeated with consumptions associated with
low culture. For instance, opera can be promoted side by side with football.
Despite the focus of Savage et al.'s (1992) account on class, a similar argument
can be made about race.

In the organisational context of the legal profession, the use of leisure and
consumption patterns could expose renegotiations of race among the different segments of the legal profession and on an individual level. This coincides
with aspects of neo-tribal sociality through exposing participation in multiple
patterns of consumption. Neo-tribal sociality presupposes participation in a
variety of consumer groups, or tribes, which could inform the construction of
race as a component of legal professional identity. This interpretation breaks
away from traditional interpretations of race in accounts of the legal profession. It suggests that the commodification of race and its renegotiation through
participation in cultural practices of consumption in the context of legal practice could potentially reveal different inequalities. The socialisation process of
young lawyers into the upper echelons of the legal profession ensures membership of a professional tribe, as reflected in the participation of cultural practices of consumption. This is not to suggest that young lawyers' professional
identities are merely a mirror of consumer habits but, as Thornton (1996)
suggests, consumption constitutes a sometimes informal and sometimes very
formal infrastructure or backbone of the legal profession capable of addressing negotiations of race in the organisational context of legal employment. In
this sense, the postmodern paradox does not lie in the commodification of
the legal profession, extending to the commodification of race, but rather in the
conceptualisation of the commodified upper echelons of the legal profession,

without addressing how the commodification of race informs young lawyers' professional identities.

The saturation of the advertising material and websites of large commercial law firms and Chambers with cultural practices of consumption alongside embracing diversity and inclusion practices sits uneasily with the theorisation of race in accounts of young lawyers in the legal profession. With few exceptions, the theorisation of the commodification of race in accounts of young lawyers in the legal profession seems to place emphasis on the socialisation processes without emphasising cultural practices of consumption.[5] This, in a sense, exposes the law's inability to incorporate cultural practices of consumption, while at the same time, as Goodrich (2001) contends, the law reinforces the construction of white spaces through these exclusionary practices. Goodrich suggests that different cultural experiences are never quite incorporated within the organisational context of the legal profession. It is in this sense that institutions and organisations remain the same and perpetuate their image. This, however, reinforces the construction of legal professional identity as a 'white space' echoing exclusionary practices in the upper echelons of the legal profession.

On the other hand, it has long been established in accounts of youth culture that young people construct their identities through participation in cultural practices of consumption. Maffesoli (2007) argues that neo-tribal sociality entails consumer-based identifications exposed in youth groups. Consumption may well provide an alternative platform which exposes the commodification of race through placing emphasis on neo-tribalism in the upper end of the legal profession. Neo-tribal sociality exposes the importance of consumption in the articulation of aspects of race in the construction of legal professional identity. Professionalisation processes amount to the socialisation of young lawyers in the legal professional culture. Although this amounts to a form of neo-tribal sociality, it would be useful to explore how consumer-based aspects of neo-tribal sociality associated with young people's identities can be played out within the organisational context of legal practice informing racial inequalities, and, most importantly, how these aspects inform the commodification of race. This is done through an analysis of advertising material and websites of large commercial law firms and Chambers.

---

[5] This point is also made by Collier (2005, 2006) in relation to the advertising material of large law firms but also by a number of accounts on race. See for example Braithwaite, J. (2010). The strategic use of demand-side diversity pressure in the solicitors' profession. *International Journal of the Legal Profession*, 17(3): 442–465; Wilkins, D. (2004). From 'separate is inherently unequal' to 'diversity is good for business: The rise of market-based diversity arguments and the fate of the black corporate bar. *Harvard Law Review*, 117: 1554; and Carbado, D. and Gulati, G. (2004). The law and economics of critical race theory. *Yale Law Journal*, 112: 1757–1828.

Promoting Diversity, Commodifying Race: The Ideal Candidates for the Upper Echelons of the Legal Profession

Recruitment literature of large commercial law firms and Chambers seems to promote diversity and inclusion and arguably exclusion in their advertising material and their websites. The commodification of race through replete references to cultural practices of consumption constitutes evidence of neo-tribal sociality. This section examines a mixture of older and more recent advertising material and websites to expose the way in which the upper end of the legal profession deals with issues of race while explicitly constructing the profile of potential candidates.

An older example of advertising material exemplifying the permeation of legal practice with cultural practices of consumptions and lifestyle, accentuating subliminal construction of race, reads as follows:

> At Mishcon, we often talk about our client relationships extending beyond that of a legal advisor, that we care beyond the call of duty and that we make our clients' problems our own. And we mean it. As evidence of our holistic approach to client care, we have teamed up with the world's leading luxury lifestyle group, Quintessentially, to offer a 24-hour, 365 days a year, global concierge service to our clients. Our partnership enables our clients to benefit from access to an unrivalled package of privileges, preferential rates and bespoke services, saving time and money at: leading hotels, premier travel services, private clubs, fine dining restaurants, concert and theatre tickets, salons, gym and spas, shopping and personal styling services. (Mishcon De Reya 2014)

The above extract is inclusive of consumptions and cultural practices of a high-end lifestyle associated with a privileged, predominantly white elite. This reproduces the exclusion of other cultural practices of consumptions associated with different social backgrounds. Furthermore, the extract depicts a commercialised and entrepreneurial legal profession that promotes the commodification of race. It amounts to an entrepreneurial neo-tribalism, which entails a series of consumer-based identifications exposing issues of race. This is also evident in the way in which the advertising material constructs the profile of potential recruits, which is also influenced by consumer-based identifications. From this perspective, firms' and Chambers' expectations of recruits are communicated through references to aspects of consumptions and lifestyles, which in turn, reflect expectations on socio-cultural background.

One of the components that features in the legal press is the communication to the potential recruit of the experience of being with the firm or Chambers. This usually involves a recently qualified lawyer narrating their personal experience.[6] It is interesting to see how issues of commodification of race are played out.

The following extract is taken from *The Plum, Trainee Guide*, a magazine published by the law firm, SJ Berwin:

> Culture? I have been to a screening of a film where the director took questions from the audience at the end; watched a mad-German contemporary dance festival; soaked up the summer-long jazz festival; sprawled in front of classic films at the free open-air cinema; revelled to the music in the streets; been to Ian Brown and Radiohead concerts; loved the office ski trip (whole office, brilliant, never been before); partied at all night French parties with the accent; been pirate sailing in Britanny and horse-riding in Sancerre; and sat by the pool on a weekend in Montpellier. But even the joy of staying in Paris at the weekend, riding one of the 20,000 free bikes full pelt down the Champs Elysees in the sun and dipping in and out of the museums and cafes is enough. (SJ Berwin 2008/9)

This passage depicts aspects of the young lawyers' experiences during the qualification stage of their career. On analysis, it becomes abundantly clear that professional life involves aspects of consumer-based lifestyles at an early stage and perhaps some elusive notions of constructing race as a component of professional identity through consumptions and personal lifestyles. The process of becoming a lawyer entails a series of identifications with consumer-based elements associated with young people's lifestyles, hinting at issues of race but not clearly exemplifying these. The specific objective of this passage is to attract and convince certain candidates. Therefore, it must narrate a lifestyle with which potential desirable candidates are able to identify. Significantly, although there is reference to traditional aspects of lawyer's lifestyles such as sporting events, office ski trips and cycling, there also is reference to aspects of lifestyle not usually associated with lawyers, like appealing to youth culture references such as a German contemporary dance festival and Ian Brown and Radiohead concerts. This signals a transition to a consumer-based lifestyle professionalism which is channelled through an interrelation of legal skills with consumer-based social skills, addressing in this sense a more culturally but not necessarily ethnically diverse audience.

An alternative interpretation of the extract is that it attempts to construct the legal professional self through cultural practices of consumptions and the

---

[6] As part of the modernised language, Matrix regards the use of the word 'trainee' as a more appropriate term to describe pupillage. One of the successful trainees/pupils describes her experience of working at the set of Chambers: 'No need to dress in a particular way … I was even forced to take regular decent holidays'. http://www.matrixlaw.co.uk/uploads/other/29_03_2011_05_43_28_Traineeship%20Brochure%2011.pdf.

interplay with social and soft skills required by modern-day legal practice. Although this constitutes just another strategy to attract potential desirable employees, it also accords with most of the literature on the organisation of the profession, stressing that businesses pay particular attention to those personal attributes exhibited by the ideal employee (Holmer Nadesan 1999. See also McDowell 1995: 75–95; and Collier 2005). In the extract, the employee communicates to potential candidates the qualities that the firm is looking for by promoting a consumer-based professional self that possesses the ability to both fit in and stand out within the overall culture of the firm, in turn, reflecting the ability of consumption to individualise and collectivise while addressing issues of race, alluding in this sense to the way race is being commodified and eventually becomes a selling point in the organisational context of legal employment. More specifically, while alluding to the commodification of race by taking a more inclusive approach on cultural practices of consumption, informing professional identity, the extract reflects distinctions as to the renegotiation of race as a component of personal identity by emphasising the neo-tribal nature of consumption and the free movement between the 'tribes' and masses.

While the expectations of large commercial law firms and Chambers from the ideal candidates are permeated with replete references to consumption in the advertising material, issues of race remain questionably dormant, or carefully sidestepped and disassociated from markers of self-identity such as race. Participation in such cultural practices serves as a medium of antagonistic tendencies in the upper echelon of the profession. This is reflected in the way in which these are communicated to new or potential recruits, emphasising the individualistic nature of the upper end of the legal profession and the individualistic nature of the professional self through consumptions. Conversely, such a technique promotes a diverse culture while silencing components of self-identity such as race, as illustrated in the following somewhat dated but pertinent examples:

> The hip media luvvies at Olswang are on the lookout for bright young lawyers and have been trying to lure them by holding a bash at the Ministry of Sound for law students and trainees. Highlight of the evening will be the finals of a student/lawyer DJ competition, just to prove that the Covent Garden trendies appreciate the sort of lawyer that can sew up the contracts by day and spin the discs by night. (Legal Week 2001)

A more simplified (front cover) example reads:

> London Calling.[7] (SJ Berwin 2012/13)

---

[7] This is another music reference used for recruitment purposes. *London Calling* is one of the tracks contained on the album, *London Calling*, produced in 1979 by a band called The Clash. It was also one of the anthems of the British Punk scene and

An example of the Bar's approach reads:

> The Honourable Society of the Middle Temple Treasury Office Celebration Ball. (Bar News 2008, July vii)

> Disco till 1.30 am. (ibid.)[8]

Notions of hip and cool (Miles 2000; Malbon 1997; and see Pini 2001; Rief 2009) are carefully depicted here as forming youth identity and as constructing legal professional identity while exhibiting some strange connotations with race. These extracts exemplify that the amalgamation of work with music rhythms is coupled with a carefully selected 'white' vocabulary comprising phraseology widely used among young white people, to describe the successful candidate. More specifically, the reference to 'London Calling' hints at connotations with the iconic album by The Clash, a punk rock British band. The majority of the youth culture accounts exemplify that the punk scene has always been associated with homogenous and predominantly 'white' middle-class but also working-class crowds (Miles 2000; Malbon 1997; McRobbie 1994). The use of cultural practices of consumption associated with youth lifestyles as a means of promoting success and competition within the context of the legal profession denotes evidence of neo-tribalism in the upper end of the legal profession and creates distinctions in terms of race in the context of legal practice.

The constant repetition of personal pronouns in the legal press and advertising material of large commercial law firms and Chambers attests to the fact that being an individual and having personality are essential requirements within the context of legal employment. The professional self is realised and achieved through recruitment by the firm or set of Chambers.[9] The promotion of the successful professional self through references to consumer-based lifestyles also alludes to the transition in the way the profession now represents, understands and promotes itself from the importance of character once associated with the legal profession, to the importance of personality attributes. This personality can also be consumer-based. The advertising material seems to be in accordance with the literature on cultural and organisational studies which suggest that the rise of consumer society concentrates on the importance of consumer-based personality, surpassing the importance of character (Sennett

---

era. Literature on youth studies accentuates the appeal of the punk music scene to upper as well as working class predominantly white youth.

[8] On how the Inns of Court advertise life at the Bar see the discussion in Rogers, J. (2012). Representing the Bar: How the barristers' profession sells itself to prospective members. *Journal of Legal Studies*, 32(2): 202–225.

[9] This is a recurring theme in the organisational literature. See by way of example Holmer Nadesan, M. (1999). The popular success literature and a brave new Darwinian workplace. *Consumption, Markets and Culture*, 3(1): 27–60.

1977). Goodrich (2001) claims that in practice, personal attributes and choices of lifestyle and of selfhood are open to magnification. The outsider is depicted in personalised terms. Through the exposure of details of lifestyle, the outsider is portrayed as tied to subjective qualities that escape the norm (ibid.).

More recent examples of advertising material refer to issues of inclusion and diversity by linking these notions to successful performance and client care, as seen in the quote below.

> Creating an inclusive environment at Freshfields, where diversity of thought is valued, and people feel they belong and can thrive is central to making us a stronger firm and delivering better outcomes for clients. This has been a focus for us for some time, and we are proud of the progress we have made, but we need to go much further. This includes tracking our progress against ambitious targets to increase the pace of change and embedding commitments across the firm so that everyone understands the role they play. (Freshfields 2018)

The advertising material attempts to construct who successful candidates are. The analysis suggests that reference is made to certain types of social and cultural traits and this, in turn, points to a particular type of candidate. Literature on the profession suggests the successful candidates are usually the ones who fit the image of the law firm and that the profession seeks to portray (Francis & Sommerlad 2009). However, the law student population, the audience for this material, is very diverse, suggesting that they have different types of social and cultural traits to the ones that the profession seeks to portray (ibid.). Statistics from the Bar and from large commercial law firms, however, confirm that they recruit from the pool of young, predominantly white, male and middle-class, despite progress on issues of diversity (Boon et al. 2005; Whyte 2023; Shiner 2000). In accordance with the literature on the issue, the construction of the ideal candidate in the advertising material might not be as inclusive and diverse as the material suggests (Collier 2005, 2006). Another example portraying similar rhetoric as to the association of inclusion and diversity and its interplay with business and the way business is done reads as follows:

> At Herbert Smith Freehills, we do not expect our people to be or think the same – indeed, diversity and inclusion drive our success and the innovative solutions we deliver with our clients. That's why fostering an inclusive culture where our people can be themselves, contribute their perspectives and perform roles which are meaningful and aligned to our shared values is a core business priority. (Herbert Smith Freehills 2022)

The way that the profiling of potential successful candidates is constructed in advertisements from large commercial law firms is explicitly linked to recruitment, revealing evidence of Maffesoli's neo-tribal sociality in the legal profession.[10] Although profiling is linked to recruitment, representations of race are ambiguous in the advertising material. More specifically, the persistence in the all-inclusive rhetoric amounts to the disappearance of race rather than the realisation of race as a component of self-identity in a Maffesolian sense. Instead, the professional self is realised through the logic of identifications with an all-inclusive and diverse culture of the firm, in the course of business. References to race are reduced to mere expression of firms' and Chambers' diversity policies, reflecting adherence to the SRA standards and Equality Act 2010 with which they must comply. One example from a top barristers' Chambers reads:

> Matrix is committed to creating a safe environment where everyone is able to be themselves. (Matrix 2018)

Using images of lawyers of diverse racial backgrounds creates the impression that black and ethnic minority people are fairly represented in the profession and that self-identity matters. Analysis of images and text, however, creates scepticism and invites comparison with the reality of everyday legal practice (Vaughan 2014, 2017) as to whether or not initiatives such as scholarship schemes have the potential to challenge the stereotypical composition of the upper end of the legal profession at partnership (Whyte 2023) and QC levels.

> 39 Essex Chambers is deeply committed to the implementation and promotion of equal opportunities. We are particularly proud of the number of female QCs we have and the diverse socio-economic background of our barristers. (39 Essex Chambers 2018/2023)

A closer look at the statistics provided by the Chambers suggests that the gender ratio is 33% which translates to 58 women barristers as opposed to 67% for male barristers, which translates to 118 male barristers. The advertising material portrays a willingness to embrace changes in the legal profession in terms of its social composition, which constitutes an element of neo-tribalism in law as it reflects distinctions within the sectors of the legal practice. When compared to studies of the racial makeup of the profession, it becomes apparent that black and ethnic minority lawyers are underrepresented in the higher echelons of the profession, in large law firms and Chambers in particular (Shiner 2000) and are overrepresented in less prestigious branches of the profession (Vignaendra et al. 2000). An example of the willingness to embrace diversity as reflecting not just the core values of the firm but also the change in society comes from Clifford Chance:

---

[10] According to the Maffesolian interpretation, neo-tribal sociality entails a series of identifications that emerge out of participation in different consumer groups performing cultural practices of consumption.

At Clifford Chance we see inclusion as a core value of the firm and also of the law. We understand that diversity and inclusion are good for our staff and their families, our firm and our clients, and society. We believe that to help achieve these values we have to be champions of, and campaigners for them across our firm, with our clients, and in the world.

We see inclusion as an intrinsic value of our firm. It is a matter of justice. It is also a core part of our identity. Our history as a firm has been anchored in innovative and diverse cultures and approaches which have both disrupted traditional attitudes and set global standards. (Clifford Chance 2022)

Statistically if compared to other large commercial law firms, Clifford Chance appears in the UK top 25 UK law firms with the highest percentage in BAME partners, with only 1.2% (this compares with Freshfields at 2% and Linklaters at 1%) (Patel 2021a). These findings are supported by the Law Society's Report (2022: 8, 11) on diversity in the legal profession which, while acknowledging changes in composition and matters of inclusion, concludes that the proportion of black and ethnic minority lawyers in higher positions remains low (see also Sommerlad et al. 2010; and Whyte 2023). Recruitment literature suggests that the upper echelons of the profession prefer graduates from certain universities (Vignaendra et al. 2000; Sommerlad et al. 2010; Webley et al. 2016) whose student body is predominantly white. This raises further concerns about the advertising material examined above, as to whether issues of race are truly tackled in the material, or whether they constitute just another commodity in the legal services market, reflecting the commodified character of the legal profession (Wilkins 2004; Collier 2005; Braithwaite 2010). Although this challenges certain issues on the inclusion of diversity, it concurs with the suggestion that race has become commodified within recruitment and within selection processes in the upper echelons of the profession (ibid.; and see Carbado & Gulati 2004).

The example above taken from Clifford Chance exemplifies how issues of race and ethnicity are kept at a distance from cultural practices of consumption. The stance taken in the material is that legal professional identity is negotiated through issues of consumer-based identifications, which constitute evidence of neo-tribalism in legal practice. What seems to be at odds with this portrayal is that race does not seem to be included in issues of consumption in the same way that other markers of social identity are. The material creates the impression that issues of race are usually treated as promoting social sensitivity and awareness coupled with an acceptance of difference. Socialising plays a significant role in the neo-tribalism of the profession, and a key part of this revolves around the consumption of alcohol. Nevertheless, the material is entirely silent on what the experience will be like for those who, for cultural or religious reasons, abstain from alcohol (Francis & Sommerlad 2009). This echoes a similar suggestion put forward by Goodrich (2001) that cultural practices of consumption can create white spaces within the legal profession and legal practice. Goodrich suggests that different cultural experiences are never quite incorporated within the organisational context of the legal profession. It is in this sense that institutions and organisations remain the same. This, however, reinforces the construction of legal professional identity as a 'white space' (ibid.) and is also reminiscent of the exclusionary practices of the legal professional project.

Criticisms, Absences and Contradictions in the Advertising Material of Large Commercial Law Firms and Chambers

The analysis of the advertising material has shown that cultural practices of consumption and lifestyle and their interplay with issues of race are closely associated with the ways in which the upper echelons of the legal profession promote themselves. It has also demonstrated that the upper end of the profession seemingly encompasses the promotion of diversity and inclusion rhetoric. The commodification of race, diversity and inclusion as portrayed in their advertising materials raises several issues. Firstly, despite the constant reference to an all-inclusive culture, reference to cultural practices of consumption persist in the construction of large commercial law firms and Chambers as predominantly 'white' spaces. Secondly, these references to cultural practices of consumption need to be examined within the parameters of the everyday reality of legal practice at the upper echelons, in order to expose the performance and performativity of race in this legal employment context.

The advertising material provides information on the social life of the firm and Chambers, creating the impression that the working environment is highly sociable and friendly, and promotes close cooperation between members of the firm or set of Chambers. An analytical narration of what these events include, with particular emphasis on certain cultural practices of consumption, usually associated with youth culture, creates the appealing impression of an all-inclusive workplace and culture. The advertising material presents an overall contrast to most of the major studies of the legal profession. These studies fail to address the importance of cultural practices of consumption and the way in which they inform negotiations of race. The advertising material is inextricably linked to the way in which the high end of the profession now promotes, understands and presents itself as a diverse profession, more specifically as leaders for inclusion, whereas statistics suggest that less than 2% are BAME partners in these firms. An illustrative example of how diversity is sold by one of the top large commercial law firms reads as follows:

> Our approach to diversity and inclusion is driven by the principle of 'Leading for Inclusion', a strategy which sets out our vision to be the leading global law firm for diversity and inclusion. We recognise

the power of diversity and inclusion as a driver of innovation, collaboration and positive business outcomes. By enabling our people to be their
unique selves every day – we are Leading for Inclusion. (Herbert Smith
Freehills 2022)

Nevertheless, the advertising material of large commercial law firms and
Chambers is exactly that, merely advertising material. As such, it is designed
to allure and impress, but it is not necessarily designed to portray the reality of
the high end of the legal profession regarding its social composition. For example, the advertising material focuses largely on certain aspects of lifestyles and
cultural practices of consumption rather than others, which sit at odds with
the constant references to the rhetoric of the promotion of inclusion and diversity selling an ethnically diverse working environment to the potential recruits.
Similarly, the absence of reference to the use of these aspects of lifestyles in
legal practice challenges the relationship between the image the high-end
sector of the legal profession would like to portray and the reality of the performance and negotiation of race in everyday legal practice. Narratives describing
the reality of race in everyday legal practice suggest that black and other racial
minority lawyers are deliberately included on client pitches and are then later
excluded, or are merely used as a selling point on advertising materials of the
firm in order to attract clients from a diverse ethnic background (see for example, Patel 2021b).

Although the advertising material seems to promote cultural practices of
consumptions associated with the upper end of the legal profession, these
remain confined to the portrayal of predominantly 'white' aspects of lifestyles.
This again promotes the construction of 'white' spaces through the tactful
avoidance of reference to different lifestyles which would eventually challenge
that 'whiteness'. This could mean that certain lifestyles hinting at certain social
characteristics are more acceptable in the profession than others. Alternatively,
it could indicate that the search for eclectic, postmodern new recruits that large
commercial law firms and sets of Chambers so desperately seem to pursue,
merely constitutes another advertising trick. This complements the recent
findings of the Advertising Standards Authority report (2022a) on the reproduction and reinforcement and even creation of new stereotypes through
advertising (2022b), amounting to what Myers-Lamptey (2021), when referring to the process of inclusion of race as a selling point in advertising, sums up
as mere 'race-washing'.

Current advertising material only portrays the large commercial law firms'
and Chambers' perspective emphasising the promotion of their all-inclusive
policies on diversity and inclusion, therefore converting race to a commodity. However, scant attention is paid to how it is used by lawyers regarding
networking or their progression in the profession and how this exposes ethnically diverse communities within the context of everyday legal practice. In a
profession obsessed with hierarchies, the advertising material does not offer

information on how consumerism challenges or simply conforms to normative patterns of race. More importantly, although filled with constant references to success and progression, the material provides limited information
on the impact of consumer-based lifestyles on the progression and success of
those who have alternative lifestyles and bear social characteristics different to
the norm. One of the few examples on this comes from Linklaters, the first large
commercial law firm hinting at lifestyle choices, in addressing issues of race
by signing up for the Halo Code, a UK campaign advocating for ending hair
discrimination for black employees:

> At Linklaters we are committed to being home to a culture and environ-
> ment in which racial, ethnic, cultural and religious identities are cel-
> ebrated and individuals feel comfortable to bring their whole selves to
> work. We pride ourselves on our values of respect, integrity and inclusion
> and stand against all forms of racism and discrimination. (Edwards 2021)

Yet again the above example provides limited information on how these aspects
of lifestyle are viewed by the ones who exercise control over the appointment of
others to their overwhelming white majority. This makes the attempt of the
upper echelons of the legal profession to assert the importance of the interplay
between issues of race and cultural practices of consumption and lifestyles in
legal practice even weaker. At the same time, it exposes once again the inability
of law to address, accept and expose different individualities and collectivities,
which consider social markers of individual and collective identities such as
race.[11] From this perspective, the reproduction of law in its predominantly white
image, at least at the top of the profession, is based upon the subtle erasure of
race through the very commodification and promotion of race portrayed in the
diversity and inclusion policies of large commercial law firms and Chambers.

Conclusion

This chapter explored how the upper echelons of the legal profession, large
commercial law firms and commercial Chambers, promote and deal with
issues of race, diversity and inclusion in recent and slightly older advertising
material. The analysis of the chapter examined alternative ways of theorising
race through the dynamics of cultural practices of consumption evident in
their advertising material. It also examined the transition in the advertising
material from an emphasis on cultural practices of consumptions and issues
of lifestyles to a rhetoric of the promotion of diversity and inclusion of these
bodies. The analysis of the advertising material coupled with accounts of the

---

[11] This is also reminiscent of Goodrich's argument as to whether or not law can successfully address the question of lifestyles.

organisational literature on the upper echelons of the legal profession exposed exclusionary practices and racial inequalities as they are subliminally and occasionally emphatically played out in the way these entities now understand and promote themselves. More specifically, this chapter suggested that the commodification of race through the incorporation of cultural practices of consumption reinforces exclusionary practices suggestive of racial inequalities in the organisational context of modern-day legal practice. Arguably, these reinforce the ability of the upper echelons to promote and reproduce their own image, predominantly white, while seen as persistently promoting diversity and inclusion and adhering to legal standards. Even more importantly, this chapter revealed the law's inability to fully address the question of cultural practices of consumptions and lifestyles and the way they express different lived cultural experiences at the top end of the profession. This again alludes to exclusionary practices reminiscent of the creation of a white legal professional project and legal professional identity at the pinnacle of the profession.

References

39 Essex Chambers. (n.d.). Diversity and Inclusion. https://www.39essex.com/about-us/social-responsibility

Advertising Standards Authority. (2022a). ASA summary report on tackling harmful racial and ethnic stereotyping in advertising. https://www.asa.org.uk/resource/asa-summary-report-on-tackling-harmful-racial-and-ethnic-stereotyping-in-advertising.html

Advertising Standards Authority. (2022b). Findings on racial and ethnic stereotyping in ads. https://www.asa.org.uk/news/findings-on-racial-and-ethnic-stereotyping-in-ads.html

Baker, C. (2003). Chain reaction. *Law Gazette*, November.

Bar News. (2008). July vii, a supplement to *Counsel Magazine*.

Boon, A., Duff, L. and Shiner, M. (2001). Career paths and choices in a highly differentiated profession: The position of newly qualified solicitors. *The Modern Law Review*, 64(4): 563–594. https://doi.org/10.1111/1468-2230.00339

Boon, A., Flood, J. and Webb, J. (2005). Postmodern profession? The fragmentation of legal education and the legal profession. *Journal of Law and Society*, 34(2): 473–492. https://doi.org/10.1111/j.1467-6478.2005.00333.x

Boon, A. and Whyte, A. (2005). From public service to service industry: The impact of socialisation and work on the motivation and values of lawyers. *International Journal of the Legal Profession*, 12(2): 229–260. https://doi.org/10.1080/09695950500226599

Bourdieu, P. (1990). *The logic of practice*. Cambridge: Polity Press.

Braithwaite, J. (2010). The strategic use of demand-side diversity pressure in the solicitors' profession. *International Journal of the Legal Profession*, 17(3): 442–465. https://doi.org/10.1111/j.1467-6478.2010.00514.x

Carbado, D. and Gulati, G. (2004). The law and economics of critical race theory. *Yale Law Journal*, 112: 1757–1828. http://dx.doi.org/10.2139/ssrn.409360

Chronopoulou, A. (2014). Neo-tribal socialities in the legal profession: The role of consumption in forming legal professional identities (unpublished PhD thesis), Birkbeck College, University of London.

Chronopoulou, A. (2015). From a professional tribe to a business neo-tribe: Towards a theory of consumer-based lifestyles in the legal profession. *Athens Journal of Law*, 1(1): 64–84. https://doi.org/10.30958/ajl.1.1.5

Clifford Chance. (n.d.). Inclusion and Diversity. https://www.cliffordchance.com/about_us/inclusion-and-diversity.html

Collier, R. (2005). Be smart, be successful, be yourself...? Representations of the training contract and trainee solicitors in advertising by large law firms. *International Journal of the Legal Profession*, 12(1): 51–92. https://doi.org/10.1080/09695950500081366

Collier, R. (2006). Peter's choice: Issues of identity, lifestyle and consumption in changing representations of corporate lawyers and legal academics. In: Greenfield, S. and Osborne, G. (eds.) *Readings in Law and Popular Culture*. London: Routledge. pp. 31–64. https://doi.org/10.4324/9780203963838

Crenshaw, K. (1989). Demarginalising the intersection of race and sex: A black feminist critique of antidiscrimination doctrine, feminist theory and antiracist politics. *University of Chicago Legal Forum*, 1: 139–167. http://chicagounbound.uchicago.edu/uclf/vol1989/iss1/8

Edwards, B. (2021). Linklaters becomes first magic circle firm to support Afro hairstyle campaign. *Global Legal Post*, 11 March. https://www.globallegalpost.com/news/linklaters-becomes-first-magic-circle-firm-to-support-afro-hairstyle-campaign-57418054

Evans, D. (1997). Michel Maffesoli's sociology of modernity and postmodernity: An introduction and critical assessment. *The Sociological Review*, 45(2): 221–243. https://doi.org/10.1111/1467-954X.00062

Francis, A. and Sommerlad, H. (2009). Access to legal work experience and its role in the (re)production of legal professional identity. *International Journal of the Legal Profession*, 16(1): 63–86. https://doi.org/10.1080/09695950903204961

Freshfields, Bruckhaus and Deringer. (n.d.). Diversity and inclusion. https://www.freshfields.com/en-gb/about-us/responsible-business/diversity-and-inclusion/

Goodrich, P. (2001). The law of the white spaces: Race, culture and legal education. *Journal of Legal Education*, 5(1): 15–38. https://doi.org/10.1080/1752 1483.2007.11423724

Harris, C. (1993). Whiteness as property. *Harvard Law Review*, 106(8): 1707–1791. https://doi.org/10.2307/1341787

Herbert Smith Freehills. (n.d.). *Diversity and inclusion*. https://www.herbertsmithfreehills.com/content/diversity-and-inclusion

Holmer Nadesan, M. (1999). The popular success literature and a brave new Darwinian workplace. *Consumption, Markets and Culture*, 3(1): 27–60. https://doi.org/10.1080/10253866.1999.9670329

Legal Week. (2001). Where the cool kids hang out. https://www.law.com /international-edition/2001/11/07/where-the-cool-kids-hang-out/

Maffesoli, M. (1996). *The time of the tribes: The decline of individualism in mass society*. London: Sage. https://doi.org/10.4135/9781446222133

Maffesoli, M. (1996). *The contemplation of the world: Figures of community style*. Minneapolis: University of Minnesota Press.

Maffesoli, M. (2007). Tribal Aesthetic. In: Cova, B., Kozinets, R. V. and Shankar, A. (eds.) *Consumer tribes*. Oxford: Butterworth-Heinemann. pp. 27–34. https://doi.org/10.4324/9780080549743

Malbon, B. (1999). *Clubbing: Dancing, Ecstasy and vitality*. London: Routledge. https://doi.org/10.4324/9780203026458

Matrix Chambers. (n.d.). Core values https://www.matrixlaw.co.uk/csr/core -values/

Miles, S. (2000). *Youth lifestyles in a changing world*. Buckingham: Open University Press.

McDowell, L. (1995). Body work: Heterosexual gender performances in city workplaces. In: Bell, D. and Valentine, G. (eds.) *Mapping desire: Geographies of sexualities*. London: Routledge. pp. 75–95. https://doi.org/10.1177 /0309132515585

McRobbie, A. (1994). Shut up and dance: Youth culture and changing modes of femininity. In: McRobbie, A. (ed.) *Postmodernism and popular culture*. London: Routledge. pp. 155–176.

Mishcon De Reya (2014). Quintessentially.

Myers-Lamptey, D. (2021). Time to ditch the 'race-washing' in ads. *Campaign*, 27 October. https://www.campaignlive.co.uk/article/time-ditch-race-washing -ads/1731554

Nicholson, D. (2005). Demography, discrimination and diversity: A new dawn for the British legal profession. *International Journal of the Legal Profession*, 12(2): 201–227. https://doi.org/10.1080/09695950500246522

Patel, V. (2021a). 'They used me for a pitch, then excluded me': How major law firms are using their black lawyers to mislead on diversity. Law.com, 16 November. https://www.law.com/international-edition/2021/11/16/they -used-me-for-a-pitch-then-excluded-me-how-major-law-firms-are-using -their-black-lawyers-to-mislead-on-diversity/

Patel, V. (2021b). Rankings reveal which law firms have the most black lawyers in the UK. Law.com, 25 May. https://www.law.com/international -edition/2021/05/25/rankings-reveal-which-law-firms-have-the-most -black-lawyers-in-the-uk/

Pini, M. (2001). *Club cultures and female subjectivity: The move from home to house*. Basingstoke: Palgrave Macmillan. https://doi.org/10.1057/9781403914200

Rogers, J. (2012). Representing the Bar: How the barristers' profession sells itself to prospective members. *Journal of Legal Studies*, 32(2): 202–225. https://doi.org/10.1111/j.1748-121X.2011.00213.x

Rief, S. (2009). *Club cultures: Boundaries, identities and otherness*. London: Routledge.

Rolfe, H. and Anderson, T. (2003). A firm choice: Law firms' preferences in the recruitment of trainee solicitors. *International Journal of the Legal Profession*, 10(3): 315–334. https://doi.org/10.1080/0969595042000228784

Savage, M., Barlow, J., Dickens, P. and Fielding, T. (1992). *Property bureaucracy and culture: Middle class formation in contemporary Britain*. London: Routledge. https://doi.org/10.4324/9781315884349

Sennett, R. (1977). *The fall of the public man*. London: Penguin.

Shiner, M. (2000). Young gifted and blocked! Entry to the solicitors' profession. In: Thomas, P. (ed.) *Discriminating lawyers*. London: Cavendish. https://doi .org/10.4324/9781843140184

SJ Berwin. (2008–9). *The Plum*.

SJ Berwin. (2012–3). *The Plum*.

Skeggs, B. (2004a). *Class, self and culture*. London: Routledge. https://doi .org/10.4324/9781315016177

Skeggs, B. (2004b). Context and background: Pierre Bourdieu's analysis of class, gender and sexuality. In: Adkins, L. and Skeggs, B. (eds.) *Feminism after Bourdieu*. Oxford: Blackwell, pp. 19–34.

Sommerlad, H., Duff, L., Webley, L., Muzio, D. and Tomlinson, J. (2010). *Diversity in the legal profession in England and Wales: A qualitative study of barriers and individual choices*. Legal Services Board.

Sommerlad, H. (2011). The commercialisation of law and the enterprising legal practitioner: Continuity and change. *International Journal of the Legal Profession*, 18(1–2): 73–108. https://doi.org/10.1080/09695958.2011.619852

The Counsel Bar News. July 2008.

The Law Society Report. March 2022.

Thornton, M. (1996). *Dissonance and distrust: Women in the legal profession*. Melbourne: Oxford University Press.

Vaughan, S. (2014). Going public: Diversity disclosure by large UK law firms. *Fordham Law Review*, 82: 2301. https://ir.lawnet.fordham.edu/flr/vol83 /iss5/6

Vaughan, S. (2017). Prefer not to say: Diversity and diversity reporting at the Bar of England and Wales. *International Journal of the Legal Profession*, 24(3): 207–226. https://doi.org/10.1080/09695958.2016.1181076

Vignaendra, S. (2001). Social class and entry into the solicitors' profession. *Research Study 41*. London: The Law Society.

Vignaendra, S., Williams, M. and Garvey, J. (2000). Hearing Black and Asian voices – An exploration of identity. In: Thomas, P. (ed.) *Discriminating lawyers*. London: Cavendish Publishing. pp. 121–154. https://doi.org /10.4324/9781843140184

Webley, L. and Duff, L. (2007). Women solicitors as a barometer for problems within the legal profession: Time to put values before profits? *Journal of Law and Society*, 34(3): 374–402. https://doi.org/10.1111/j.1467-6478 .2007.00397.x

Webley L., Tomlinson, J., Muzio, D., Sommerlad, H. and Duff, L. (2016). Access to a career in the legal profession in England and Wales: Race, class and the role of educational background. In: Headworth, S., Nelson, R. L., Dinovitzer, R. and Wilkins, D. B. (eds.) *Diversity in practice*. Cambridge: Cambridge University Press. https://doi.org/10.1017/CBO9781316402481 .007

Whyte, A. (2024). Do prizes have any point? The potential for diversity initiatives to change the ethnic profile of the solicitors' profession. In: Whyte, A., Tuitt, P. and Bourne, J. (ed.) *The long walk to equality: Perspectives on racial inequality, injustice and the law*. London: University of Westminster Press, pp. 77–112.

Wilkins, D. (2004). From 'Separate is Inherently unequal' to 'Diversity is good for business': The rise of market-based diversity arguments and the fate of the black corporate bar. *Harvard Law Review*, 117: 1554. https://doi .org/10.2307/4093260

Zimdars, A. (2010). The profile of pupil barristers at the Bar of England and Wales 2004–2008. *International Journal of the Legal Profession*, 17(2): 117–134. https://doi.org/10.1080/09695958.2010.530881

CHAPTER 5

Do Prizes Have Any Point? The Potential for Diversity Initiatives to Change the Ethnic Profile of the Solicitors' Profession

Avis Whyte

Introduction

When it comes to the ethnic makeup of commercial law firms, the industry isn't as representative of contemporary society as it could be. Firms are replete with white men and women, but individuals from ethnic minority backgrounds can ... be few and far between. Where, I hear you ask, are the Black rainmakers? (Dikko 2018)

At the culmination of three decades of change, we have a solicitors' profession which is more representative of ethnic diversity in the general population (Aulakh et al. 2017: 11–12). Yet despite changes the profession remains stratified. It is dominated at its top by white graduates from higher socio-economic backgrounds (Bridge Group 2020; Law Society 2020a), especially white men at partnership level (Aulakh et al 2017; Fouzder 2017a). Less than one per cent of partners in large law firms are black (Extense 2022). This chapter considers what role diversity and social mobility initiatives play in increasing ethnic

How to cite this book chapter:
Whyte, A. 2024. Do Prizes Have Any Point? The Potential for Diversity Initiatives to Change the Ethnic Profile of the Solicitors' Profession. In: Whyte, A., Tuitt, P. and Bourne, J. (eds.) *The Long Walk to Equality: Perspectives on Racial Inequality, Injustice and the Law*. Pp. 77–112. London: University of Westminster Press. DOI: https://doi.org/10.16997/book63.e. License: CC-BY-NC-ND 4.0

diversity in the solicitors' profession and considers the potential of such initiatives to influence law firm structure in the future.[1] It focuses on black males
as a particularly underrepresented group,[2] and though the situation does not
appear to be much better for black women (Bindman 2020; Law Society's Fiona
Woolf Lecture 2020), their consideration is outside the scope of this chapter.
In focusing on black males, the chapter uses Freshfields Bruckhaus Deringer's
diversity initiative, the Freshfields Stephen Lawrence Scholarship (FSLS), as a
case study, although other law firms' initiatives are briefly considered by way of
comparison and contrast. The chapter considers the impact, and thus the value,
of these initiatives in promoting access by black males to elite sectors of the
'top ten' solicitors' firms.[3] The central question is then, are initiatives important
in changing the culture of large City law firms? And ultimately, do they have
potential to effect sustained change to the perceived old, white male face of the
profession more generally (University of Law 2021)?[4]

The chapter begins with mention of methodology, then considers context
and background on the profile of the solicitors' profession, before examining
the FSLS as a case study and highlighting other diversity and social mobility
initiatives. It moves on to consider the potential impact of these initiatives on
the profile of the solicitors' profession. The chapter ends with a discussion and
concluding remarks.

Method

The method employed in this chapter is that of desktop analysis of available statistical data on the legal profession and analysis of data on minorities
both in legal education and practice. I also review the reports, academic and

---

[1] The Bar faces similar issues, see for example, The Bar Council, (2021). *Race at the
Bar: A snapshot report* (www.barcouncil.org.uk/uploads/assets/d821c952-ec38
-41b2-a41ebeea362b28e5/Race-at-the-Bar-Report-2021.pdf); The Bar Standards
Board, (2022). *Diversity at the Bar 2021* (www.barstandardsboard.org.uk/uploads
/assets/be522642-160b-433b-af03a910a5636233/BSB-Report-on-Diversity-at
-the-Bar-2021.pdf); and Freer's in depth study of social mobility and the legal profession which examines access to the Bar and uses Inner Temple's Pegasus Access
and Support Scheme as a case study: Freer, E. (2018). *Social mobility and the legal
profession: The case of professional associations and access to the English Bar*. London:
Routledge.
[2] Solicitors Regulation Authority statistics for 2022 show that black lawyers make up
2% of all lawyers in law firms and that there are fewer men (46%) in the legal profession than women (52%).
[3] Considered in this chapter as firms inhabiting the magic and silver circles (see
further pp92–99).
[4] This perception is, to a great extent, borne out by the current statistics on the profession (see Context and Background, pp79–85).

professional, that examine professional widening in relation to minorities, and the regulatory changes that have occurred in the light of calls for widening diversity in the legal profession. The key part of this chapter is a close examination of the FSLS. This is based on available statistics (some of which were provided by Freshfields to universities considering entrants for the scholarship), data from social media sites such as LinkedIn, and my own involvement with students from the University of Westminster School of Law who have entered the scholarship initiative. Examination of other firm's initiatives are limited to those in the magic and silver circles with data being gathered from the firm's website and the website of the organisations with which they collaborate. The main reason for this is the finding that transformation happens when driven and facilitated by those at the top (see for example, Braithwaite 2010).

Context and Background

As indicated above lack of diversity in the legal profession is not a new issue and can be traced back to at least the mid 1970s. Before this it was rare for ethnic minority graduates to pursue careers as solicitors because, until 1974, only British subjects could enter the solicitors' profession and because overseas (mainly Commonwealth) students primarily trained for the Bar as this gave them an option to practise in their home countries (Goulbourne 1985: 5). Because of the myriad problems faced trying to practise at the Bar,[5] the trend then became for law graduates to select the solicitor route into the legal profession. According to Goulbourne, this increased pressure for access and exposed the solicitors' profession's 'conservatism' (ibid.).

By 1979, the Benson Report (1979) warned that the consequences of conservatism could be a profession bifurcated along lines of ethnicity because minorities, unsuccessful in securing positions in large law firms or Chambers for failure to fit the received profile, would set up on their own.[6] Placing responsibility on the two branches of the profession to achieve full racial integration, the

---

[5] Including the difficulties of earning a living wage during the early years and the resulting uncertainty of a long-term career at the Bar (Goulbourne 1985), see further Zander, M. (1980). *The state of knowledge about the English legal profession.* Chichester: Barry Rose. Moreover, for ethnic minority barristers finding seats in Chambers in the first instance was much more difficult than for their non-ethnic counterparts (Benson Report 1979).

[6] The report found evidence that ethnic minority barristers were the least successful in finding seats in Chambers and were conscious of the fact that there were sets of Chambers exclusively made up of ethnic minorities. Consequently, Benson was concerned that, with the increased number of ethnic minority solicitors, 'if the present pattern of events were repeated the results would be that firms of solicitors composed exclusively of members of ethnic minorities would set up in practices in areas with a substantial minority population ... there would be a clear division on

report recommended, inter alia, that they should set up procedures for keeping records on ethnicity. In turn these records would provide the evidentiary basis for future policy making. Unwilling to acknowledge racial discrimination in the profession, the Law Society did not follow this recommendation. Its reluctance was somewhat explained by a confidential report from a working party of the Professional and Public Relations Committee in 1983 which had found no evidence of racial discrimination and thus no need for remedial action, explicitly ruling out the need for ethnic monitoring (Goulbourne 1985: 12–13).

By the 1980s there was a groundswell of opinion that the composition of the profession should be more reflective of society (Twining 1989; Boon 2014), and the Law Society faced the heavy weight of adverse publicity in the media (including Legal Action, The Guardian and The New Statesman) as well as calls from campaigning groups (like The Trainee Solicitors Group and The Minority Access Project) to at least take minimal measures to demonstrate some commitment to examining racial discrimination in the profession (Goulbourne 1985: 13). Consequently, the Law Society established a working party for this task (ibid.). Then in 1984 the Law Society published its first Annual Statistics Report (ASR) on trends in the solicitors' profession. These reports aim to provide a comprehensive picture of the changing size and structure of the legal profession over time, including its ethnicity profile.

With acceptance of the need for monitoring the composition of the legal profession, the 1990s saw the Law Society act to deepen its understanding of entry into the profession by funding two research studies into training and putting further measures in place to respond to discrimination issues. In assessing the impact of the Legal Practice Course (LPC),[7] the first study (Goriely & Williams 1996) found that when assessing applicants, the main consideration for law firms was, 'are they one of us?' (ibid., as cited by Boon 2014: 579; see also Rolfe & Anderson 2003). As Boon (2014) observed, '[t]his potentially discriminated against anyone who was not male, white or middle class' (ibid.: 579). The findings of Goriely and Williams drove the second bout of research, the Law Society's longitudinal 'Cohort Studies',[8] tracing a

---

racial lines in the practice of the law and, to some observers, the administration of justice itself' (para. 35.2).

[7] The LPC was introduced in 1993 replacing the Law Society Finals as the new training schemes for solicitors. See Wallach, S. (1992). Transforming knowledge into know-how: The Law Society's finals are to be replaced with a one-year training scheme that will emphasize practical skills. The Independent, 20 August.

[8] Published from 1994 to 2000 there were six cohort study surveys conducted by different teams of academics. The first, Halpern, D. (1994). Entry into the Legal Professions: The Law Student Cohort Study Years 1 and 2. London: The Law Society. The second, Shiner, M. and Newburn, T. (1995). Entry into the Legal Professions: The Law Student Cohort Study Year 3. London: The Law Society. The third, Shiner, M. (1997). Entry into the Legal Professions: The Law Student Cohort Study Year 4, London: The

large group of undergraduates into practice (ibid.). In terms of more concrete measures the Law Society, in 1995, appointed an Equal Opportunities
Officer and introduced the Solicitors Model Anti-Discrimination Policy[9]
(ibid.: 578). The policy is noteworthy in that it obligated firms not only to take
'positive action to ensure greater representation of unrepresented groups' but
also to 'compl[y] with Law Society policy on targets for the employment of
ethnic minorities', defined as people of 'Asian, African-Caribbean, African or
Chinese origin' (ibid.).

By 2002, the Chief Executive of the Law Society declared a good record of
tackling unlawful discrimination in the legal profession but admitted considerable obstacles to achieving a representative profession remained (Boon ibid.).
This admission currently holds true, but the data does demonstrate some progress. In its ASR 1990 the Law Society found that just over 1% (n=709) of the
solicitors' profession were known to be 'from the ethnic minorities', but the
ethnic origin of 30% (n=16,622) of solicitors was unknown (Law Society 1990:
4). However, over 30 years later, known numbers have grown and Black Asian
and Minority Ethnic (BAME)[10] solicitors with practicing certificates (PCs) now
make up 18.1% of all PC holders (Law Society 2022a: 11).[11] This is higher than
the 13.4% of BAME in the wider working population (Law Society 2020b: 4).
On average the decade 1990 to 2000 saw an increase of around 400 BAME PC
holders per annum. The next two decades saw an increase of around 800 per
annum (see Figure 5.1 below).

Law Society. The fourth, Shiner, M. (1999). *Entry into the Legal Professions: The Law
Student Cohort Study Year 5*, London: The Law Society. The fifth, Duff, E., Shiner,
M., Boon, A. and Whyte, A. (2000). *Entry into the Legal Professions: The Law Student
Cohort Study Year 6*. London: The Law Society.

[9] Rooted in the Sex Discrimination Act 1975 and the Race Relations Act 1976.

[10] I am aware of the debates surrounding the use of this term and its acronym as
'masking tremendous heterogeneity' (Webley et al 2016: 202) and being unreflec-
tive of communities and their experiences, alongside calls for the term to be dis-
continued (see for example, The Commission on Race and Ethnic Disparities 2021:
32). Indeed, in answering these calls, the UK government now no longer uses the
terms BAME and BME when writing about ethnicity but instead refers to ethnic
groups individually (www.gov.uk). However, the term is used here because of its
widespread currency and application in much of the relevant research on which this
chapter relies.

[11] There remains concern about underreporting of ethnic background particularly
among newly qualified solicitors with a record 33,561 solicitors of unknown ethnic
origin in 2020, almost 5,000 more than in 2019 (Law Society March 2022b: 8). The
Law Society explains this number as likely being due to an increase of non-reporting
of ethnicity. Its report observes: 'most newly admitted solicitors do not provide their
ethnic origin on the mySRA website. Unless this data is collected through other
means, the ability to monitor diversity trends based on individuals' ethnicity will be
further impacted' (ibid.).

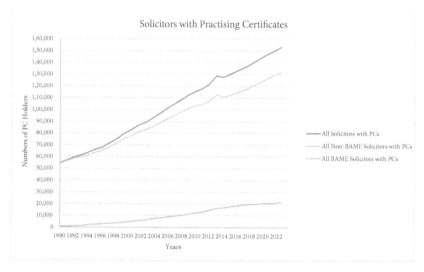

Figure 5.1: Solicitors with Practising Certificates 1990 to 2022. Source: Compiled from the Law Society Annual Statistic Reports (1990 to 2022) and tables detailing the ethnicity of solicitors holding PCs.

Furthermore, the Solicitors Regulation Authority (SRA), in its 2021 biennial survey of law firm diversity,[12] found that 17% of solicitors are of BAME origin (SRA 2022). Asian solicitors account for approximately two-thirds of this number at 12%, whereas black solicitors account for 2% (ibid.). The latter figure is roughly in line with the percentage of black people in the general working population (3%) (ibid.) whereas Asian solicitors make up near double their proportion in the working population (7%) (ibid.). Mixed/multiple ethnic groups accounted for 3% of solicitors (compared to 1% of the workforce) and 'other' ethnic groups made up 1% of solicitors (compared to 2% of the workforce) (ibid.). So, whilst other ethnic groups appear to be thriving, black groups appear to be lagging behind.

The SRA statistics (ibid.) also show that more BAME solicitors can be found in firms mainly undertaking less prestigious and remunerative criminal and private client work than those doing mainly more prestigious and remunerative corporate work. In criminal firms, 5% are black and 21% Asian (overall 30% BAME). In private client firms, 8% are black and 22% Asian (overall 33% BAME). By contrast, in corporate[13] firms, merely 18% of lawyers are BAME

---

[12] Under paragraph 1.5 of the Code of Conduct for Firms it is a regulatory requirement that all regulated firms, regardless of size, must collect, report and publish data about the diversity make-up of their workforce every two years (SRA *Reporting your Firm Data*, www.sra.org.uk/solicitors/resources/diversity-toolkit/your-data).

[13] The SRA statistics concentrate on corporate rather than commercial law, a focus of this chapter. Though they are both related to business, they are separate fields of law

(10% Asian and 2% black). Likewise qualitative studies suggest BAME lawyers are concentrated in the less prestigious and lucrative sectors of the profession (see e.g., Ouseley 2008; Aulakh et al. 2017; Hinde, Marchant & Lay 2020). The SRA's statistics further show that firms undertaking mainly corporate law have the lowest proportion of state secondary-educated solicitors at 45%, compared with 70% state educated solicitors in firms mainly undertaking criminal law (SRA 2022). Those attending private fee-paying schools dominate the corporate and arguably the commercial world. Indeed, Aulakh et al. (2017: 5) have commented:

> … the profession remains heavily stratified by class, gender and ethnicity. Large city law firms undertaking the highest paying legal work are dominated by white men, who are likely to have attended fee-paying schools and have a family background of attending university.

Although it has clearly taken time, and though some areas remain stubborn in the face of change, the profile of the profession is slowly shifting, particularly in relation to ethnic diversity. The research has identified a number of reasons for this shift. There is altruism, with law firm decision makers championing diversity and inclusion and possibly 'competitive altruism' between firms (Hull 2013). There is also belief in the business case of a strong correlation between inclusivity and profits (Hunt et al. 2015 (known as the McKinsey Report) and 2018; Parker 2017 and 2020), i.e., the 'diversity dividend' (www.Arrival Education.com).[14] Urwin et al. (2013) question, however, the limited quantitative data that evidences belief in a business case. Ely and Thomas (2020) go further by stating that none of these claims are supported by 'robust research findings', whereas there is abundant research supporting the finding that increasing the number of those traditionally unrepresented in a workforce does not *automatically* lead to notable improvement in firms' effectiveness or financial performance (ibid.). They characterise this as an 'add diversity and stir' approach which, if business continues as normal, has little effect on the bottom line (ibid.).

Legal and regulatory objectives and obligations have also contributed to the shift. The Legal Services Board (LSB) and legal service regulators (including

---

covering and governing different areas of a corporation's activities. Broadly speaking, corporate law concerns corporate governance and corporate finance. Whereas commercial law concerns the day-to-day aspects of running a business such as commercial transactions and business deals. Commercial law is therefore broader than corporate law. All the law firms considered here conduct both.

[14] The 'diversity dividend', a phrase coined by Arrival Education, expresses the commercial potential for those companies who can diversify their workforce at all levels.

the Law Society[15] and the SRA[16]) share an objective under the Legal Services Act 2007 to encourage an 'independent, strong, diverse and effective legal profession' (Legal Services Act: s.1(1)(f); and see further Braithwaite 2008 and p99 in this volume). Furthermore, the legal profession must meet its duties under the Equality Act 2010 to avoid discrimination in employment and service provision and the SRA's equality and diversity requirements and expected outcomes[17] (see further p99).

A critical role is also played by other outside parties, most importantly clients, the media and interest groups, pressuring firms to take action on diversity (Braithwaite 2008: 3). One very effective way they do this is by inventing and awarding prizes, for example, the UK Diversity Legal Awards,[18] and by running league tables. Indeed, following a study analysing a decade of information from the Black Solicitors Network (BSN) Diversity League Tables (DLT),[19] Dame Linda Dobbs DBE suggested, 'since publication of the first Diversity League Table, there has been positive change for which the DLT can take much credit' (Urwin & Gould 2017: 3).

There is, however, frustration at the pace of change which, in relation to progress at the top for black ethnic minority lawyers, the BSN has called 'painstakingly slow' (BSN in DLT 2020a: 38). This frustration centres especially on large law firms whose record on diversity is consistently problematic (Braithwaite 2010: 142) and on top commercial firms who tend to have narrow diversity profiles (Business In The Community n.d.; Tillay 2020); the frustration is often manifested in firms, alongside the profession in general, being challenged to talk less and do more about ethnic diversity (Redfield 2009; Mattu 2020). This frustration and call for action is set against a global backdrop which has seen growing and intense focus on diversity and inclusion due to the

---

[15] The independent professional body for solicitors in England and Wales. Run by and for its members, the Society is the 'voice of solicitors'.

[16] As the largest regulatory arm of the solicitor's profession, the SRA serves the public interest and protects consumers of legal services.

[17] These are set out in principle six of the SRA Principles ('you act in a way that encourages equality, diversity and inclusion' www.sra.org.uk/solicitors/standards-regulations /principles); chapter one of the SRA Code of Conduct for Solicitors, Registered European Lawyers and Registered Foreign Lawyers (www.sra.org.uk/solicitors /standards-regulations/code-conduct-solicitors/); and the SRA Code of Conduct for Firms ('you do not unfairly discriminate by allowing personal views to affect your professional relationships and the way in which you provide your services' www.sra.org.uk/solicitors/standards-regulations/code-conduct-firms).

[18] Founded in 2009 these are the only industry awards which focus solely on recognising, promoting and celebrating equality, diversity and inclusion across the legal profession.

[19] Started in 2006, The Law Society sponsored Diversity League Table is now widely considered to be one of the legal profession's leading diversity reporting initiatives and publications.

#BlackLivesMatter[20] movement and in particular the death of George Floyd, a black American man, at the hands of white police. His death swelled a worldwide tidal wave of conversations.

The legal profession took part in these conversations, with firms acknowledging the fact that the profession is not immune from charges of racial inequalities, prejudice and unfairness (Ashurst 2021: 12). Senior lawyers added their voices, characterising the circumstances of Mr Floyd's death as a catalyst for deeper change (Cohen et al. 2020).[21] Moreover, the Black Solicitors Network (2020b) wrote an open letter to all law firms and legal service providers calling on them 'to "walk the talk", to turn positive intentions into positive actions and create a level playing field for all.' The letter continued by outlining five 'action points' around which firms and providers could anchor their diversity efforts (metrics, targets and accountability; retention; promotion; organisational culture—inclusive leadership; and external diversity engagement/ social impact (ibid.)). The action points distilled by the BSN are not new. Over the years many firms have taken up these types of challenges, making conscious efforts to diversify their workforce and foster inclusivity (Dikko 2018), often covering some or all the action points. However, perhaps the times in which they are now operating and the will to engage with them are new or at least have been reinvigorated. If this is the case then there is potential for the face of the profession to darken.

The next section is an in-depth examination of the Freshfields Stephen Lawrence Scholarship (FSLS) as an example of the ways one global law firm is responding to the challenges as they relate to black men as high-status practitioners in commercial law. For comparison, context and contrast, it also highlights some of the analogous initiatives offered by other firms.

The Freshfields Stephen Lawrence Scholarship (FSLS)[22]

Black teenager Stephen Lawrence was murdered in an unprovoked racist attack while waiting at a bus stop in south-east London in 1993 (Macpherson 1999). Five years later the Stephen Lawrence Charitable Trust was founded by his mother, Doreen Lawrence, to provide support and bursaries to young people from disadvantaged backgrounds who, like Stephen, wanted to become

---

[20] See https://blaclivesmatter.com/about/ for more information.

[21] Clifford Chance issued a forthright statement from Senior Partner Jeroen Ouwehand and US Head Evan Cohen which acknowledged they could and would do more to tackle racial injustice. Other firms issuing statements included Bryan Cave Leighton Paisner, Baker McKenzie, Linklaters, and Allen & Overy.

[22] In relation to the scholarship, much of the information in this section is taken from Freshfields website pages (including its interviews with scholars) and the additional information the firm shares with the University of Westminster Law School as one of the universities from which it recruits its scholars.

architects (BBC n.d.). The trust went on to expand its horizons 'to include ambitious "Access to Professions" schemes and programmes enabling young people to challenge the confines of "Elitist Britain"' (ibid.). One such scheme was the Freshfields Stephen Lawrence Scholarship (FSLS). After a trial run in 2012, in 2013 Freshfields Bruckhaus Deringer set up the FSLS with the support of Stephen's mother (who, in the same year was made Baroness Lawrence of Clarendon OBE). Hailed as a 'first-in-kind race and social mobility scheme' (Legal Business Awards 2014) and the most innovative diversity initiative in the City (BITC n.d.), it aimed to address the disproportionate underrepresentation of black and black mixed-race males from low-income households and less socially mobile backgrounds, in large commercial law firms.[23]

The scheme is annual and is open to every UK University Law School. Since the scheme's launch Freshfields has worked with over 70 universities across the country. Universities nominate candidates they think eligible and exceptionally talented enough to be considered for a scholarship. Exceptional talent is not measured by a minimum grade requirement, it is judged in the round. Therefore, candidates must exhibit 'desk smarts' (explained as problem solving and lateral and agile thinking, the ability to identify key issues and see the 'big picture'), 'street smarts' (explained as commercial and international instinct, plus common sense and numeracy), communication skills (including the ability to clearly explain concepts), people skills (including leadership potential), resilience (including a 'can do' attitude), drive, rigour and a passion for learning (including self-awareness and the ability to learn from mistakes).[24]

The Eligibility, Application and Award Process

To be eligible not only must candidates be exceptionally talented and, of course, interested in a legal career (or one in the City) but they must also be male, black (African, African-Caribbean, or mixed-race thereof), generally speaking, in their first year of studying for a law degree at a UK university, state school educated and meet specified socio-economic criteria (for example being in receipt of a maintenance loan or having received free school meals).

Once the conditions for eligibility are established, the application proceeds in two stages. Firstly, the application itself is made by the university, which completes the application form having identified the exceptionally talented candidate(s) and having discussed the scheme with them (universities cannot nominate a scholar without first having a conversation with him about why

---

[23] In 2017 the scholarship was expanded to cover their underrepresentation in the City of London, i.e., the financial services sector.

[24] The Freshfields Stephen Lawrence Scholarship Scheme 2021, Universities Day Slides 21 Jan 2021, slide 29.

Table 5.1: FSLS Candidate Summary 2013–2020.

	2013	2014	2015	2016	2017	2018	2019	2020	Totals	Averages
Insight Day	26	36 [+10]	47 [+11]	53 [+6]	93 [+40]	110 [+17]	102 [−8]	88 [−14]	555	69
Assessment Centre	30	42 [+12]	51 [+9]	50 [−1]	68 [+18]	86 [+18]	93 [+7]	68 [−25]	488	61
Runners-up	24	36 [+12]	44 [+8]	40 [−4]	55 [+15]	74 [+19]	79 [+5]	55 [−24]	407	51
Runners-up Follow-up meetings	14	12 [−2]	26 [+14]	23 [−3]	25 [+2]	51 [+26]	55 [+4]	41 [−14]	247	31
Runners-up work shadowing	5	5	10 [+5]	21 [+11]	19 [−2]	35 [+16]	28 [−7]	30 [+2]	153	19
Scholars	6	7* [+1]	7	10 [+3]	13 [+3]	12 [−1]	14 [+2]	13 [−1]	82	10

Note: The figures in brackets represent movement in numbers from the previous year.
* The number of candidates attending each stage of the scholarship process and becoming scholars is taken from the information Freshfield provides to universities. There is an error here as, based on the number attending the Assessment Centre (42) and becoming runners-up (12), six (not seven) scholarships were to be awarded.

they think him exceptional enough to be put forward). Secondly, candidates submit a two-minute supporting video.

Prior to the university making applications on the behalf of eligible students, they are all invited to an *insight meeting* at Freshfield's offices in London (Freshfields 2022). Financed by Freshfields, the meeting takes about a day and students gain an understanding of the purpose and content of the scheme and what Freshfields looks for in its scholars, as well as what the firm does. Not only do candidates meet staff from Freshfields and those from other City organisations but also previous scholars. Candidates have the opportunity to ask questions and discuss the Assessment Centre stage of the process. Though attendance is voluntary, and does not form part of the application process, the insight meeting presumably allows candidates to make an informed decision about their nomination and allay any fears they might have about the next stage of the process. However, as the insight meeting is not mandatory it is not possible to substantiate these assumptions from the available data or quantitively assess the impact the meeting has in driving candidates to the Assessment Centre (see Table 5.1).

Candidates whose nominations are successful are next invited to attend an *Assessment Centre*, which is also fully funded by Freshfields (Freshfields 2022). Attendance is compulsory and over two in-person days, followed by some further virtual assessments via Microsoft Teams. Candidates learn and are tested, individually and in groups, on competencies covering not merely intellectual ability but skills such as critical thinking and problem solving. Personal characteristics are also tested. The tests are aimed at assessing exceptional talent and gauging potential across many areas. Hence there are exercises covering all the exceptional talent competences as explained above and including 'desk smarts' and 'street smarts'. This type of aptitude testing for disadvantaged groups may be seen as a more efficient and objective method of selection than traditional interviews and exams, which are possibly more biased in favour of more privileged groups (Twining 1989: 279). Indeed, there is much evidence to suggest that assessment centres are perceived as fair (Thornton & Byham 1982; Robertson et al.1991) and that their procedures do not disproportionately reject candidates from any particular social group (Huck & Bray 1976; Ritchie & Moses 1983).

Characterised as being 'fun, challenging and constructive', regardless of whether candidates are ultimately selected as scholars (Freshfields 2022: 9), the Assessment Centre process is clearly very influential as it is after this that candidates are selected for scholarships. Scholarship support then begins in the summer of the year in which the application was submitted.

The scholarship lasts 15 months and its benefits are bespoke, so tailored to meet the needs of each individual scholar. They include a £5,000 contribution towards course and associated study-related costs; skills workshops; an alternative route to a guaranteed interview for a Freshfields training contract; mentoring; work shadowing; and development opportunities such as careers advice, interview coaching and support with job applications, networking and commercial awareness. Freshfields collaborates with clients and partners, e.g., Goldman Sachs and the Bank of England, to deliver aspects of the scheme.

A vital component of the scholarship, worth final mention is *Project Week* wherein scholars are given an 'authentic experience of working in a high-pressure corporate environment' (Danby 2020). Without prior notice, at the beginning of the week scholars are given a brief on an important topical issue and, by the end of the week, must produce a comprehensive report and present their strategies and findings (ibid.). The week enables scholars to get as close as possible to real client work without being qualified lawyers (Danby 2020). In reflecting on his experiences of the FSLS one scholar commented:

> One of the best highlights would be when we did the project week … we got a taste of the hours that people do here. I quite enjoyed that myself … you're working midnight hours and you're in this group of people all coming together to try and just get it done. (Bingham 2018)

From this explanation of the FSLS we move on to measure its effectiveness at a micro level, i.e., from the perspective of nominees, runners-up, scholars and the firm. This is done by analysing the numbers passing through the scheme and their career destination as well as the effect the scholarship has on the firm and its members.

Measuring the Effectiveness of the Scholarship

When the FSLS started in 2013 six scholarships were awarded. Almost triple that number were awarded in 2022 bringing the total to 111 with an average of approximately 11 scholars each year (see Table 5.1). There is no maximum intake but clearly this is not, and does not aim to be, a volume scheme. Rather it is about exposing high performing black males to an environment they may be unfamiliar with or may have self-selected out of, on the assumption their face would not fit. Though there are relatively few scholars the numbers going through the scholarship process has generally increased year on year (ibid.).

When the scheme first began there were 15 participating universities. Currently 31 universities take part. Information on the number of candidates each university puts forward is not publicly available. However, bearing in mind the eligibility requirements, the numbers attending the insight meeting and the Assessment Centre, and personal knowledge of the numbers put forward from University of Westminster Law School, it is possible to estimate that each university nominates one to four students. An estimated yearly average of nominees would therefore be 108.

The numbers going to the insight meeting and through the Assessment Centre have increased reasonably steadily over the years (see Table 5.1). There was a huge jump in 2017 when an extra 40 students came to gain an insight into life at Freshfields (ibid.). This was due, at least in part, to the scheme being opened up to non-law students. In 2020, numbers were down at each stage of the scholarship process, probably due to the Covid-19 pandemic. However, this did not impact the number of scholarships awarded which, at 13, was above average. Overall, Freshfields has assessed 488 candidates since 2013, one in six of whom secures a scholarship (c.17%).

Though the numbers are small the scheme is successful at the micro level. Nominees who do not progress to the Assessment Centre stage report a boost in confidence and motivation in having been identified as 'exceptionally talented' and thus nominated – a fact which has appeared on disappointed nominees' LinkedIn profiles.[25] From the insight meeting, candidates get a glimpse of a world that has not been part of their vision, which encourages them to challenge and reset their low expectations. As a 2017 runner-up put it:

> Initially I didn't have a clue about what went on in the professional legal world. The process has helped me to understand how a large successful

---

[25] LinkedIn describes itself as the world's largest professional network on the internet. As a social networking site, it is designed specifically for the business community, allowing professionals to connect, share and learn from each other.

firm operates. I had vague ideas about employment, but my sights were set quite low. The Stephen Lawrence Scholarship process opened my eyes to the scope of legal roles and helped me to focus where I want to be when I enter the profession. (Daliel 2017)

Runners-up value the Assessment Centre experience for giving them a better understanding of working in a corporate environment and for learning about the skills, attributes and experience they need to pursue a commercial law career or one in the City. Participation also provides valuable experience for future assessments. Furthermore, runners-up receive feedback, are invited to follow-up meetings and are given the opportunity of work shadowing. The benefits of participating in the process are encapsulated in the words of a 2013 runner-up thus:

I came out of the scheme with newfound energy to strive for more [and] made friends ... I didn't think I was good enough and now I know I am good enough. Often you feel inferior when you come up against people from certain backgrounds but when you recognise your own strengths that is no longer a factor. I earned it. He's there by merit. (Colas 2013)

And in the words of a 2018 scholar thus:

I think one good thing about this whole programme is that even if you don't win it, you are part of that family regardless. We still keep in contact. I heard back from some other scholars who may not have won the scholarship but they're still excited because they just got off doing their one week work experience, so everybody is appreciative of what's going on regardless. (Biney 2018)

One concrete measure of the scheme's success is the career destinations achieved by its scholars. At present, some scholars have still to reach recruitment stage. Of those who have, two-thirds have roles at leading commercial law firms or barristers' chambers and investment banks, or are studying for their Master's degree (see Table 5.2). To scholarship year 2019, 16 scholars had accepted training contracts at Freshfields, an average of two trainees per year.

Overall, there is substantial attrition in numbers from nomination to award. It is conceivable that participation in the process confers the main benefit, as candidates change their vision of the possibilities open to them and have opportunities to network. Indeed, many scholars use the professional networking site LinkedIn to connect with one another[26] and some have set up networks

---

[26] For example, Freshfields Bruckhaus Deringer Scholars: Kamso Nwokolo (2022), Tyron Denton (2022), Idris Noor (2022), Yemi Adeboyejo (2022), Jason Mbuku (2021), Jeante Nero (2021), Theo Duah (2020) and Curtley Bale (2019).

Table 5.2: FSLS Career Trajectory by year (and number of scholars).

	2013 [6]	2014 [7]	2015 [7]	2016 [10]	2017 [13]	2018 [12]**	2019 [14]
Continuing studies	1		1		3	6	13***
Legal analyst	1						
Civil Service (fast stream)	1						
Training contracts: qualified		2	2	7	4	3	1
Goldman Sachs contract		1		1	2	2	
Qualified Lawyer		4*					
The Bar			2				
Leaving FSLS with a first-class degree			1				
Business			1				
In work/recruiting	3			2	4	2	

* One at Freshfields and three elsewhere.
** These figures were taken from the information Freshfields provides to universities. There appears to be an error as 12 scholarships were awarded in 2018, however, 13 destinations are noted.
*** Includes one defer/resume studies.

of their own to support aspiring commercial lawyers with their insights and advice (e.g., www.thelegallineup.com).

Success can also be looked at from the perspective of Freshfields and its staff. Indeed, Urwin and Maatwk found that the FSLS has had 'significant impact on Freshfields' culture, particularly in the way it views and addresses inclusion' (2021: 23). The scholarship is clearly an important part of the firm's social mobility activities and practically demonstrates its commitment to equality, diversity and inclusion. This commitment was recognised in 2016 at the UK Diversity Legal Awards, when Freshfields won the law firm award for the FSLS, as the Diversity and Inclusion Initiative of the Year (www.diversitylegalawards .org). It is noteworthy that all stages of the scholarship are solely financed, organised and operated by the firm, which is unusual as typically firms outsource at least one stage of the process (Legal Business Awards 2014). Over 230 Freshfields volunteers are involved in the scholarship at various stages. Benefits include gaining unique insights from the type of black males they might not typically have encountered. Such publicity and kudos are obviously beneficial to the firm. Before and since the introduction of the FSLS other initiatives have emerged with similar aims. The next section considers some of these.

'Magic and Silver Circle' Law Firms
and Internal Diversity Initiatives

Freshfields is one of five 'magic circle' firms, the others being, Allen & Overy, Clifford Chance, Linklaters, and Slaughter and May (Chambers Student n.d.). These firms are global leaders and deemed 'the best' at corporate, banking and finance work (ibid.). Claims are also made of a 'silver circle', the band of five law firms falling just below those in the 'magic circle' (ibid.).[27] All these firms typically rank highly in the Social Mobility Index (Social Mobility Foundation, 2022: 3).[28] Figures from the latest index show over one third of the top 75 social mobility employers are law firms (n.35 ≅ 48%) and of these 23% (n.8) are magic and silver circle (ibid.).[29] As firms in a position to make real changes, it is worth taking time to consider their commitment to diversity and in particular to bringing more black males from low-income backgrounds into their ranks.

All these firms have *internal* mechanisms, groups and networks addressing inequalities of ethnicity, diversity and inclusion (EDI) (see Table 5.3). For example, Ashurst has the Ashurst Black Network, the Social Inclusion and Mobility Network and the Race and Ethnicity Equality Group (Ashurst 2021: 30). However, none of the firms have initiatives precisely the same as the FSLS, though, some have some similar attributes (see Table 5.3). In particular Linklaters' Making Links Scholarship and Herbert Smith Freehills' Roger Leyland Memorial Excel Scholarship are both aimed at black and minority ethnic students interested in a career in commercial law (ibid.).

'Magic and Silver Circle' Law Firms and External Drivers

Magic and silver circle firms, in addition to or instead of internal initiatives often partner with *external* organisations to deliver on their EDI promises (see Table 5.3). For instance, Clifford Chance partners with Aspiring Solicitors, which aims to increase diversity in the legal profession (www.aspiringsolicitors .co.uk) and Slaughter and May partner with upReach, which works to assist undergraduates from less-advantaged backgrounds to access and sustain high profile graduate positions (https://upreach.org.uk).

---

[27] They are Ashurst, Bryan Cave Leighton Paisner, Herbert Smith Freehills, Macfarlanes and Travers Smith.

[28] Established in 2017 it highlights employers doing the most to change how they find, recruit and advance talented employees from different social class backgrounds.

[29] Four magic circle (MC) firms and four silver circle (SC) firms are in the Index. At no.3 is Herbert Smith Freehills (SC), no.9 is Byran Cave (SC), no.24 is Allen & Overy (MC), no.27 is Slaughter and May (MC), no.28 is Linklaters (MC), no.37 is Freshfields (MC), no.52 is Macfarlanes (SC), and no.69 is Ashurst (SC).

Table 5.3: Magic Circle and Silver Circle Law Firms Initiatives on Ethnic Minorities and Diversity.

	Magic Circle					Silver Circle				
	Allen & Overy	Clifford Chance	Freshfields	Linklaters	Slaughter and May	Ashurst	Bryan Cave Leighton Paisner	Herbert Smith Freehills	Macfarlanes	Travers Smith
Scholarships										
Name and (year established)	Allen & Overy Scholarship (2022)	Clifford Chance Scholarships for Diverse Students in Europe (2022) Part of REACH Race Equality and Celebrating Heritage network	Freshfields Stephen Lawrence Scholarship (2013)	Making Links Scholarship (2019)	Slaughter and May Scholarship Scheme (2021) NB: Law Springboard Programme (upReach)	None but note Access Ashurst Award	Diversity Scholarship Program (USA only)	Roger Leyland Memorial Excel Scholarship (2014)	Macfarlanes Training Scholarship (2022)	None
Internal Diversity Initiatives, Networks, Groups etc.										
Race & Ethnicity	Race & Ethnicity Network (including REACH & Smart Start Mentoring 2009)	Ethnicity (Includes REACH)	Race & Ethnicity (including their global Black Affinity Network (2015))	Race & Ethnicity (includes INspire 2018 and the Race Action Plan 2020)	Employee Networks (Includes DIVERSE ethnic, racial & social diversity)	Inclusion, Diversity and Belonging: Multiculturalism (includes Ashurst Black Network (2020) and the Race & Ethnicity Equality Group)	Internal Diversity Networks: BAME (including Race for Change)	Internal Diversity Networks: Reverse Mentoring	Inclusion: Ethnicity (includes REACH and the BME Reverse Mentoring Programme)	Internal Diversity Networks: BAME inclusion

(continued)

Table 5.3: Continued.

	Magic Circle					Ashurst	Silver Circle			
	Allen & Overy	Clifford Chance	Freshfields	Linklaters	Slaughter and May		Bryan Cave Leighton Paisner	Herbert Smith Freehills	Macfarlanes	Travers Smith
Internal Diversity Initiatives, Networks Groups etc.										
Others	Disability Gender Health/Wellbeing LGBTQ+ Social Mobility Working Families	Disability Faith Gender Inclusion and Diversity LGBT+ Social Mobility Wellbeing	Disability Gender Health/Wellbeing LGBTQ+ Social Mobility Working Families	Diversity, Equity & Inclusion Age & Lifestyle Diversabilities Gender LGBT+ Social Mobility	Empowered (disability & health) Family Network GEN (gender equality & equal opportunities for people of all gender identities) PRISM (LGBTQ+) Thrive (mental health & wellbeing) J-Net (Jewish Network) Muslim Network Christian Network	Caring Responsibilities Disability & Wellbeing Gender Equality LGBTI+ Social Inclusion & Mobility	Disability Gender Health/Wellbeing LGBTQ+ Social Mobility Working Families	Ability Family Gender Equity LGBT+ Multi-culturalism Military Social Mobility	Gender Health/Wellbeing Social Mobility	Disability Gender Health/Wellbeing LGBTQ+
External Diversity Initiatives, Partnerships and Committments										
#10000 Black Interns (2020)	✗	✗	✗	✓	✓	✗	✗	✗	✗	✓
Aspiring Solicitors (2014)	✓	✗	✓	✗	✗	✓	✓	✓	✓	✓

(continued)

Table 5.3: Continued.

	Magic Circle					Silver Circle				
	Allen & Overy	Clifford Chance	Freshfields	Linklaters	Slaughter and May	Ashurst	Bryan Cave Leighton Paisner	Herbert Smith Freehills	Macfarlanes	Travers Smith
External Diversity Initiatives, Partnerships and Committments										
Bright Network (2013)	✓	✓	✓	✓	✓	✓	✓	✓	✓	✓
Law Firm Antiracism Alliance (2020)	✓	✓	✓	✓	✗	✓	✓	✓	✗	✓
Legal Core (2021)	✓	✓	✓	✓	✓	✓	✗	✓	✓	✗
Mansfield Rule (2021)	✓	✓	✓	✗	✗	✗	✓	✗	✗	✗
NOTICED (2013)	✓	✓	✓	✗	✓	✓	✗	✓	✓	✗
PRIME (2011)	✓	✓	✓	✓	✓	✓	✓	✓	✓	✗
Rare Recruitment (2005)	✓	✓	✓	✓	✓	✓	✓	✓	✓	✓
Rare Race Fairness Commitment (2020)	✓	✓	✓	✓	✓	✓	✓	✓	✓	✓

(continued)

Table 5.3: Continued.

	Magic Circle						Silver Circle			
	Allen & Overy	Clifford Chance	Freshfields	Linklaters	Slaughter and May	Ashurst	Bryan Cave Leighton Paisner	Herbert Smith Freehills	Macfarlanes	Travers Smith
External Diversity Initiatives, Partnerships and Committments										
Social Mobility Pledge (2018)	✓	✓	✓	✓	✓	✗	✓	✓	✗	✓
upReach (2012)	✓	✓	✗	✗	✓	✗	✗	✗	✓	✗

Source: Firms websites and external partners website (information as posted by April 2023).

#**10000 Black Interns:** Large companies (including law firms) have promised to cumulatively hire 10,000 black interns, offering paid work experience, providing training and development opportunities and creating a sustainable cycle of mentorship and sponsorship for the black community to improve the diversity of the UK's professional industries (www.10000blackinterns.com/sectorlist/legal-services).

Access Ashurst Award: Recognises one student each year, from their Access Ashurst programme, who has demonstrated outstanding commitment and passion for commercial law over the course of the programme. The recipient receives an annual bursary of £2,000 for the duration of their undergraduate course (www.ashurst.com/en/careers/students-and-graduates/uk/work-experience/access-ashurst/access-ashurst-award/).

Allen & Overy Scholarship: Supports the education of four students from lesser privileged backgrounds while studying law at the National Law School of India University (www.allenovery.com/en-gb/global/news-and-insights/news/ao-encourages-social-mobility-in-the-legal-community-in-india-by-collaborating-with-nlsiu-on-scholarships#:~:text=B%20(Hons)%20and%20LLB%20(,ratio%20in%20the%20scholarship%20candidates).

Aspiring Solicitors: Is a legal diversity platform focused on increasing diversity and inclusion within the legal industry. It partners with firms helping them hire diverse aspiring solicitors by targeting diverse undergraduates, postgraduates and graduates aiming to enter the legal profession through a combination of mentoring and coaching services, diversity specific events, placements and competitions (https://www.aspiringsolicitors.co.uk).

Bright Network: A free membership network designed to help university students and recent graduates across the UK connect with employers and get the support they need to fulfil their potential (www.brightnetwork.co.uk).

Clifford Chance, Scholarship for Diverse Students in Europe: Part of the firm's Race Equality and Celebrating Heritage (REACH) diversity and inclusion initiative, the scholarship aims to improve social mobility within the legal sector and ensure the firm's workforce better represents the social and economic diversity across continental Europe. The Scholarship (three per annum) targets university students with a diverse cultural or social economic background, in their final years of law studies, majoring in business law and interested in pursuing a career in an international law firm (https://careers.cliffordchance.com/spain/your-career/reach-scholarship.html).

(continued)

Table 5.3: Continued.

INspire: This Minority Ethnic Talent programme is designed as a career accelerator to progress talent from minority ethnic backgrounds helping them to overcome progression barriers and ensure that the Linklater's working environment is inclusive for all (https://careers.linklaters.com/en-us/early-careers/diversity#:~:text=Our%20INspire%20Minority%20 Ethnic%20Talent,environment%20is%20inclusive%20for%20all).

Legal CORE: A collective of firms across the UK's legal industry, collaboratively addressing and tackling the lack of representation of ethnic minority talent, to substantively increase the representation of ethnic minorities in private practice. Working collectively firms aim to drive action and facilitate a fundamental shift across the legal sector, more substantial and sustainable in impact than could be achieved by acting individually (www.legalcore.co.uk).

Macfarlanes Training Scholarship: A programme developed within the firm, delivered in partnership with Brunel Law School at Brunel University London and using Rare Recruitment's contextual recruitment system. It is designed to tackle the socio-economic barriers that discourage talented students from joining the legal profession. The firm supports three Brunel law students annually, through a fully funded programme from the first year of their law degree onwards. This includes tuition fees, paid work experience, a paid placement year at the firm, and mentoring from senior lawyers throughout (www.macfarlanes.com/join-us/early-legal-careers/macfarlanes-training-scholarship).

Making Links Scholarship: Designed to help talented university students from underrepresented groups (from a social mobility background) succeed in their early careers. The scholarship offers coaching, work experience and £6,000 in financial support to students committed to pursuing a career in commercial law (https://careers.linklaters.com/en/early-careers /making-links).

Mansfield Rule: Introduced in 2021 the Mansfield Rule is a 12-month certification process that measures whether law firms have considered at least 30% women, racial and ethnic minorities, LGBTQ+ lawyers, and lawyers with disabilities for leadership and governance roles, equity partner promotions, formal client pitch opportunities, and senior lateral positions (see https://www.diversitylab.com/pilot-projects/mansfield-overview/).

NOTICED: The UK's legal profession's first inter-firm diversity network aimed at promoting networking opportunities to integrate, celebrate and educate on diversity across the legal sector and to work towards resolving issues faced by ethnic minority individuals. The network is supported by The Law Society (https://noticed.org.uk).

PRIME: An alliance of law firms across the UK and Republic of Ireland determined to improve access to, and socio-economic diversity within, the legal profession. Every firm involved in PRIME makes 'the PRIME Commitment', of which there are nine, including providing fair access to high-quality work experience for young people who have least opportunity (https://primecommitment.co.uk/about-us).

Race for Change: A annual event (recruitment initiative) run by the Bright network with Bryan Cave Leighton Paisner aimed at supporting black aspiring lawyers (undergraduates and recent graduates) to enter the legal profession and increasing their number in private practice law firms. It offers access to role models and networks, along with practical tips and advice on how to succeed when applying for law firm training contracts and vacation scheme places (https://trainee.bclplaw.com/media/BCLP_London_Apprentice_ Booklet_2021_36pp_DIGITAL.pdf).

Rare Recruitment: Helps drive social mobility in graduate trainee selection. Their Contextual Recruitment System helps put candidates' achievements into context, measuring them against a classification system they have developed, and thus identifying outperformers others may have missed (www.rarerecruitment.co.uk).

Rare Race Fairness Commitment: A signed mutual pledge to strive for racial equality within legal organisations using specific data points, which signatories are mandated to calculate and strongly encouraged to publicise. This internal monitoring of aggregated data measures the signatories' records in hiring black and other ethnic minority lawyers, plus their progress up the career ladder when compared to white colleagues. It also ensures that race and racism are talked about in every induction and every exit interview, and that junior ethnic minority staff have access to the most senior management (www.racefairnesscommitment.com).

(continued)

Table 5.3: Continued.

REACH Network (Clifford Chance): The Race Equality and Celebrating Heritage network focusing on ethnicity, culture, race and heritage that reflect the wide variety of people who make up the firm (www.cliffordchance.com/about_us/inclusion-and-diversity/ethnic-diversity.html).

REACH Programme (Allen & Overy): An internal network which aims to support ethnic minority employees and those from disadvantaged socio-economic backgrounds in their career progression (Urwin & Maatwk 2021).

Roger Leyland Memorial Excel Scholarship: Developed by Rare and Herbert Smith Freehills to provide exceptional black and minority ethnic students with a high level of financial support and unique access to work experience opportunities. It is open to first year BAME students interested in a career in commercial law. Students must be Rare candidates in order to apply. One scholar each year receives £9,000, over three years of study, paid work experience and a guaranteed spot on the summer vacation scheme (www.rarerecruitment.co.uk/excel).

Slaughter and May Scholarship Scheme: Provides bursaries to high-potential undergraduates from less advantaged backgrounds interested in a legal career. Working with upReach, the Scheme provides tailored leadership development opportunities in addition to financial support. The firm funds three cohorts of 10 students per year, for three years of university study (www.slaughterandmay.com/news/slaughter-and-may-announces-new-bursary-scheme-to-support-increased-diversity-in-the-legal-sector).

Smart Start: A work experience and skills programme for Year 12 or equivalent students from disadvantaged backgrounds. It is designed to give students who might not have considered a legal career an insight into the legal environment and potential career opportunities (https://www.allenovery.com/en-gb/global/about_us/responsible_business/our_pro_bono_and_community_work/who_we_support#eligibility).

Social Mobility Pledge: A coalition of 550 businesses globally, as well as more than 50 universities, pledging commitment to social mobility by committing to outreach, access and recruitment by working with local schools and colleges, offering work placements and apprenticeships and adopting open recruitment policies (www.socialmobilitypledge.org/about).

SPARK: Open to exceptional first year law students, second year students of a four-year law degree or penultimate year non-law students, this is a five-day paid scheme during which students experience an intensive schedule of classroom-based learning, complemented with time spent shadowing Clifford Chance lawyers, gaining hands-on work experience. Students are exposed to a variety of networking opportunities and receive a weekly salary of £450.00 (https://careers.cliffordchance.com/london/what-we-offer/spark.html).

upReach: A social mobility charity which, through partnerships with top employers and universities, uses an intensive programme of tailored career support to help disadvantaged UK students access to a comprehensive range of opportunities and activities to broaden their horizons, understand career pathways and develop the skills, networks and experiences needed for professional success and ultimately to access, secure and sustain top graduate jobs (https://upreach.org.uk). One example is upReach's Law Springboard exclusively sponsored by Slaughter and May. It is a two-year programme of personalised careers support, designed to help eligible university students looking to join the commercial law sector.

All the circle firms are signatories to PRIME. Launched in 2011 it is an alliance of UK (and Republic of Ireland) law firms determined to improve access to and socio-economic diversity within the legal profession (https://primecommitment.co.uk). More recently all circle firms have signed up to the RARE Race Fairness Commitment (launched July 2020), which is a series of commitments for the recruitment, progression and retention of black and all ethnic minority talent for businesses operating in the UK (https://racefairnesscommitment.com). By signing, the firms are mandated to calculate specific data points on race as a means of measuring their efforts to eradicate institutional racism, and are strongly encouraged, though not obliged, to make their data public (ibid.). All circle firms (Ames 2015) use RARE's real time, Contextual Recruitment System, which integrates with their recruitment system and measures disadvantage (e.g., qualifying for free school meals) as well as performance (i.e., outperformance against students at the same school) (GC Magazine—The Legal 500, n.d.). As a result, firms can identify exceptional candidates they may otherwise have missed and improve workplace diversity. Furthermore, seven of the ten firms have signed up to the Social Mobility Commission's first sector specific toolkit, launched in 2020 (https://socialmobilityworks.org).[30] By exploring best practices in the sector, the toolkit seeks to supplement and boost current initiatives and provide new insights into best ways of levelling the playing field for the socially disadvantaged, driving positive and impactful change while retaining organisations competitive advantage (ibid.).

Regardless of what firms do under their own steam, they must comply with legal and regulatory requirements on equality and diversity. First, the overarching Equality Act 2010 provides a comprehensive legal framework to avoid discrimination in employment, to protect individuals' rights and to advance equality of opportunity for all. The Act, as a matter of good business practice, permits employers to take *positive action* as a means of alleviating disadvantage experienced by people with a protected characteristic(s), such as race and sex, without that action being classed as unlawful discrimination (see s.158).[31] It also introduced a specific exemption for positive action in relation to recruitment and promotion (see s.159).[32] Secondly, and specific to the field of law, there are the key provisions under the LSA 2007, mentioned earlier, encouraging an independent, strong, diverse and effective legal profession (s.1.(1)(F)).

---

[30] At the time of writing, Clifford Chance, Ashurst and Travers Smith have not signed up.

[31] S.158 *allows*, rather than requires, 'any action' to be taken to support those with a protected characteristic, as long as it is a 'proportionate means'.

[32] S.159 *allows*, rather than requires, an employer to take a protected characteristic into consideration when deciding whom to recruit or promote, where people having the protected characteristic are at a disadvantage or are underrepresented. This positive action can be taken only where the candidates are 'as qualified as' each other.

Meanwhile, the Law Society's and the SRA's commitments and actions in this area must be examined if we are to fully appreciate the potential of initiatives to open doors to the world of commercial law to black males from unrepresented backgrounds, and also, more broadly, their potential impact on the profile of the solicitors' profession. The Law Society demonstrates its commitment to a more diverse legal profession with its Diversity Access Scheme (DAS), Solicitors for Social Mobility: The Ambassadors scheme and its new Diversity and Inclusion Framework.[33] Ten DAS awards are given annually and support promising entrants to the solicitors' profession facing exceptional social, educational, financial or personal hurdles to qualification (www.lawsociety.org .uk/campaigns/diversity-access-scheme). The scheme provides LPC or SQE scholarships, mentoring by practising solicitors and work experience (ibid.). The Ambassador's scheme promotes role models from non-traditional backgrounds who, having achieved their ambitions, are willing to support up and coming youngsters (www.lawsociety.org.uk/law-careers/Becoming-a-solicitor /equality-and-diversity/social-mobility-ambassadors). The Framework encourages and guides firms in taking a systematic approach to embed diversity and inclusion in a sustained and meaningful way. This is done using the Society's three-step action plan and accompanying resources. If firms are already taking action the Framework helps with reviewing that action and identifying gaps or areas for continuing improvement (www.lawsociety.org.uk/topics/diversity -and-inclusion-framework).

The SRA runs a significant programme of work on EDI,[34] work which necessarily accords with the LSA 2007 s.1(1)(f) objective and with the Legal Services Board's (LSB) diversity outcomes. These involve building a better understanding of diversity in the profession, using *evidence* on diversity to inform and evaluate its regulatory arrangements and operational processes, working collaboratively and being more accountable about its diversity work (https://legalservicesboard.org.uk/about-us/diversity-and-inclusion). Specifically, the LSB's requirement for evidence, mandates collection and publication of data on diversity in the legal profession. This is the first and only direct regulatory intervention with regard to diversity in the profession (Vaughan 2015)

---

[33] The framework builds on and replaces the Diversity and Inclusion Charter which was a public statement of its signatories' commitment to promote the values of diversity and inclusion throughout their business. Signatory firms represented over a third of the profession and included all members of the magic and silver circle. The framework represents a practical way of accomplishing action rather than a commitment to act.

[34] See, for example, StaRs (Standards and Regulations) launched in November 2019, where the SRA sets out key obligations placed on firms in respect of encouraging EDI (see Principle 6) and prohibiting discriminatory behaviour (see chapter one of the SRA Code of Conduct for Solicitors, RELs and RFLs and the SRA Code of Conduct for Firms) (SRA n.d.).

and highlights how critical data collection is in developing an effective race and ethnicity strategy. Consequently, biennially, the SRA obliges every law firm in England and Wales to conduct a demographic survey of the makeup of its workforce, then publishes its diversity profile of the profession (www.sra.org .uk/sra/equality-diversity/key-findings/diverse-legal-profession/). Undeniably, the publication is important as it allows the Authority to better understand diversity in the profession and how/whether it is changing. It allows firms to better understand and assess how different groups are represented and making progress, whether the actions they take to address imbalances are having an impact, and to benchmark themselves against others in their sector. The obligation does not carry with it any accountability though. So, the SRA does not impose any sanctions on firms with poor diversity records.

The foregoing suggests that, at least at a micro level, these schemes may be measured as successful and effective for participants and for firms providing them with opportunities. It is more difficult to measure their effectiveness over time and at a macro-level in terms of changing the profile of the solicitors' profession. A macro-level view may suggest they will not cause perceptible alteration in the profile of the solicitors' profession, especially in the commercial law field. However, there may be an extent to which they change perceptions and attitudes towards further action. The next section goes on to explore these suggestions.

Discussion and Conclusions: The Potential and Future of Diversity Initiatives to Change the Profile of the Profession

Research makes it incontrovertible that ethnically diverse lawyers are under-represented in some sectors and at some levels of the legal profession. This is particularly the case for black male lawyers in the fields of commercial and corporate law.[35] As this chapter illustrates, many firms have now recognised the need to put in place measures to counteract their deficit of minority ethnic lawyers and to change the profession's profile towards more inclusivity and diversity (see Table 5.3); but the pace of change is slow despite the many actions taken to address the issues. A reason for this may be the lack of comprehensive and sustained longitudinal quantitative data allowing law firms to evaluate the impact of their initiatives and say what does and does not work. Such data may provide a key to unlocking the potential for increased diversity in the field of commercial law and in the 'upper echelons' of the legal profession (see also in this volume Chronopoulou: Chapter 4) more generally, because it would allow firms to identify any gaps in diversity, concentrate on areas requiring action and gauge progress. Therefore, rather than firms' data gathering merely being about collating numbers, they could leverage that information with a purpose

---

[35] Though black women may fare no better – see p78.

(MacArthur 2020). Indeed, the Legal Services Board) (2021) recently commissioned an independent research report (Bridge Group 2021) to, *inter alia*, investigate the degree to which regulators assess the impact of their diversity and inclusion initiatives. The report findings led to the Board's call for regulators to use the data they collect about legal professions to do more to understand what programmes and initiatives are the most successful at improving diversity and inclusion in the legal sector and as a result to focus on those which make a 'meaningful difference for professionals ...' (LSB 2021). Like Hinde et al. (2020) this research found but few instances where the direct impact of individual initiatives was being measured, though admittedly they may be measured privately but not publicly declared. For instance, by internally keeping track of its scholars' career progression, Freshfields is able to monitor its success in facilitating and fostering entry of black males from low-income backgrounds into the world of commercial law. By contrast the alliance of firms signing up to the PRIME commitment (which includes Freshfields, see Table 5.3) did not focus on data and how to track the progression of teenage work experience students, so 'evidence' of impact is more anecdotal (GC Magazine – The Legal 500, 2019).

The FSLS and similar initiatives, potentially have important parts to play in changing the profession's profile at the junior level. The more schemes and initiatives that embed, the more likely the presence of ethnic minorities, such as black males, will become normalised. This may in turn increase their general access to the fields of law typically viewed as the preserve of the 'privileged'. Indeed, there are 'good' levels of ethnic minority representation at trainee solicitor stage, but the further ethnic minority solicitors move up the profession's ladder, the higher the attrition rate (Urwin & Gould 2017: 15). So, at the peak of the 'diversity pyramid', i.e., partnership, levels of ethnic minority (and female) representation drops substantially (ibid.). Consequently, when measuring the success of schemes and initiatives in increasing diversity, we need to do so, as Tomlinson et al. (2019) state, by focussing on career progression to senior lawyer or partnership roles.

Much qualitative research has been done on the reasons for lack of progression, suggesting a variety of factors as barriers. These include aspirant lawyers not possessing 'the right' educational backgrounds, which is of course one of the factors used to measure socio-economic diversity,[36] itself a barrier to progression (Bridge Group 2018). There is no denying the ethnic diversity in our body of law students or the entrenched stratification of our Higher Education institutions (HEI) between the elite/'old' HEIs and 'new' universities (see

---

[36] Socio-economic status (SES) is a combined (economic and social factors) measure of a person's or family's social and economic position in relation to others in the community, the social hierarchy. Not only is your level, amount and type of education a factor but so too is your level of income and wealth, your type of occupation, your access to good nutrition (including whether you receive free school meals) and where you reside (Baker 2014)

further Bourne: Chapter 6 in this volume). The latter has contributed to the fact that diversity at the stage of legal education has not directly translated into sustained diversity throughout all levels of the legal profession. The bias for leading firms, including large commercial firms, to recruit from elite HEIs has long been acknowledged (Rolfe and Anderson 2003) and as more ethnic minority students can be found at new universities, they are obviously less likely to be recruited. Prior to attending an elite HEI, lawyers in the upper echelons of the profession will typically have attended an independent school. One study called the lack of socio-economic diversity among a group of partners at leading firms in England and Wales 'acute', finding that 48% of those partners were white male and 52% of those white males had attended an independent school (Bridge Group 2020: paragraph d.). The study went on to describe the pipeline to progression for state school attendees as 'disproportionately narrow' (ibid.: paragraph g.).

High socio-economic status (SES) often correlates to the upper classes, middle SES to the middle classes and lower SES to the working classes and the poor. While Ashley and Emspon (2013) concede that SES cannot be directly mapped onto class position their '… research has identified a relationship whereby relatively privileged individuals, based on socio-economic factors, are more likely to gain access to leading law firms' (ibid.: 223). They note a marked preference in these firms for the relatively privileged in terms of material advantage and the privately educated at an 'old' university, preferably Oxbridge (ibid.). Social stratification based on class does have an exclusionary role to play in career progression (Skeggs 1997; Goldthorpe 2000).

Finally, the interplay between class and race is a significant obstacle to climbing the career ladder. If ethnic minority members from a lower social class do not, for instance, possess social capital, have parents who are professionals (parental occupation can be a proxy for class) and attend high status schools, they may not be seen long term, as the right fit for the law firm (see Chronopoulou: Chapter 4). Obstacles to progression can also be internal. For instance, minority ethnic middle-class participants in Archer's study (2011), constructed 'middle-classness' in a range of ways but generally regarded it as unachievable because of its association or conflation with 'whiteness' (ibid.: 148–9). This led to feelings of exclusion from 'authentic' middle-classness (ibid.), and may mean individuals do not aspire to join elite law firms in which they do not see themselves truly belonging or, if they overcome these feelings and clear the external hurdles to join this elite, they leave to join smaller firms or other parts of the legal profession they see as more inclusive (Hinde et al. 2020; RARE 2020). It is worth noting that currently there is nothing embedded in the law which prevents discrimination based on class, i.e., there is no legal framework to tackle it. Consequently, individuals may be denied opportunities based on their accent, their postcode, or any other marker of their socio-economic status (Rickett et al. 2022). This has led to calls for social class to be made a protected characteristic under the Equality Act 2010 (ibid.).

By contrast with the qualitative research highlighted above, and as Tomlinson et al. (2019) and Urwin and Gould (2017) found, there is limited quantitative evidence permitting the accurate mapping of career trajectories of ethnic minority (and women) employees in UK professions. Moreover, even if the data is being gathered it is most likely not being shared publicly. For instance, the Race Fairness Commitment (see Table 5.3) obliges firms to internally collect and monitor the aggregate measure of very specific data points in hiring black (and other ethnic minority) lawyers as well as their career progress in comparison to their white colleagues. However, firms are *encouraged* but not mandated to make this data public, and though RARE (n.d.) produces an aggregate report of data points this is available only to the signatory firms. Consequently, it is difficult to 'differentiate between … possible relevant drivers/barriers to identify which one "bites" and when' (Urwin & Gould 2017: 16). Though, one quantitative finding Urwin and Gould made, which is of particular relevance to this chapter, is that diversity policy and practices have 'no significant impact … on subsequent levels of gender and ethnic diversity' (ibid.: 13). In looking at trajectory rather than less revealing yearly proportions, they concluded firms 'with higher policy scores[37] do not experience a significant upward "diversity trajectory" (ibid.: 46). So, despite implementation of policy and practices which would be classed as diversity good practice, levels of representation at the peak of the profession remain quite stagnant (ibid.: 25). Thus, the increasing numbers of ethnic minorities entering the profession are doing so with 'very little prospect of moving to the top (when compared to their white and/or male counterparts)' (ibid.: 25). One suspects that this is true, however, contextually speaking the FSLS has only been running for a relatively short time. Beginning in 2013 with scholars in the first year of academic study these scholars would, roughly speaking, be in their fifth year post-qualification as solicitors. Therefore, they would not be expected to meet senior lawyer status as yet. If the beneficiaries of these types of schemes do progress in the profession they will act as role models and have the potential to become advocates for, and mentors to, new generations, and their success might further break down bias and prejudice.

While diversity initiatives may make a difference to the profession's profile, legislation possibly deters law firms from engaging with them in any event. For instance, despite its good intentions, the Equality Act 2010 has done little to quicken the pace of change. As illustrated in Table 5.3, employers are willing to use, and are open about using, scholarships, internships, outreach measures and more, to redress disadvantage but may be wary of taking direct positive action as envisaged by s.159[38] (Davies & Robison 2016). Being highly sensitive

---

[37] This was made up of points scored for a range of equality and diversity 'policy' questions including those surrounding monitoring information, leaders championing these issues, the firms external/public face, staff development and support, and recruitment, promotion and retention (see Urwin & Gould 2017: 64–65).

[38] See footnote 31.

to risk they are concerned about actions that could expose them to claims of reverse discrimination (ibid.).

Boon (2022) argued that lawyers' constitutional duty to the rule of law embraced principles of equality and rights. I argue that these duties apply to lawyers' collegial obligations to each other and to society just as much as they do to the rights of clients. Therefore, whatever view one might take on the effectiveness of initiatives, in order to sustain change in the profession's profile, it must deploy every available resource. Additionally, firms must question and publicly *evidence* how their initiatives, practices and policies, work on the ground and fundamentally whether their workplace culture actually supports, promotes and sustains ethnic diversity.[39] This chapter therefore ends with three suggestions. The first is that the legal profession and its associated professional bodies should expand the research in this field. A single case study is reported here and others are referred to but we need sustained research across access to the legal profession. While ad hoc studies have been made, generally it is difficult to draw strong conclusions on the progress, or lack of it, in this particular field. Longitudinal research, perhaps analogous to the 'After the JD' study by the American Bar Foundation,[40] and The Law Student Cohort Study' by the Law Society,[41] would lay the groundwork for real substantive change to occur by providing constant scrutiny of the legal profession's ideals and actions. The second suggestion is that the array of regulators remain committed to change by funding research and using it to ensure the appropriate regulatory framework exists. The third is not so much a suggestion but more of an important appeal. Change within the legal profession and law is slow, perhaps rightly, but nevertheless change must occur. The rule of law (Boon 2022) depends on a fair and just system that believes in access for all in all areas of the legal system. Our treatment of minorities is a good index for change and adherence to the rule of law.

References

Ames, J. (2015). Contextual recruitment hits magic circle: Firms to consider students' economic background and personal circumstances. *Legal Cheek*, 3 September. https://www.legalcheek.com/2015/09/contextual-recruitment -hits-magic-circle-linklaters-to-consider-students-economic-background -and-personal-circumstances

---

[39] Indeed, it may be possible to measure law firm culture using cultural inventory tools which can give firms better understanding of their culture and how to manage it (Henry 2023).

[40] See After the JD Series at https://www.icpsr.umich.edu/web/ICPSR/series/1560. See also ABF Learning and Practicing Law Projects at https://www.americanbar foundation.org/research/learning-and-practicing-law/.

[41] See footnote 8.

Archer, L. (2011). Constructing minority ethnic middle-class identity: An exploratory study with parents, pupils and young professionals. *Sociology*, 4(11): 134–151.

Ashley, L. and Empson, L. (2013). Differentiation and discrimination: Understanding social class and social exclusion in leading law firms. *Human Relations*, 66(2): 219–244. https://journals.sagepub.com/doi/epub/10.1177/0018726712455833

Ashurst. (2021). *Diversity and Inclusion Annual Report 2020*. London: Ashurst.

Aulakh, S., Charlwood, A., Muzio, D., Tomlinson, J. and Danat, V. (2017). *Mapping advantages and disadvantages: Diversity in the legal profession in England and Wales. Final Report for the Solicitors Regulation Authority*. University of Leeds and Newcastle University Business School: Centre for Employment Relations and Innovation and Change.

Baker, E. H. (2014). Socioeconomic status. In: Cockerham, W.C., Dingwall, R. and Quah, S. R. (eds.) *The Wiley Blackwell Encyclopedia of Health, Illness, Behavior and Society*. Oxford: Wiley Blackwell.

Bar Council. (2021). *Race at the Bar: A snapshot report*. https://www.barcouncil.org.uk/uploads/assets/d821c952-ec38-41b2-a41ebeea362b28e5/Race-at-the-Bar-Report-2021.pdf

Bar Standards Board (2022). *Diversity at the Bar 2021*. https://www.barstandardsboard.org.uk/uploads/assets/be522642-160b-433b-af03a910a5636233/BSB-Report-on-Diversity-at-the-Bar-2021.pdf

BBC. (n.d.). Stephen Lawrence Charitable Trust. https://www.bbc.co.uk/programmes/b0547v6h

Benson, Sir H. (1979). The Royal Commission on Legal Services: Final Report. Cmd 7648. London: HMSO.

Bindman, D. (2020). Black women lawyers outline struggles of succeeding at City firms. *Legal Futures*, 1 December. https://www.legalfutures.co.uk/latest-news/black-women-lawyers-outlines-struggles-of-succeeding-at-city-firms

Biney, I. *The Experience: 2018 Scholars Stories*. Video. https://www.freshfields.com/en-gb/about-us/responsible-business/freshfields_stephen_lawrence_scholarship/

Bingham, S. (2018). *The Experience: 2018 Scholars Stories*. Video. https://www.freshfields.com/en-gb/about-us/responsible-business/freshfields_stephen_lawrence_scholarship/

Black Solicitors Network. (2020a). *Diversity league table: Profiling successful change in change in diversity & inclusion: Law firm case studies, 12th edition A report from the BSN*. https://www.1kcloud.com/edlv_qQGTu/#38

Black Solicitors Network. (2020b). *BSNs' Open letter: A call to action for racial diversity*. 22 June. https://www.blacksolicitorsnetwork.co.uk/bsns-open-letter-a-call-to-action-for-racial-diversity/

Boon, A. (2014). *The ethics and conduct of lawyers in England and Wales*. Oxford: Hart Publishing.

Boon, A. (2022). *Lawyers and the rule of law*. London: Hart Publishing.

Bourne, J. (2024). The colour of shame: The lack of ethnically diverse university senior academics and professors – can, and should we, expect the law to provide equality? In: Whyte, A. et al. (eds.) *The long walk to equality: Perspectives on racial inequality, injustice and the law*. London: University of Westminster Press.

Braithwaite, J. (2008). *Power, prizes and partners: Explaining the diversity boom in City law firms*. (PhD), Queen Mary University of London.

Braithwaite, J. (2010). Diversity staff and the dynamics of diversity policy-making in large law firms. *Legal Ethics*, 13(2): 141–163.

Bridge Group. (2018). *Socio-economic background and early career progression in the law*. London: Bridge Group.

Bridge Group. (2020). *Socio-economic background and progression to partner in the law*. London: Bridge Group.

Bridge Group. (2021). *Legal regulation to promote diversity and inclusion: literature review*. https://legalservicesboard.org.uk/wp-content/uploads/2021/05/Bridge-Group-Legal-Regulation-Literature-Review.pdf

Business in the Community. (n.d.). Race Equality Awards 2016 – Recruiting Diverse Talent (private org) – Freshfields Bruckhaus Deringer. https://race.bitc.org.uk/all-resources/impact-stories/race-equality-awards-2016-recruiting-diverse-talent-private-org

Chambers Student. (n.d.). Magic circle law firms. https://www.chambersstudent.co.uk/law-firms/types-of-law-firm/magic-circle-law-firms

Chambers Student. (n.d.). The silver circle. https://www.chambersstudent.co.uk/law-firms/types-of-law-firm/the-silver-circle

Chronopoulou, A. (2024). Neo-tribal sociality in the upper echelons of the legal profession: Issues of race. In: Whyte, A. et al. (eds.) *The long walk to equality: Perspectives on racial inequality, injustice and the law*. London: University of Westminster Press.

Cohen, E., Ouwehand, J., Layton, M. and Brady T. (2020). A call to action for racial equality. www.cliffordchance.com/news/news/2020/06/a-call-to-action-for-racial-equality.html

Colas, C. (2013). *Freshfields scholars stories*. Video. https://www.freshfields.com/en-gb/about-us/responsible-business/freshfields_stephen_lawrence_scholarship/

Commission on Race and Ethnic Disparities. (2021). *The Commission on race and ethnic disparities: The report*. London: The Commission on Race and Ethnic Disparities.

Daliel, J. (2017). UWE law students say, 'magic circle' scheme opens up a whole new world. *Bristol Law School Blog*, 5 May. https://info.uwe.ac.uk/news/uwenews/news.aspx?id=3591

Danby, T. (2020). Stephen Lawrence Scholarship project: Empowering future sustainability experts. https://sustainability.freshfields.com/post/102g7m3/stephen-lawrence-scholarship-project-empowering-future-sustainability-experts

Davies, C. and Robison, M. (2016). Bridging the gap: An exploration of the use and impact of positive action in the United Kingdom. *International Journal of Discrimination and the Law*, 16(2–3): 83–101.

Dikko, H. (2018). How the legal industry is tackling its diversity head-on. *The Lex100*. https://www.lex100.com/2018/12/04/how-the-legal-industry-is -tackling-its-diversity-issue-head-on/

Diversity Legal Awards. (2016). Freshfields Bruckhaus Deringer. https:// diversitylegalawards.org/law-firm-diversity-inclusion-initiative-of-the -year-winner-freshfields-bruckhaus-deringer/

Duff, E., Shiner, M., Boon, A. and Whyte, A. (2000). *Entry into the legal professions: The law student cohort study year 6*. London: Law Society.

Ely, R. J. and Thomas D. A. (2020). Getting serious about diversity: Enough already with the business case. It's time for a new way of thinking. *Harvard Business Review*, November-December. https://hbr.org/2020/11/getting-serious -about-diversity-enough-already-with-the-business-case#:~:text=The%20 Context,results%20in%20better%20financial%20performance

Extense. (2022). *The 1% study*. https://www.extense.co.uk/#study

Fouzder, M. (2017a). White men dominate law firm partnerships. *The Law Society Gazette*. 31 October. https://www.lawgazette.co.uk/practice/white -men-dominate-law-firm-partnerships-sra-research/5063473.article

Fouzder, M. (2017b). Law school tackles profession's dearth of black men. *The Law Society Gazette*. 12 September. https://www.lawgazette.co.uk/practice /law-school-tackles-professions-dearth-of-black-men/5062756.article

Freer, E. (2018). *Social mobility and the legal profession: The case of professional associations and access to the English Bar*. London: Routledge.

Freshfields. (2022). *The Freshfields Stephen Lawrence Scholarship Scheme 2022*: Connecting exceptional talent with great opportunity. https://www.law .ox.ac.uk/sites/default/files/migrated/fslss_2022_brochure_-_final.pdf

GC Magazine—The Legal 500. (n.d.). Interview: Raphael Mokades, founder, Rare Recruitment. https://www.legal500.com/gc-magazine/interview/interview -raphael-mokades-founder-rare-recruitment/#:~:text=In%202015%2C%20 we%20launched%20the,get%20to%20about%2040%20clients

Goldthorpe, J. (2000). Rent, class conflict, and class structure: Commentary on Sørensen. *The American Journal of Sociology*, 105(6): 1572–1582.

Goriely, T. and Williams, T. (1996). *The Impact of the new training scheme: Report on a qualitative study*. London: The Law Society.

Goulbourne, S. (1985). *Minority entry to the legal profession: A discussion paper*. Policy Papers in Ethnic Relations No.2. Coventry: Centre for Research in Ethnic Relations.

GOV.UK. (n.d.). Writing about ethnicity. https://www.ethnicity-facts-figures .service.gov.uk/style-guide/writing-about-ethnicity#bame-and-bme

Halpern, D. (1994). *Entry into the legal professions: the law student cohort study years 1 and 2*. London: The Law Society.

Henry, J. (2023). Everyone talks about their law firm's culture, but is it possible to measure it? *The American Lawyer*, 15 March. https://www.law.com /americanlawyer/2023/03/15/everyone-talks-about-their-law-firms-culture -but-is-it-possible-to-measure-it/?slreturn=20230311100150

Hinde, J., Marchant, D. and Lay, E. (2020). *Race for inclusion: The experiences of black, Asian & minority ethnic solicitors.* DJS Research. London: The Law Society.

Huck, J. R. and Bray, D. W. (1976). Management assessment center evaluations and subsequent job performance of black and white females. *Personnel Psychology*, 29: 13–30.

Hull, H. (2013). Diversity in the legal profession: Moving from rhetoric to reality. *Columbia Journal of Race and Law*, 4(1): 1–22.

Hunt, V., Dennis, L. and Prince, S. (2015). *Diversity Matters*, 2 February. New York: McKinsey & Company. https://www.mckinsey.com/capabilities /people-and-organizational-performance/our-insights/~/media/2497d4ae 4b534ee89d929cc6e3aea485.ashx

Law Society. (1990). *Annual statistical report 1990.* London: The Law Society.

Law Society. (2016). *Trends in the solicitors' profession annual statistical report 2015.* London: The Law Society.

Law Society. (2019). Increasingly diverse solicitor profession more closely reflects society. https://www.lawsociety.org.uk/en/contact-or-visit-us/press -office/press-releases/increasingly-diverse-solicitor-profession-more -closely-reflects-society

Law Society. (2020). Fiona Woolf lecture: The challenges of intersectionality – why are there so few black women lawyers in senior leadership roles in the legal profession and what can we do to change this? https://www.lawsociety .org.uk/topics/women-lawyers/fiona-woolf-lecture-2020-the-challenges -of-intersectionality

Law Society. (2020a). *Diversity profile of the legal profession 2019.* London: The Law Society.

Law Society. (2020b). *Trends in the solicitors' profession annual statistical report 2019.* London: The Law Society.

Law Society. (2022a). *Trends in the solicitors' profession annual statistical report 2021.* London: The Law Society.

Law Society. (2022b). *Trends in the solicitors' profession annual statistical report 2020.* London: The Law Society.

Legal 500. (2019). Whatever happened to PRIME? https://www.inhouselawyer .co.uk/feature/whatever-happened-to-prime

Legal Business Awards. (2014). CSR Programme of the Year, Freshfields Bruckhaus Deringer. https://www.legalbusinessawards.com/wp-content/uploads /sites/23/2019/09/lbas14_csr.pdf

Legal Services Board. (2021). Legal regulators must better understand the impact of diversity programmes if we are to drive meaningful change, 28 May. https:// legalservicesboard.org.uk/news/legal-regulators-must-better-understand -the-impact-of-diversity-programmes-if-we-are-to-drive-meaningful-change

Loury, G., Modood, T. and Teles, S. (eds.) (2005). *Ethnicity, social mobility and public policy: A comparison of the US and UK.* Cambridge: Cambridge University Press.

MacArthur, H.V. (2020). Data and diversity: How numbers could ensure there's a genuine change for the better. *Forbes*, 27 August. https://www.forbes.com /sites/hvmacarthur/2020/08/27/data-and-diversity-how-numbers-could -ensure-theres-a-genuine-change-for-the-better/?sh=3ce3011d6907

Mastin, P. (2020). BSN – 25 years of striving for equality. *The Law Society Gazette*, 26 October. https://www.lawgazette.co.uk/features/bsn-25-years -of-striving-for-equality/5106121.article

Mattu, R. (2020). Law firms urged to talk less and do more on ethnic diversity. *Financial Times*, 2 October. https://www.ft.com/content/e4eeef88-e994 -4fdd-8b9d-0d02b647ee45

Macpherson, W. (1999). The Stephen Lawrence inquiry. Cm 4262-I. London: The Stationery Office.

Nicholson, D. (2015). Demography, discrimination and diversity: A new dawn for the British legal profession? *International Journal of the Legal Profession*, 12(2): 201–228.

Ouseley Report. (2008). *Independent review into disproportionate regulatory outcomes for black and minority ethnic solicitors*. London: Solicitors Regulatory Authority.

Parker Review Committee. (2020). *Ethnic diversity enriching business leadership: An update report from the Parker Review*, 5 February. https://www .nedaglobal.com/assets/files/New_site_PDFs/NEDA%20-%20Review%20 -%20EY-parker-review-2020-report-final.pdf

Parker Review Committee. (2017). *A report into the ethnic diversity of UK boards*. https://assets.ey.com/content/dam/ey-sites/ey-com/en_uk/news/2020/02 /ey-parker-review-2017-report-final.pdf

RARE. (2020). *Closing the ethnicity stay gap: Why firms are failing to retain ethnic minority talent and what to do about it*. https://www.rarerecruitment.co.uk /static/research/2020_Closing_the_ethnicity_staygap_v2.pdf

RARE. (n.d.). Race Fairness Commitment—FAQs. https://www.racefairness commitment.com/static/downloads/faqs.pdf

Redfield, S. (2009). *Diversity realized: Putting the walk with the talk for diversity in the legal profession*. Lake Mary: Vandeplas Publishing.

Rickett, B., Easterbrook, M., Sheehy-Skeffington, J., Reavey, P. and Woolhouse, M. (2022). *Psychology of social class-based inequalities: Policy implications for a revised (2010) UK Equality Act*. The British Psychological Society. https:// explore.bps.org.uk/binary/bpsworks/b5c9f3afe2f3b45b/c831f5664 ba3cea5cfa8e9b372e809c81bd380dc0a801d18dd383b32b57f5abf/bpsrep _rep167.pdf

Ritchie, R. J. and Moses, J. L. (1983). Assessment center correlates of women's advancement into middle management: A 7-year longitudinal analysis. *Journal of Applied Psychology*, 68: 227–231.

Robertson, I. T., Iles, P. A., Gratton, L. and Sharpley, D. (1991). The impact of personnel selection and assessment methods on candidates. *Human Relations* 44: 693–982.

Robinson, M. (2020). This is what a lawyer looks like. *The Law Society Gazette*, 6 May. https://www.lawgazette.co.uk/commentary-and-opinion/this-is-what-a-lawyer-looks-like/5108390.article

Rolfe, H. and Anderson, T. (2003). A firm choice: Law firms' preferences in the recruitment of trainee solicitors. *International Journal of the Legal Profession*, 10(3): 315–334.

Shiner, M. and Newburn, T. (1995). *Entry into the legal professions: The law student cohort study year 3*. London: The Law Society.

Shiner, M. (1997). *Entry into the legal professions: The law student cohort study year 4*. London: The Law Society.

Shiner, M. (1999). *Entry into the legal professions: The law student cohort study year 5*. London: The Law Society.

Shiner, M. (2000). Young, gifted and blocked! Entry to the solicitors' profession. In: Thomas, P. (ed.) *Discriminating lawyers*. London: Cavendish, pp. 87–120.

Skeggs, B. (1997). *Formations of class and gender*. Thousand Oaks: Sage Publications.

Social Mobility Foundation. (2022). *Employer index report 2022*. London: Social Mobility Foundation.

Solicitors Regulation Authority. (n.d.). *Reporting your firm data*. https://www.sra.org.uk/solicitors/resources/diversity-toolkit/your-data

Solicitors Regulation Authority. (n.d.). *SRA code of conduct for firms*. https://www.sra.org.uk/solicitors/standards-regulations/code-conduct-firms

Solicitors Regulation Authority. (n.d.). *SRA code of conduct for solicitors, registered European lawyers and registered foreign lawyers*. https://www.sra.org.uk/solicitors/standards-regulations/code-conduct-solicitors

Solicitors Regulation Authority. (n.d.). SRA standards and regulations. https://www.sra.org.uk/solicitors/standards-regulations/

Solicitors Regulation Authority. (2020). Five year review of our equality, diversity and inclusion work. https://www.sra.org.uk/sra/equality-diversity/diversity-work/promote-equality-five-year-summary/

Solicitors Regulation Authority. (2022). How diverse if the legal profession? www.sra.org.uk/sra/equality-diversity/key-findings/diverse-legal-profession/

Sommerlad, H. (2008). 'What are you doing here? You should be working in a hair salon or something': Outsider status and professional socialization in the solicitors' profession. *Web Journal of Current Legal Issues* 2. http://webjcli.ncl.ac.uk/2008/issue2/sommerlad2.html

Thornton, G. C. and Byham, W. C. (1982). *Assessment centers and managerial performance*. New York: Academic Press.

Tillay, M. (2020). Which law firms have the most black lawyers in the UK? *The American Lawyer*, 12 June. https://www.law.com/international-edition/2020/06/12/which-law-firms-have-the-most-black-lawyers-in-the-uk/

Tomlinson, J., Valizade, D., Muzio, D., Charlwood, A. and Aulakh S. (2019). Privileges and penalties in the legal profession: An intersectional analysis of career progression. *The British Journal of Sociology*, 70(3): 1043–1066.

Twining, W. (1989). Access to legal education and the legal profession: A Commonwealth perspective. In: Dhavan, R., Kibble, N. and Twining, W. (eds.) *Access to legal education and the legal profession*. London: Butterworths, pp. 237–279.

Webley, L., Tomlinson, J., Muzio, D., Sommerlad, H. and Duff, L. (2016). Access to a career in the legal profession in England and Wales: Race, class and the role of educational background. In: Headworth, S., Nelson, R. L., Dinovitzer, R. and Wilkins, E. (eds.) *Diversity in practice*. Cambridge: Cambridge University Press, pp. 198–225.

Wright Edelman, M. (2015). It is hard to be what you can't see. *Child Watch Column*. https://www.childrensdefense.org/child-watch-columns/health/2015/its-hard-to-be-what-you-cant-see/

University of Law. (2021). Is this the face of the legal industry? Half of Brits assume someone working in law will be white. https://www.law.ac.uk/about/press-releases/assumed-face-of-law/

Urwin, P. and Gould, M. (2017). *Barriers and drivers of diversity: Analysis of 10 years of the BSN DLT diversity survey sample of firms*. London: Black Solicitors Network. https://www.blacksolicitorsnetwork.co.uk/the-findings/

Urwin, P. and Maatwk, F. (2021). *Profiling successful change in diversity and inclusion: Law firm case studies*. London: Black Solicitors Network.

Urwin, P., Parry, E., Dodds, I., David, A. and Karuk, V. (2013). *The business case for equality and diversity: A survey of the academic literature*. London: London Department for Business, Innovation and Skills.

Vaughan, S. (2015). Going public: Diversity disclosures by large UK law firms. *Fordham Law Review*, 83(5): 2301–2324.

Wallach, S. (1992). Transforming knowledge into know-how: The Law Society's finals are to be replaced with a one-year training scheme that will emphasize practical skills. *The Independent*, 20 August. https://www.independent.co.uk/news/uk/law-transforming-knowledge-into-knowhow-the-law-society-s-finals-are-to-be-replaced-with-a-oneyear-training-scheme-that-will-emphasize-practical-skills-writes-sharon-wallach-1541673.html

Zander, M. (1980). *The state of knowledge about the English legal profession*. Chichester: Barry Rose.

CHAPTER 6

The Colour of Shame: The Lack of Ethnically Diverse University Senior Academics and Professors – Can, and Should We, Expect the Law to Provide Equality?

Judith Bourne

Academia looks like a pint of Guinness to me – diverse below, but not at the top.

(Wilson 2020)

Introduction

The UK's university sector has a reputation for excellence, which enables it to attract some of the world's finest academics and students (Howell 2014: 98); its system is steeped in a rich history and almost 1,000 years of tradition.[1]

---

[1] For example, the University of Oxford has evidence of teaching since feudal times, 1096.

How to cite this book chapter:
Bourne, J. 2024. The Colour of Shame: The Lack of Ethnically Diverse University Senior Academics and Professors – Can, and Should We, Expect the Law to Provide Equality? In: Whyte, A., Tuitt, P. and Bourne, J. (eds.) *The Long Walk to Equality: Perspectives on Racial Inequality, Injustice and the Law*. Pp. 113–140. London: University of Westminster Press. DOI: https://doi.org/10.16997/book63.f. License: CC-BY-NC-ND 4.0

At the heart of university culture lies the pursuit of objective inquiry and transformative education. In order to thrive and advance, universities need to continue to generate critical and analytical inquiry, but this requires diversity of thought, which can only be achieved by a diversity of academics. On the surface it appears that academics in universities are ethnically diverse, as statistics evidence that, save for black academics, almost all other ethnic groups are well represented at a 'junior' academic level when compared (crudely) to the general population.[2] However, these figures are inconsistent with the disproportionate numbers of ethnically diverse students entering university when compared to white students,[3] and meaningless in light of the statistics that show 88% of university professors[4] and 86% of senior academics[5] are white. These statistics matter, as professors and senior academics are the people who lead universities and who are ultimately responsible for the management, education, curriculum design and research direction of those institutions. The statistics suggest that universities may be institutionally racist, with discriminatory recruitment strategies, and retaining barriers that prevent career progression for academics from an ethnically diverse heritage.

Universities should be meritocracies, providing curricula fit for the twenty first century and representative of not just different races, but also different social classes, ages, abilities, sexes, genders, sexualities and religions. This chapter acknowledges that race is not the only diversity issue within academia, but focuses on the issue of race, the topic upon which this volume based, and is impenitent in its premise that ethnic diversity is good, and worth striving for (Mor Barak 2013: 228). Moreover, as numerous studies show (Page 2008: 335; Dizikes 2014), diversity is good for business (Hunt et al. 2015; Fulp 2018: 30). The lack of ethnically diverse staff at professorial and senior academic levels is a cause for concern, and has consequences, not just for students, other academics and university staff, but also for society and the acquisition of knowledge itself. This chapter will examine whether the law can effect equality in relation to ethnic diversity in professorial and senior academic positions, and whether it is a fair expectation. It will begin with a consideration of the statistics and law, and then move on to consider why, given the 'changing' university, we are not seeing a 'trickle up' of ethnically diverse students into senior roles; the chapter will conclude with possible solutions to this problem.

---

[2] See Table 6.3 below.

[3] See Table 6.4 below.

[4] See Table 6.2 below. 'Professor' is defined by the Higher Education Statistics Authority (HESA) as 'senior academic appointments which may carry the title of professor but which do not have departmental line management responsibilities' (HESA 2022).

[5] See Table 6.2 below. 'Senior academic' is defined as 'senior management' and 'Head of Schools/Senior Function Head' (ibid.).

Table 6.1: Senior academics (Source: HESA 2022).

Ethnicity	Numbers	Total academic staff	% compared to the total academic staff
White	5,490 (86%)	144,255	3.81
Black	75 (1%)	5,940	1.26
Asian	330 (5%)	23,105	1.43
Mixed	80 (1%)	5,675	1.41
Other	85 (1%)	5,445	1.56
Not known	265 (4%)	19,660	1.35
Total	6325	204,080	0.26

Part I: The Statistics

Negative press attention has attached to statistics on academic ethnic diversity within universities with headlines such as 'Minister criticises lack of senior black UK academics' (Adams 2020), 'Racism in UK universities is blocking BAME academics from the top' (Sian 2019), 'British universities employ no black academics in top roles, figures show' (Adams 2017) and 'Only 1% of UK university professors are black' (Coughlan 2019; White 2022). Statistical evidence shows that whilst the numbers of ethnically diverse academics in British universities have risen, ethnic diversity in senior academic positions remain low and unrepresentative (see Table 6.1). White academics are three times more likely to become senior academics than their Asian colleagues and four times more likely than their black colleagues.

Professorial statistics paint a similar picture (see Table 6.2), with white academics four times more likely to become professors than black academics; white professors make up 88% of all professorial appointments.

The statistics on professorial and senior academic numbers are difficult to understand when viewed in context; we will see from Table 6.3 that, save for black academics, almost all other ethnic groups are well represented at a 'junior' academic level, particularly when compared to their numbers in the general population.

Whilst these statistics are hopeful, with numbers appearing to move in a more representative direction, the most recent available statistical report (Advance HE 2021) at time of writing found other areas of concern beneath the veneer of these statistics. For instance, although there has been an increase in 'Black, Asian and Minority Ethnic' academic staff (as defined by ibid.: 12), white academic staff benefit from open-ended or permanent contracts, hold senior management positions and receive higher salary bands compared to their ethnic minority counterparts. Conversely, compared to white academics,

Table 6.2: Professors (Source: HESA 2022).

Ethnicity	Numbers	Total academic staff	% compared to the total academic staff
White	19,130 (88%)	144,255	13.3
Black	165 (1%)	5,940	2.8
Asian	1,705 (8%)	23,105	7.4
Mixed	365	5,675	6.4
Other	85	5,445	1.6
Not known	385	19,660	
Total	21,835	204,080	10.7

Table 6.3: Academic staff (excluding atypical) by personal characteristics. Academic years 2017/18 to 2021/22 (Source: HESA 2022).

Ethnicity	Numbers	Census 2021	% compared to the general population
White	144,255	45.8m (81.0%)	0.315
Black	5,940	2.4m (4.2%)	0.248
Asian	23,105	5.4m (9.6%)	0.428
Mixed	5,675	1.7m (3.0%)	0.334
Other	5,445	1.2m (2.2%)	0.454
Not known	19,660		
Total	204,080	56.5m	0.361

ethnically diverse academics hold more temporary contracts, have higher leaving rates (ibid.: 130), are under-represented in the highest contract levels and are over-represented in the lowest salary bands (ibid.: 131). The report did, however, find that ethnic minority academics are on average paid more than UK white staff (ibid.: 132). So, although diversity has increased and the wage gap decreased, serious problems remain.

As Table 6.4 demonstrates, people from a diverse background are more likely to enter higher education (HE) than their white counterparts and take HE qualifications (Connor, Tyers & Modood 2004: xiii). Therefore, we should be seeing a 'trickle up' of more ethnically diverse staff in senior academic and professorial positions by now. For example, in the five years to July 2020, the number and percentage of white undergraduate entrants went down, but all other ethnic groups undergraduate entrants went up, with the Asian ethnic group having the biggest increase.

Table 6.4: Students entering university (Source: HESA 2021, Table 27).

Year	Asian		Black		Mixed		White		Other	
	%	Number	%	Number	%	Number	%	Number	%	Number
2015/16	10.5	61,545	8.2	48,335	3.8	22,125	76	446,040	1.5	8,715
2016/17	11	63,540	8.5	49,140	4	22,925	75	434,580	1.6	9,290
2017/18	11.3	65,335	8.6	49,860	4.1	23,565	74.2	428,565	1.8	10,345
2018/19	11.5	66,635	8.5	49,300	4.2	24,460	73.9	427,040	1.8	10,175
2019/20	12.2	70,660	8.7	50,655	4.5	25,840	72.6	421,730	2	11,635

In summary, it is therefore possible to say that diverse junior academic staff are becoming more representative of society, but not as representative as their numbers entering university. Senior academic and professorial staff remain predominantly and unchangeably white. University culture remains discriminatory, despite numerous diversity and inclusivity initiatives and not-withstanding over half a decade of race discrimination legislation. We will next consider the law's ability to effect equality in universities and thus change these statistics in the future.

Part II: Equality and Discrimination Legislation

The UK has had almost 60 years of protective legislation against racial inequality and discrimination, perhaps not a long period of time in legal history, but long enough to have expected parity between races in institutions such as universities. This legislation was piecemeal and arose slowly and incrementally over time. Indeed, the Race Relations Act (RRA) 1965 was the UK's first legislation prohibiting discrimination on racial grounds in places of 'public resort',[6] making it a civil wrong. The RAA 1965 did not prohibit direct discrimination in employment, so could not have been used by ethnically diverse academics to challenge non-appointment to senior positions. Overall, the 1965 Act was toothless, representing a failed attempt to remove formal inequality.[7]

---

[6] Section 1 (2) defined public resort as hotels, restaurants, cafes, pubs or other places where food was supplied for consumption; theatres, cinemas, dance halls; sports grounds, swimming pools or other places for entertainment, public transport; and places maintained by a local authority.

[7] It could also be described as simple, if a somewhat naïve, response to a country in which immigrants were arriving in ever increasing numbers, often in reply to government invitation but against the backdrop of a collapsed empire.

Therefore, in 1968 a new Race Relations Act was introduced. The RRA 1968 extended the 1965 Act to cover both public and private employment, as well as other areas of life, such as housing. In theory this legislation would have assisted anyone challenging their non-appointment to a senior academic or professorial position. However, the 1968 Act had little impact, mainly because it was difficult to enforce, but it did send out a powerful public information message that racial discrimination was not an acceptable form of behaviour.

Eight years later, and replacing the 1965 and 1968 Acts, the RRA 1976 was introduced in an attempt to eradicate more subtle indirect discrimination and to make enforcement of the law easier. Later, the Race Relations (Amendment) Act 2000 placed a general duty on schools, universities and public authorities to rid themselves of racist practices, and to promote equality and good relations between different races. In light of the statistics on senior and professorial academic staff discussed in Part I, it is evident that this legislation was not entirely successful.

The present law on race discrimination is contained within the Equality Act 2010 (EA 2010), which replaced previous anti-discrimination laws (including repeal of the RAA 1976), putting all equality legislation within a single Act.[8] It offers legal protection to people if they fall within one or more of the nine categories of protected characteristics.[9] It protects against indirect[10] and direct discrimination,[11] as well as harassment and victimisation. Race is one of those nine protected characteristics and defined within section 9 (1) as: (a) colour; (b) nationality; and (c) ethnic or national origins.

The 2010 legislation also introduced the notion of 'positive action', a way for employers (in theory) to encourage and assist people with a protected characteristic in relation to recruitment and promotion in employment. These provisions are contained within sections 158 and 159 of the Act.[12] This is positive action and *not* positive discrimination,[13] which remains both discriminatory and unlawful. Section 158 lawfully allows employers to take

---

[8]   It brought together over 116 separate pieces of legislation, including the Race Relations Act 1976.

[9]   Section 4 contains the protected characteristics: age; disability; gender reassignment; marriage and civil partnership; pregnancy and maternity; race; religion or belief; sex; and sexual orientation.

[10]   According to section 19 EA 2010, indirect discrimination is for example, where an organisation, such as a university, puts a rule/policy/way of doing something in place that has a worse impact on someone with a protected characteristic, in our case, race, than someone without one.

[11]   According to section 13 EA 2010, direct discrimination is where a person is treated worse than another person because of a protected characteristic, in our case, race.

[12]   Positive action acknowledges that in order to overcome disadvantage, a person with a protected characteristic should be given equality of opportunity.

[13]   Positive discrimination would treat the person with the protected characteristic more favourably than candidates who do not fall into any of the protected characteristic categories – this would be direct discrimination.

proportionate action where they believe a protected group suffers a disadvantage, has particular needs or does not participate enough in an activity. The employer can take proportionate action to reduce the disadvantage, meet the particular needs or increase their participation. If the employer has evidence of employee disadvantage they can take positive action, such as ensuring bias is removed from recruitment processes, reviewing their recruitment strategies, reviewing their promotion practices, providing mentoring for and/or coaching for protected groups and raising awareness of the issues. However, although there are examples of action employers may take, positive action is not actually defined by the legislation. As a result, many employers are wary of falling foul of the law and having to defend themselves in an employment tribunal. Section 159 concerns recruitment and promotion. It allows for the (mythical) 'tiebreaker' situation, which is where employers can recruit or promote a person with a protected characteristic if they are equally qualified as the other candidate. There have been few cases on this, and it is difficult to use because it is rare for two candidates to be identical. Both sections are unclear and thus usually legally meaningless and unhelpful.

Additionally, from 2011 all publicly funded authorities, such as universities, have been placed under a public sector equality duty (PSED) which requires them to pay due regard to the need to eliminate harassment (pursuant to section 149 of the Equality Act 2010). Universities, are required, in carrying out their functions, to have due regard to the need to achieve the objectives set out under s149 of the Equality Act 2010 to:

(a) eliminate discrimination, harassment, victimisation and any other conduct that is prohibited by or under the Equality Act 2010;
(b) advance equality of opportunity between persons who share a relevant protected characteristic and persons who do not share it;
(c) foster good relations between persons who share a relevant protected characteristic and persons who do not share it.

It does not place a positive duty on universities to take all reasonable steps to prevent racial harassment; rather, the onus is on individual academics to make a challenge via litigation, but litigation is expensive, time-consuming and difficult (Equality and Human Rights 2019).

However well-intentioned and protective the EA 2010 (and previous legislation) set out to be, it has been passed against a continuing backdrop of restrictive immigration legislation and political anti-immigration rhetoric which has, and will always, produce confusion and tension within society, negating the positives of equality law. The EA 2010 has failed to make any noticeable difference to the diversity statistics for professors and senior academics within universities. Had they done so we should, by now, be able to see some 'trickle up' from an ethnically diverse student body to an ethnically diverse body of senior academics. The next part considers this conundrum.

Part III: 'Trickle Up'? – The Changing University

As the statistics in Table 6.4 illustrate, students from an ethnically diverse heritage are more likely to attend university than white students (Dearing Report 1997: Chapter 7; Connor, Tyers & Modood 2004: xiii; Crawford & Greaves 2015: 7). This over-representation of ethnically diverse students can be explained by a number of factors, and we will examine each in turn.

Firstly, evidence suggests ethnically diverse communities place a higher value on HE in comparison to white communities. For most students, be they from an ethnic minority or the white majority, a degree or a higher degree has currency; students pay for and consume education, and in return they expect higher paid employment than their non-university educated counterparts. For their investment, most students expect a 'good' degree. Indeed, government university policies have been designed to encourage student participation in undergraduate study, thus expanding opportunities and reducing unemployment. As a result, universities have become market driven, seeking to provide students with the skills and qualifications that make them more employable; universities have become mass, competitive models of education.

The suggested reasons for increased participation particularly by students from an ethnically diverse background are twofold: one, the idea that qualifications have more value to these groups because it allows them to progress economically (Law & Swann 2016); and two, that such students are given a stronger 'push' to attend university and gain further qualifications by their families (Connor et al. 2004: 17). If it is true that such high value is placed on education, then we would expect to see more senior and professorial ethnically diverse academics moving up the academic ladder.

A further explanation for the over-representation of ethnic minority students in universities is a regulation system which has been designed to promote inclusivity. Universities are heavily regulated by many bodies. For example, Universities UK regulates all universities, requiring them to offer consistent and comparable services. The Quality Assurance Agency (QAA) safeguards standards and seeks to improve the quality of UK higher education. The independent regulator, the Office for Students (OfS), aims to ensure that every student has a fulfilling experience of higher education that enriches their lives and careers. Outside of this is Advance HE which sets industry standards.

A key priority in the regulation of universities has been the 'widening participation' (WP) initiative. It was a priority for the Dearing Report (1997) and was introduced as a policy in 2013 when WP became an amalgamation of the old 'Access Agreements and Widening Participation Strategic Assessments' (Department for the Economy 2019). WP aims to:

> [E]nsure that all those who have the ability to benefit from higher education have the opportunity to do so. Higher education and the

opportunities that it brings should be available to all, regardless of their background. (Department for the Economy 2019)

In order to achieve WP, in 2017 for example, a legal duty was placed on universities to widen participation (Harwood et al. 2017: 70), with section 2(3) of the Higher Education and Research Act 2017 (HERA) requiring the OfS to 'have regard to the need to promote equality of opportunity in connection with access to and participation in higher education' in performing its functions (Department for Education 2018: 3).

Whilst it might seem that WP has been partly responsible for the increase in ethnically diverse student numbers (Table 6.4 in this chapter; Gov.UK 2020: para. 1), the Dearing Report (1997: para. 7.16) found that even before WP policies were in place, ethnic minorities were as a whole more than proportionally represented in higher education, compared to the general population. Yet, to reiterate, they are far from proportionally represented at senior level academic positions such as professor or manager.

Another explanation for the statistics is the student loan system which (in theory) enables students to study at university independently of their parents. The past 60 years have seen many changes to how universities are funded. The pursuit of knowledge and the expansion of university numbers is expensive. Before 1962 students had to pay to go to university, but after the enactment of the 1962 Education Act, full-time university education was free to domestic students. The system changed again in 1998 to fulfil the Labour Party's vision of expanding university student numbers following the Dearing Report (1997), and the enactment of the Teaching and Higher Education Act 1998 required students to pay £1,000 towards their tuition fees. Consequently, the 2004 Higher Education Act sanctioned variable tuition fees, and made student fees one of three vital sources of university funding.[14] The Higher Education Act of 2004 enabled universities to charge up to £3,000 in tuition fees. Then, following the Browne Review in 2010, the cap was raised to £9,000 a year, and in 2016 it rose to its current maximum of £9,250. These fees have enabled the expansion of degree-awarding providers,[15] therefore increasing student numbers. It has also resulted in some universities using tuition fees to make up to half or more of their funding.

---

[14] The other two sources of income are the Office for Students which distributes government higher education funding to more than 300 providers in England, and Research England distributes funding for research (see: https://www.officeforstudents .org.uk/advice-and-guidance/funding-for-providers/annual-funding/ and https:// re.ukri.org/).

[15] Ibid., the 2020–21 total for teaching is 78% below the 2010–11 figure in real terms. The large increase in fee income (from home and EU students) since 2012 has meant that the total funding for institutions through regulated fees and funding council allocations increased in real terms in each year from 2011–12 to 2019–20.

With these regulatory and funding changes has developed a university culture from one of learning to a more business-focused model, with students now as consumers. Whilst student loans theoretically enable students to be financially independent of their parents and provide access to education, there are student concerns about costs and debt. Yet these concerns have not translated into students rejecting undergraduate study (Department for Education 2018: 6); rather, student numbers have increased (Brown & Carasso, 2013: 30–31). Regardless of our views on student fees, there is an argument that the loan system has made education more accessible for all. However, we should have reservations, as US research suggests that many American students from an ethnically diverse background have been deterred from prestigious four-year programmes and have chosen less prestigious two-year programmes because of debt fears (Parry, Gallacher & Scott 2017: 120). Recent UK research suggests that proposed changes to the loan system will affect 'poor and minority ethnic people harder' (Adams 2022). We have seen that more ethnically diverse people are choosing to go to university and attending in ever-increasing numbers. We have also examined some of the contributory factors for this; next we will consider the barriers to progression from student to junior academic to senior academic and beyond.

Part IV: Barriers to the 'Trickle Up' – From Student to Junior Academic, to Senior Academic to Professor and Beyond

There are many barriers to progression to senior academic, professor or higher (Vice Chancellor etc.). Some of these barriers begin before undertaking an undergraduate degree and follow the ethnically diverse academic throughout their studies and after university into their career(s). Therefore, we will examine the barriers at each of these stages.

Before university studies

The attainment gap[16] begins long before the student enrols in university and will prevent some students from continuing into HE; for example, for black students, 'the black penalty'[17] becomes evident at secondary school (Social

---

[16] This is where pupils living in deprived communities do significantly worse at all levels of the education system than those from our least deprived communities.

[17] The 'black penalty' was defined as: A black penalty in secondary and higher education. Despite starting school ahead with performance largely in line with national averages, black children fail to show this advantage higher up the age range. They are the ethnic group most likely to fail their Maths GCSE, most likely to be excluded from school and one of the least likely groups to achieve a good degree at university. Black boys do substantially less well than their female peers particularly

Mobility Commission 2016: 3). The attainment gap starts at pre-school and widens with GCSE and A Levels. The Education Policy Institute (2020) found that attainment varied significantly between school ethnic groups. For example, Gypsy/Roma pupils were almost three years (34 months) behind white British pupils at GCSE level. However, Chinese pupils were two whole years ahead of white British pupils. Some ethnic groups continue to experience growing inequalities: black Caribbean pupils were 6.5 months behind white British pupils in 2011, but the gap has now increased to 10.9 months. Other black groups have also seen the attainment gap widen, for example, other black backgrounds and pupils who do not have English as a first language (ibid. 2020).

If ethnically diverse students manage to attain despite these gaps, then the next step to a senior career in academia is the need to attend the 'right' university. GSCE grades affect the student's choice of A Levels, and both A Level choices and subsequent grades affect the student's choice of university. The problem can be further compounded by a lack of good information, advice and guidance when making GCSE and A Level subject choices, as well as university choice. Aspirations may also be set too low at an early stage.

In theory *all* universities are the same and therefore a degree from one is as good as another, in as much as universities *all* work to the same quality standards (as set by the QAA), *all* strive to ensure students have fulfilling university experiences (OfS) and *all* work towards the same standards set by Advance HE. In reality, the academy prefers to recruit and promote staff who possess qualifications from those universities perceived as 'kite marks' of academic excellence (Hay 2017: Chapter 12), i.e., from Russell Group universities.[18] These universities are held up as offering a gold standard of research and teaching (Anderson 2006:186; Palfreyman & Tapper 2014). Whilst ethnically diverse student numbers are rising at Russell Group universities (Adams 2022a), students from ethnically diverse backgrounds tend to congregate in the 'new' universities, i.e., the post-1992[19] universities (Runnymede 2015:12).[20] Indeed, in 2006 it was reported that more black Caribbean students studied at London Metropolitan University than at all the Russell Group universities put together (Curtis

---

at Key Stage 4. Furthermore, granular analysis of different black sub-groups (for example black African cf. black Caribbean) has also shown distinctive patterns in achievement (Social Mobility Commission: 3).

[18] These are the 24 universities known as the 'Russell Group'. For more information see: www.russellgroup.ac.uk.

[19] Post-1992 universities are former polytechnics or institutions that were given university status through the Further and Higher Education Act 1992, or an institution that has been granted university status since 1992 without receiving a royal charter (Scott 2021: ix).

[20] In 2015, 25% of students from an ethnically diverse background studied at 30 post-1992 universities compared to an institutional average in the UK of 16% (Runnymede 2015: 12).

2006).[21] Whilst these figures are now over 15 years old and seemingly out of date, they may provide an explanation for the lack of ethnically diverse senior academics and professors today: there may not have been enough candidates from an ethnically diverse background for institutions to promote or appoint in their own image to senior academic/professorial positions.

At university

Once a student has progressed to university, there are other barriers they will face, primarily a risk of non-continuance of studies and the university attainment gap. Although we have seen that students from an ethnically diverse background are more likely to attend university than their white counterparts, the Office for Fair Access (OFFA) reported that the non-continuation rate for black students is almost 1.5 times higher than it is for white and Asian students (OFFA, June 2017/02). These statistics have a bearing on the lack of diversity at senior academic and professorial level today.

Furthermore, there is an attainment gap[22] which not only affects student transition from undergraduate to postgraduate study but is another area of serious concern. In 2017/18, 80.9% of white students attained a 2:1 or first class degree compared to 67.7% of 'BAME' students (Universities UK & NUS 2019: 17). Further analysis of these figures demonstrated that 57.5% were black, 70.5% Asian, 77.2% mixed and 67.8% 'other', with students achieving a first or 2:1 (Universities UK & NUS, 2019:17a). Such an attainment gap prevents diversity in the senior levels of academia.

Universities are aware of and have been tackling the attainment gap, for example many have adopted initiatives such as 'cultural awareness' training for staff and anonymous marking procedures (Broughan et al. 2013).[23] However, initiatives do not always have the intended results. One illustration of this is the use of alternative forms of assessment. Many post-1992 universities use different forms of assessment to minimise the negative impact of traditional exams on their students. These assessments take the form of oral presentations, vivas, groups presentations, vodcasts and podcasts for example (Bloxham & Boyd 2007). The problem with these 'alternative' methods is that they are unavoidably assessed in a non-anonymous way and risk the danger of biased

---

[21] For a detailed explanation of the reasons for the attainment gap see Universities UK & NUS, 2019: 16–19, & 22.

[22] This is where a student's ethnicity can affect their degree outcome (Universities UK & NUS 2019: 6).

[23] Anonymous marking in summative assessments is designed to counter any unconscious bias the marker may have and to address systemic discrimination. It matters that, like justice, marking is fair and seen to be done fairly. The literature on anonymous marking shows that it is the best way of avoiding bias.

marking or perceived biased marking. So, in attempting to equalise assessment, it may have increased the risk of bias (Office for Students 2019).

Bias is the not the only explanation for the attainment gap. It has been suggested that some students do not come to university equipped with the necessary academic skills to study their chosen discipline. For example, in Law, students do not come with the ability to write or read analytically. This problem is known as the 'deficit' model; this model places all culpability on the student (Valencia 2021: 2): it is their attributes and characteristics that are seen as the problem, not the education system or the society in which they have matured. No accountability is placed on how schools or colleges are organised, or the structural discrimination that may lie in the society in which the student has lived. Though the deficit model attempts to explain the problem, it does not solve it. It has been suggested that institutions fail to take responsibility for the problem of the attainment gap (African Caribbean Achievement Project 2020).

After university

Without a 'good' degree, a student cannot progress to postgraduate studies, a qualification essential to progress to senior academic roles. A person may teach without a postgraduate degree, but that lack of qualification may later bar academic promotion and progression. The 2018/19 policy briefing from the UK Council for Graduate Education (UKCGE 2020) demonstrated that students from an ethnic minority are under-represented in postgraduate study. They highlighted that the proportion of Black, Asian and Minority Ethnic (BAME) students enrolled in UK HE dropped from 24.81% at undergraduate level to 18.07% at postgraduate research level. Further, in the same period, 48.19% of postgraduate research students (PGRs) received no award or financial backing for their tuition fees, as compared with 32.66% of white PGRs. There was a gap of almost 2% in the qualification of white and ethnic minority PGRs: 18.91% of white PGRs qualified in 2018/19, as opposed to 16.13% of BAME PGRs. The UKCGE concluded that greater diversity in PGR participation could only be improved with direct intervention. They noted that the growth rate was so small that it would take more than half a century for 'BAME' participation in postgraduate research to reach its equivalent proportion at undergraduate level. To tackle this issue, the OfS announced a funding competition to improve access and participation for black, Asian and minority ethnic groups in postgraduate research study (OfS 2020). We will wait to see the success of this initiative.

Even if a candidate from an ethnic minority background has achieved the necessary GCSE and A Level qualifications, attended a good university, achieved a 'good' degree and passed a postgraduate qualification, the next hurdle they must successfully jump in order to start or progress in their academic career is being selected for interview and subsequently being appointed. Research has demonstrated that when white and ethnic minority candidates are considered for the same post at application stage, the ethnically diverse candidate is not selected as often as the white candidate even when they have the same qualifications. The explanation for this discrimination is 'implicit' prejudice or bias (Bhopal 2015: 7–8; Deaux & Snyder 2018: 116).[24] Bhopal stated that although interviews are designed to be neutral, as they progress, they become 'negotiated' and 'contextual' (Bhopal 2015: 53), which can be detrimental to an ethnically diverse candidate. Representatives of the institution may wish consciously or unconsciously to appoint in their own (white) image (Calvard & Cornish 2018: 89).

One constant theme from reports on universities is that many academics from an ethnically diverse background feel that promotion pathways are not as transparent as that of their white colleagues (Universities UK & NUS 2019: 4 & 36). UCU found that black female professors reported four significant barriers to promotion: being overtaken by less qualified and less experienced white female colleagues in appointments to new posts and in the promotion process, poor feedback after interviews, a lack of rigour and transparency in the promotion process, and being delayed in applying for promotion as a result of unsupportive or bullying Heads (UCU 2019: 4).

Once suitably qualified, the ethnically diverse person has to find a position within a university in which to work as an academic and in which to progress their academic career. We will see below that problems may arise when trying to work within these institutions.

Part V: An Unchanging University Culture

This comparative lack of progress of ethnically diverse academics to the top of the 'ivory tower' is reflective of the embedded/entrenched culture of universities. Despite changes to funding, regulation and student diversity, universities essentially remain culturally unchanged. These traditions may stymie the recruitment and progression of ethnically diverse academics. The first UK university was the University of Oxford, founded around 1096 (Brockliss 2019: 75). In or about 1249, Oxford student lodgings evolved into what are now known as Oxford colleges, when University College came into being; thus the white, male, middle-class academic culture was born. It is into this established culture that all academics must fit (Gabriel & Tate 2017; Gabriel 2020). If an academic does not fit into this image they may find it difficult to find employment; if they reject or feel uncomfortable within that university culture they may feel compelled to leave, disengage or de-emphasise their cultural identity.

---

[24] A standard description of implicit biases is that they are unconscious and/or automatic mental associations made between the members of a social group and one or more attributes or a negative evaluation (FitzGerald, Martin & Berner 2019: 7).

Indeed, it is probable that the structure was formulated to exclude those who did not conform. It was designed to suit the dominant culture, i.e., the white and privileged male.

The dominant image of an academic is still a white and male one (Maylor 2018: 350–51). By contrast, women and ethnically diverse academics are a recent invention. However, white women academics are enjoying the labours and fruits of diversity and inclusion initiatives (Bhopal 2020). So although the British university system is almost a thousand years old, it was just over one hundred years ago, in 1908, that it acquired its first female professor, Edith Morley (Fraser 2004);[25] it was not until 40 years later, in 1947, the black economist, Sir William Arthur Lewis, became the first black professor, Professor of Economics at the University of Manchester (see Tignor 2020: 268). Another 73 years later, in 2020, Professor Charles Egbu became one of the first black VCs in the UK (Dacey 2021) when he was appointed to Leeds Trinity University.

This resistance to change in academia's cultural landscape may be viewed through a prism of institutional racism.[26] Authors such as Alexander and Arday (Runnymede 2015) and Miller (2016) have argued that universities remain institutionally racist, with policies and practices that, at the very least, take 'whiteness' to be the norm (Bhopal 2020; 2022). This institutional racism affects ethnically diverse academics progress within the academy. Coupled with this institutional racism are incidents of a racist nature.

There have been many reported racist incidents in British universities. For example, in November 2020, Zac Adan, a student at Manchester University, was wrongly accused by university security staff of 'looking like a drug dealer'. He was held against a wall and a demand to see his university identification was made (Halliday & Walker 2020). In 2018 a recording of racist student chants

---

[25] Her professorship was not a benign gift for her academic skills, nor was it graciously given. Her employer, Reading College, in preparation for their university status, made all Heads of Department Professors – except for Morley, because she was a woman. After a battle, she was, in 1908, promoted to Professor of English Language.

[26] Defined as 'the collective failure of an organisation to provide an appropriate and professional service to people because of their colour, culture or ethnic origin, it can be seen or detected in processes, attitudes and behaviour which amounts to discrimination through unwitting prejudice, ignorance, thoughtlessness and racist stereotyping which disadvantage minority ethnic people' (MacPherson 1999: para. 6.34). Such racism is pervasive in society (see Windrush Review 2020; Lammy 2017). It is detrimental to society in many ways, for example in damaging the economy up to £24bn (see Gov.UK 2017). Black people in England were more than three times more likely to be a victim of murder (Equality and Human Rights Commission 2016: 41) and four times more likely to be stopped and searched by the police (2016: 40). In 2016 the Equality and Human Rights Commission reported that black workers with degrees earned over 23% less on average than white workers with degrees (2016: 21).

made the newspapers (Bouattia 2018), as did the infamous banana incident at Warwick University in 2016 (Guardian Students 2016). Coupled with this blatant racism is the more common casual racism that is part and parcel of everyday life; this hostile environment makes life as an ethnically diverse academic difficult, as well as making it difficult for such students to study and attain a good degree.

Racial harassment is a common experience for many students and staff in UK universities. A total of 24% of students from an ethnically diverse background, compared to 9% of white students, said they had experienced racial harassment (Equality and Human Rights 2019: 6). This equates to 13% of all students (ibid.). In all, 56% of students who had been racially harassed had experienced racist name-calling, insults and jokes (ibid.). Other experiences included microaggressions, exclusion and exposure to racist material. The harasser was predominantly another student but in some cases a tutor or another academic (ibid.). It is within these institutions and cultures that academics from an ethnically diverse culture have to work. The same report found that approximately 3 in 20 ethnically diverse academics reported racial harassment which then caused them to leave their jobs, with many more saying they were considering, or had considered, doing so (ibid.). Others expressed a fear of reporting discrimination issues for fear of being branded a 'troublemaker' (ibid.), and others lacked the confidence to bring complaints against racial harassment (ibid).

We have now examined the statistics, law and some suggested reasons for the lack of ethnically diverse senior academics and professors. What then are the possible solutions? We will now give consideration to this question.

Part VI: Towards True Inclusion – Solutions

There have been many studies into ways of improving inclusion, as well reports more generally on racial discrimination and institutional racism; all have suggested ways of fixing the problems, and yet the problem remains stubbornly unresolved. This chapter does not attempt to review all the report literature, but highlights below themes emerging from some of those reports.

Government assistance

The government has passed equality legislation, alongside inclusive university regulation and policy. However, whilst government anti-immigration rhetoric remains, we will not be able to tackle issues of racism; inclusivity cannot be achieved whilst this contradictory rhetoric remains. Likewise, politicians must stop using false narratives; for example, in 2016, the then Prime Minister, Theresa May MP, remarked, 'If you're a white, working-class boy, you're less likely than anybody else in Britain to go to university' (GOV.UK July 2016). This observation may have been true, but is more nuanced. The actual outcome is that white working-class boys with lower educational qualifications and a lower likelihood of going to university still have higher employment rates and higher social mobility than those from an ethnically diverse background (Aoki, Battu & Mass 2019).

For almost 60 years, legislation has tried to resolve race discrimination, and yet it still remains a problem. The Equality Act 2010 was a positive step towards protecting people from discrimination, but to be more effective it requires additional measures. For example, litigants require quick, affordable expert legal advice which a change on government policy in regard to legal aid would resolve.

A coherent university approach

Despite legislation, policy and regulation, the government needs to provide better guidance on how to tackle racism (including institutional racism: see Equality and Human Rights 2019). There are so many reports and recommendations that it results in a lack of coherence and clear messaging. A more streamlined approach is needed (Universities UK Taskforce 2016), as is a university sector joint approach to the problem (ibid.), as well as the sharing of applicable data (UCU 2019: 36) and the dissemination of appropriate research (ibid.). Universities are not precluded from sharing such information (and it has been questioned whether they fully understand the Data Protection Act 2018 (see Advance HE 2021)).

Individual universities

Individual universities need strong leaders. Vice Chancellors and the senior leadership teams they command should be transparently appointed on excellence. They should lead by example and take responsibility for change, putting in place robust policies, plans, key performance indicators and progress reports on diversity. Strong leadership teams should be able to hold brave and honest conversations about race.

Human Resources (HR) departments should have policies that are clearly communicated, with meaningful resources and support dedicated to ensuring that recruitment is fair (and anonymous up until the time of interview). Unconscious bias training needs to be more than a typical HR multiple-choice test prescribed for mandatory training. Staff training is required on white privilege, as well as cultural awareness training. Universities need to be confident in talking about, and tackling, racial harassment.

Harassment and complaint processes must be clear, and robustly carried out. There has to be accountability. It has been recommended that universities have a clear and transparent complaints process (Equality and Human Rights 2019:

8–10, 12–13). Complainants need to understand their rights, and feel able to complain to HR without fear of losing their job, or being branded as 'difficult'. HR needs to help ethnically diverse staff with issues of fatigue (Withers 2020), feelings of being brow-beaten or with fighting a system that is structurally racist. The law alone cannot resolve all these problems, and universities have to put in place structures and procedures to help such staff. Universities should have zero tolerance towards racism (Universities UK Taskforce 2016), and all university 'bystanders' should understand their role in 'calling out' racism or racist behaviour (ibid.).

Creating an inclusive culture

Discussing race would stimulate an inclusive curriculum. Britain had an 'Empire', which at its height was the largest in world history, covering around 25% of the world's land surface (Burton 2015). It has shaped not only British history, but world history. The ripples of that imperialism are still visible and as a result have relevance to all parts of the curriculum. By decolonising the curriculum, universities will help challenge racism and racial discrimination. Unfortunately, in the past many of these attempts for an honest debate have been met with a negative press or outright hostility (see for example: Mitchell 2020; Harding 2021); the UK has a problem discussing its colonial past and legacy (Brookfield 2018). Decolonisation will provide an inclusive curriculum and therefore an inclusive university. Problems with funding mean that many university academics have little time to redesign courses, so a strategy to deal with this is also needed. If universities are unable to speak to an inclusive curriculum, then university culture will remain stagnant and unable to tackle racial discrimination.

Conclusion: 'Deeds not Words'

UK universities lack ethnically diverse senior academics and professors despite almost six decades of race discrimination legislation. This suggests that the law alone cannot resolve the problems of deep-seated discrimination that is prevalent in UK society. Both UK culture and government policy require change. The government could help change UK culture by abolishing its anti-immigration rhetoric and policy. Other change could be assisted via education, and universities are well placed to lead the way. Universities should continue to be the stronghold of objective and research-led inquiry and be at the centre of re-examining British colonialism and empire. This is a both nuanced and complicated history, exactly the sort of inquiry and research that universities should be leading and teaching, but this cannot be done without diverse research and diverse academic leadership.

The law alone cannot effect equality, or single-handedly improve the statistics on the lack of ethnically diverse senior academic leaders and professors, but it should be able to protect people from discrimination and the corresponding harm that discrimination causes. The law should be the last resort for people who have been discriminated against, as universities should resolve issues before recourse to law (as you 'dig two graves' when you litigate, your own and the defendant's). The time to merely talk about race and the under-representation of academics from an ethnically diverse background is over, since we need 'deeds' and not more words; there have been so many reports with excellent data and recommendations that need to be implemented. Action does not need to be taken in a sentimental fashion or within a culture of 'victimhood' (or sympathy); we just need to act in an objective manner, so favoured by academia, and driven by data. All academics, especially senior and professorial, have a duty to speak up against racial injustice as the law alone cannot resolve the lack of ethnically diverse professors and senior academics.

References

Alexander, M. (2010). *The new Jim Crow: Mass incarceration in the age of color-blindness*. New York: New Press.

Anderson, R. (2006). British universities past and present. London: Bloomsbury.

Apena, F. (2007). 'Being black and in trouble: The role of self-perception in the offending behaviour of black youth. *Youth Justice*, 7(3): 211–228. https://doi.org/10.1177/147322540708251

Arday, J. (2021). 'Race, education and social mobility: We all need to dream the same dream and want the same thing. *Educational Philosophy and Theory*, 53(3): 227–232. https://doi.org/10.1080/00131857.2020.1777642

Back, L. and Solomos, J. (eds.) (2000). *Theories of race and racism: A reader*. Didcot: Routledge.

Mor Barak, M. E. (2013). *Managing diversity, toward a globally inclusive workplace*. Thousand Oaks: Sage.

Barkan, E. (1992). *The retreat of scientific racism: Changing concepts of race in Britain and the United States between the world wars*. Cambridge: Cambridge University Press.

Bess, J. L. and Dee, J. R. (2012). *Understanding college and university organization, theories for effective policy and practice*. Sterling: Stylus.

Bhambra, G. K., Gebrial, D. and Nişancıoğlu, K. (eds.) (2018). *Decolonising the university*. London: Pluto Press.

Bhatia, M. (2015). Turning asylum seekers into 'dangerous criminals': Experiences of the criminal justice system of those seeking sanctuary. *International Journal for Crime, Justice and Social Democracy*, 4(3): 97–111. https://doi.org/10.5204/ijcjsd.v4i3.245

Bhopal, K. (2015). *The experiences of black and minority ethnic academics. A comparative study of the unequal academy.* Didcot: Routledge.

Bhopal, K. (2018). *White privilege, the myth of a post-racial society.* Bristol: Policy Press.

Bhopal, K. (2022). Academics of colour in elite universities in the UK and the USA: The 'unspoken system of exclusion'. *Studies in Higher Education,* 47:11, 2127–2137. https://doi.org/10.1080/03075079.2021.2020746

Biko, A. (2003). *Counter colonial criminology. A critique of imperialism reason.* London: Pluto Press.

Bloch, A. and Solomos, J. (eds.) (2009). *Race and ethnicity in the 21st century.* Basingstoke: Palgrave Macmillan.

Bloxham, S. and Boyd, P. (2007). *Developing assessment in higher education: A practical guide.* Maidenhead: Open University Press.

Bolognani, M. (2009). *Crime and Muslim Britain: Race, culture and the politics of criminology among British Pakistanis.* London: IB Tauris.

Bosworth, M., Hoyle, C. and Zedner, L. (eds.) (2016). *Changing contours of criminal justice.* Oxford: Oxford University Press.

Bosworth, M. and Flavin, J. (2007). *Race, gender, and punishment: From colonialism to the war on terror.* New Brunswick: Rutgers University Press.

Bowling, B. and Phillips, C. (2002). *Racism, crime and justice.* Harlow: Pearson Education.

Brady, P. (2020). *Internationalisation of post-1992 UK universities.* London: Anthem Press.

Brockliss, L. (2019). *The University of Oxford: A brief history.* Oxford: Bodleian Library Press.

Brookfield, S. (2018). *Teaching race: How to help students unmask and challenge racism.* San Francisco: John Wiley & Sons, Inc.

Broughan, C., Steventon, G., Clouder, L. and Jewell, S. (eds) (2013). *Improving student engagement and development through assessment, theory and practice in higher education.* Oxford: Oxford University Press.

Brown, R. and Carasso, H. (2013). *Everything for sale? The marketisation of UK higher education.* Didcot: Routledge.

Bucerius, S. M. and Tonry, M. H. (eds.) (2014). *The Oxford handbook of ethnicity, crime, and immigration.* Oxford: Oxford University Press.

Burton, A. (2015). *The trouble with empire.* Oxford: Oxford University Press.

Cacho, L. M. (2012). *Social death: Racialized rightlessness and the criminalization of the unprotected.* New York: New York University Press.

Calvard, T. and Cornish, T. (eds.) (2018). *The psychology of ethnicity in organisations.* London: Macmillan Education UK.

Camp, J. T. and Heatherton, C. (eds.) (2016). *Policing the planet: Why the policing crisis led to Black Lives Matter.* London: Verso Books.

Chick, M. (2020). *Changing times, economics, policies, and resource allocation in Britain since 1951.* Oxford: Oxford University Press.

Cohen, S. (2017). *Against criminology.* Didcot: Routledge.

Connor, H., Tyers, C., Modood, T. and Hillage, J. (2004). *Why the difference? A closer look at higher education minority ethnic students and graduates.* Department for Education and Skills, Research Report RR552, p. xvi. http://www.bristol.ac.uk/media-library/sites/ethnicity/migrated/documents/educationreport.pdf

Cook, D. and Hudson, B. (eds.) (1993). *Racism and criminology.* London: Sage.

Crawford, C. and Greaves, E. (2015). *Socio-economic, ethnic and gender differences in HE participation.* London: Department for Business, Innovation and Skills. https://ifs.org.uk/publications/socio-economic-ethnic-and-gender-differences-he-participation

Crenshaw, K. (1996). *Critical race theory.* New York: The New Press.

Crimmins, G. (2020). *Strategies for supporting inclusion and diversity in the academy: Higher education, aspiration and inequality.* London: Palgrave Macmillan.

Cunneen, C. and Tauri, J. (2016). *Indigenous criminology.* Bristol: Policy Press.

Deaux, K. and Snyder, M. (2018). *The Oxford handbook of personality and social psychology.* Oxford: Oxford University Press.

Dizikes, P. (2014). Workplace diversity can help the bottom line, MIT economist scrutinizes firm data suggesting diverse offices function more effectively. *MIT News Office,* 7 October. https://news.mit.edu/2014/workplace-diversity-can-help-bottom-line-1007

FitzGerald, C., Martin, A., Berner, D. and Hurst, S. (2019). Interventions designed to reduce implicit prejudices and implicit stereotypes in real world contexts: A systematic review. *BMC Psychology* 7(29). https://doi.org/10.1186/s40359-019-0299-7

Fraser, P. (2004). Lewis, Sir (William) Arthur (1915–1991), economist. *Oxford dictionary of national biography.* https://www.oxforddnb.com/view/10.1093/ref:odnb/9780198614128.001.0001/odnb-9780198614128-e-49872

Fulp, C. (2018). *Success through diversity: Why the most inclusive companies will win.* Boston: Beacon Press.

Gabriel, D. (2020). *Transforming the ivory tower: Models for gender equality and social justice.* London: Trentham Books.

Gabriel, D. and Tate, S. A. (2017). *Inside the Ivory Tower: Narratives of women of colour surviving and thriving in British academia.* London: Trentham Books.

Goldberg, D. T. (1993). *Racist culture: Philosophy and the politics of meaning.* Oxford: Blackwell.

Goldberg, D. T. (2002). *The racial state.* Oxford: Blackwell.

Harwood, V., Hickey-Moody, A., McMahon, S. and O'Shea, S. (2017). *The politics of widening participation and university access for young people making educational futures.* Didcot: Routledge.

Hay, I. (2017). *How to be an academic superhero: Establishing and sustaining a successful career in the social sciences, arts and humanities.* Cheltenham: Edward Elgar.

Hepple, B. (2014). *Equality: The legal framework.* London: Bloomsbury.

Hunt, V., Layton, D. and Prince, S. (2015) Diversity matters. McKinsey. https://www.mckinsey.com/~/media/mckinsey/business%20functions/people%20and%20organizational%20performance/our%20insights/why%20diversity%20matters/diversity%20matters.pdf

Jackson, S. A. (2014). *Routledge international handbook of race, class, and gender*. Didcot: Routledge.

Kendall, F. E. (2013). *Understanding white privilege: Creating pathways to authentic relationships across race*. Didcot: Routledge.

Law, I. and Swann, S. (2016). *Ethnicity and education in England and Europe: Gangstas, geeks and gorjas*. Didcot: Routledge.

Maylor, U. (2018). Leadership for race and social justice in HE. In: Mirza, S. and Arday, J. (eds.) *Dismantling race in higher education, racism, whiteness and decolonising the academy*. London: Palgrave Macmillan, pp. 349–364.

Miles, R. (1989). *Racism*. London: Routledge.

Miller, P. (2016). 'White sanction', institutional, group and individual interaction in the promotion and progression of black and minority ethnic academics and teachers in England. *Power and Education*, 8(3): 205–221. https://doi.org/10.1177/175774381667288.

Morris, L. (2002). *Dangerous classes: The underclass and social citizenship*. London: Routledge.

Museus, S. (2014). The culturally engaging campus model: A new theory of success among racially diverse college student populations. In: Paulsen, M. B. (ed.) *Higher education: Handbook of theory and research volume 29*. Cham: Springer Nature, pp. 189–229.

Page, S. E. (2008). *The difference: How the power of diversity creates better groups, firms, schools, and societies*. Princeton: Princeton University Press.

Palfreyman, D. and Tapper, T. (2014). *Reshaping the university: The rise of the regulated market in higher education*. Oxford: Oxford University Press.

Rees, J., Pomati, M. and Elke, H. (2020). *Social policy review 32: Analysis and debate in social policy*. Bristol: Policy Press.

Sanger, S. and Gleeson, N. (2020). *Diversity and inclusion in global higher education*. London: Palgrave Macmillan.

Scott, P. (2021). *Retreat or resolution? Tackling the crisis of mass higher education*. Bristol: Policy Press.

Scott, P., Gallacher, J., and Parry, G. (eds.) (2017). *New languages and landscapes of higher education*. Oxford: Oxford University Press.

Tignor, R. W. (2020). *Arthur Lewis and the birth of development economics*. Princeton: Princeton University Press.

Valencia, R. (1997). *The evolution of deficit thinking: Educational thought and practice*. Didcot: Routledge.

Wellman, D. (ed.) (2012). *Portraits of white racism*. Cambridge: Cambridge University Press.

Willetts, D. (2017). *A university education*. Oxford: Oxford University Press.

Withers, M. F. (2020). *Black fatigue: How racism erodes the mind, body, and spirit*. Oakland: Berrett-Koehler Publishers.

Reports

The African Caribbean Achievement Project. (2020). *Why the attainment gap has stopped closing for the first time in ten years*. https://acap.org.uk/why -the-attainment-gap-has-stopped-closing-for-the-first-time-in-ten-years/

Advance HE. (2021). *Equality + higher education. Staff statistical report 2021*. AdvHE_Equality in higher education_Saff_stats_2021_1635342217.pdf

Advance HE. (2020). *Advance HE statement about tackling inequalities*, 31 May. https://advance-he.ac.uk/news-and-views/advance-he-statement -about-tackling-inequalities

Census. (2021). 29 November 2022 *Office for National Statistics (ONS) statistical bulletin, ethnic group, England and Wales: Census 2021*. https://www.ons.gov .uk/peoplepopulationandcommunity/culturalidentity/ethnicity/bulletins /ethnicgroupenglandandwales/census2021#:~:text=%22Black%2C%20 Black%20British%2C%20Caribbean,was%202.2%25%20(1.2%20million)

Commission on Race and Ethnic Disparities. (2021). *Commission on race and ethnic disparities: The report*, March. https://assets.publishing.service .gov.uk/government/uploads/system/uploads/attachment_data/file /974507/20210331_-_CRED_Report_-_FINAL_-_Web_Accessible.pdf

Dearing Report. (1997). *Higher education in the learning society. Main report*. London: Her Majesty's Stationery Office.

Department for Business Innovation and Skills. (2015). *Research paper no. 186: Socio-economic, ethnic and gender differences in HE participation*, November. https://assets.publishing.service.gov.uk/government/uploads/system /uploads/attachment_data/file/474273/BIS-15-85-socio-economic-ethnic -and-gender-differences.pdf)

Department for Education. (2018). *Access and participation. Secretary of State for Education guidance to the Office for Students (OfS)*, February. https://www .officeforstudents.org.uk/media/1112/access-and-participation-guidance.pdf

The Education Policy Institute. (2017). *Closing the gap? Trends in education attainment and disadvantage*, August. https://epi.org.uk/wp-content /uploads/2017/08/Closing-the-Gap_EPI-.pdf

The Education Policy Institute. (2020). *Education in England annual report 2020*. https://epi.org.uk/wp-content/uploads/2020/09/EPI_2020_Annual _Report_.pdf

Equality and Human Rights Commission. (2016). *Healing a divided Britain: The need for a comprehensive race equality strategy*, 18 August. https://www .equalityhumanrights.com/en/publication-download/healing-divided -britain-need-comprehensive-race-equality-strategy

Equality and Human Rights Commission. (2019). *Tackling racial harassment: Universities challenged*, 23 October. https://www.equalityhumanrights.com/en/publication-download/tackling-racial-harassment-universities-challenged

GOV.UK. (2016). *Speech, statement from the new Prime Minister Theresa May: Theresa May delivered her first statement as Prime Minister in Downing Street*, 13 July. https://www.gov.uk/government/speeches/statement-from-the-new-prime-minister-theresa-may

GOV.UK. (2017). *Increase in BME workplace progression could give UK economy a £24bn boost – Baroness McGregor-Smith review finds*, 28 February. https://www.gov.uk/government/news/increase-in-bme-workplace-progression-could-give-uk-economy-a-24bn-boost-baroness-mcgregor-smith-review-finds#:~:text=Work-,Increase%20in%20BME%20workplace%20progression%20could%20give%20UK%20economy%20a,Baroness%20McGregor%2DSmith%20Review%20finds&text=The%20UK%20economy%20could%20benefit,government%2Dbacked%20review%20has%20found.

GOV.UK. (2020). *Further education participation*, 2 October. https://www.ethnicity-facts-figures.service.gov.uk/education-skills-and-training/a-levels-apprenticeships-further-education/further-education-participation/latest

GOV.UK Department for the Economy. (2019). *Higher education widening participation*. https://www.economy-ni.gov.uk/articles/higher-education-widening-participation#:~:text=Widening%20Access%20and%20Participation%20Plans%20(WAPPs)%20were%20introduced%20in%202013,and%20Widening%20Participation%20Strategic%20Assessments

Great Britain: Parliament: House of Lords (Lord David Arthur Russell Howell of Guildford) March 2014 *Select Committee on soft power and the UK's influence*. London: Her Majesty's Stationery Office.

HESA. (2021). *UK domiciled first year students by ethnicity: Higher education provider tariff grouping and academic year*, DT051 Table 27, UK, AY: 2014/15 to 2021/22, HESA, 051 Table 27. Table 27 – UK domiciled first year students by ethnicity and higher education provider tariff grouping 2014/15 to 2021/22 | HESA

HESA. (2022). *Higher education staff statistics: UK, 2020/21. Statistical bulletin, SB261*, 1 February. Higher Education Staff Statistics: UK, 2020/21.

Lammy, D. (2017). *An independent review into the treatment of, and outcomes for, Black, Asian and Minority Ethnic individuals in the criminal justice system*. GOV.UK. https://www.gov.uk/government/publications/lammy-review-final-report

MacPherson, W. (1999). *The Stephen Lawrence inquiry*. Cm 4262-1. 4262.pdf (publishing.service.gov.uk)

Office for Fair Access (OFFA). (2017/02). *Outcomes of access agreement monitoring for 2015–16.* https://dera.ioe.ac.uk/29489/1/OFFA-Monitoring-Outcomes-Report-2015-16-Final.pdf

Office for Students. (2019). *Annual review, English higher education.* https://www.officeforstudents.org.uk/annual-review-2019/

Office for Students. (2020). *Funding competition to improve access and participation for black, Asian and minority ethnic groups in postgraduate research study,* 22 October. https://www.officeforstudents.org.uk/publications/improving-access-and-participation-for-minority-ethnic-groups-in-pgr-study/

Oxford University. (2019). *Annual statistical report,* May. https://www.ox.ac.uk/sites/files/oxford/Admissions%20Report%202019.pdf

Oxford University. (2022). *Annual statistical report,* May.https://www.ox.ac.uk/sites/files/oxford/AnnualAdmissionsStatisticalReport2022.pdf

Royal Historical Society. (2018). *Race, ethnicity & equality in UK history: A report and resource for change,* October. https://royalhistsoc.org/racereport/

Runnymede Trust. (2015). *Aiming higher: Race, inequality and diversity in the academy.* https://assets.website-files.com/61488f992b58e687f1108c7c/617bcf1cd124685da56a014c_Aiming%20Higher.pdf

Social Metrics Commission. (2020). *Poverty and Covid: Measuring poverty 2020.* https://socialmetricscommission.org.uk/wp-

Social Mobility Commission. (2016). *Ethnicity, gender and social mobility,* 28 December. https://assets.publishing.service.gov.uk/government/uploads/system/uploads/attachment_data/file/579988/Ethnicity_gender_and_social_mobility.pdf

University of Aberdeen. (Aoki, Y., Battu, H. and Massa, P. V.) (2019). *The intergenerational mobility of white working-class boys: A quantitative analysis,* April. Discussion paper no. 19–2. https://aura.abdn.ac.uk/bitstream/handle/2164/12563/DP_2019_2.pdf?sequence=1&isAllowed=y

UCU. (2019). *Staying power. The career experiences and strategies of UK Black female professors,* February. https://www.ucu.org.uk/media/10075/Staying-Power/pdf/UCU_Rollock_February_2019.pdf

UCU. (2020). *Universities' £2.5bn 'black hole' will cost economy £6bn and 60,000 jobs, warns report,* 23 April. https://www.ucu.org.uk/article/10759/Universities-2.5bn-black-hole-will-cost-economy-6bn-and-60000-jobs-warns-report

UCU/LE London Economics. (2020). *Impact of the Covid-19 pandemic on university finances. Report for the university and college union,* April. https://www.ucu.org.uk/media/10871/LE_report_on_covid19_and_university_finances/pdf/LEreportoncovid19anduniversityfinances

UK Council for Graduate Education (UKCGE). (2020). *Access and participation of black, Asian and minority ethnicities in UK postgraduate research – policy briefing,* 22 June. http://www.ukcge.ac.uk/article/bame-pgr-access-participation-459.aspx

Universities UK. (2016). *Changing the culture: Report of the Universities UK Taskforce examining violence against women, harassment and hate crime affecting university students.* https://www.universitiesuk.ac.uk/sites/default/files/field/downloads/2021-07/changing-the-culture.pdf

Universities UK. (2022). *Tackling racial harassment in higher education.* https://www.universitiesuk.ac.uk/what-we-do/policy-and-research/publications/tackling-racial-harassment-higher

Universities UK & NUS. (2019). *Black, Asian and Minority Ethnic student attainment at UK universities: #CLOSINGTHEGAP,* May. https://www.universitiesuk.ac.uk/policy-and-analysis/reports/Documents/2019/bame-student-attainment-uk-universities-closing-the-gap.pdf

Windrush Review GOV.UK. (2020). *Independent report, Windrush Lessons Learned Review by Wendy Williams.* Home Office, March. https://www.gov.uk/government/publications/windrush-lessons-learned-review

Newspapers

Adams, R. (2017). British universities employ no black academics in top roles, figures show. *The Guardian,* 19 January. https://www.theguardian.com/education/2017/jan/19/british-universities-employ-no-black-academics-in-top-roles-figures-show

Adams, R. (2020). Minister criticises lack of senior black UK academics. *The Guardian,* 23 January. https://www.theguardian.com/education/2020/jan/23/minister-criticises-lack-of-senior-black-uk-academics

Adams, R. (2022a). Record number of black and Asian students accepted at top UK universities. *The Guardian,* 27 January. https://www.theguardian.com/education/2022/jan/27/record-number-of-black-and-asian-students-accepted-at-top-uk-universities#:~:text=The%20number%20of%20Black%20students,to%20figures%20released%20by%20Ucas.

Adams, R. (2022). IFS: England's student loan change to hit poor and minority ethnic people harder. *The Guardian,* 27 April. https://www.theguardian.com/education/2022/apr/27/student-loan-change-england-hits-poor-minority-ethnic-people-harder-ifs-analysis

Adams, R. and Batty, D. (2019). Black female professors must deal with bullying to win promotion, report finds. *The Guardian,* 4 February. https://www.theguardian.com/education/2019/feb/04/black-female-professors-report

Ames, J. (2023). Midwife wins racism claim over bag theft 'joke'. *The Times,* 3 March. https://www.thetimes.co.uk/article/midwife-wins-racism-claim-over-bag-theft-joke-gsfzw5g8j

Barnes, L. and Hicks, V. (2022). Covid: Uni students' legal action over pandemic education. *BBC News,* 1 November. https://www.bbc.co.uk/news/uk-england-nottinghamshire-63434284

Bhopal, K. (2020). UK's white female academics are being privileged above women – and men – of colour. *The Guardian*, 28 July. https://www.theguardian.com/education/2020/jul/28/uks-white-female-academics-are-being-privileged-above-women-and-men-of-colour

Bouattia, M. (2018). Racist incidents at universities show they aren't as tolerant as we think. *The Guardian*, 11 March. https://www.theguardian.com/commentisfree/2018/mar/11/racist-universities-not-tolerant-rugaro-chisango-nottingham-trent

Coughlan, S. (2019). Only 1% of UK university professors are black. *BBC News*, 19 January. https://www.bbc.co.uk/news/education-55723120

Curtis, P. (2006). Black students failing to get into top universities. *The Guardian*, 3 January. https://www.theguardian.com/uk/2006/jan/03/highereducation.race

Dacey, R. (2021). Leeds Trinity University Vice-Chancellor Professor Charles Egbu on how higher education can be more diverse. *The Yorkshire Post*, 13 February. https://www.yorkshirepost.co.uk/education/leeds-trinity-university-vice-chancellor-professor-charles-egbu-on-how-higher-education-can-be-more-diverse-3131674

Easton, M. and May, C. (2021). Hong Kong citizens to be given 'support' to come to UK. *BBC News*, 8 April.

Guardian Students. (2016). 'Bananagate' highlights racism among Warwick students. *The Guardian*, 8 April. https://www.theguardian.com/education/2016/apr/08/bananagate-highlights-racism-among-warwick-students

Halliday, J. and Walker, A. (2020). Calls for Manchester University Vice-Chancellor to quit after racism row: Protests after first-year student is accused of 'looking like a drug dealer' by security officers. *The Guardian*, 17 November. https://www.theguardian.com/education/2020/nov/17/calls-for-manchester-university-vice-chancellor-to-quit-after-racism-row

Harding, E. (2021). Only 23% of adults support 'decolonising' university courses, poll finds as lecturers try to make reading lists less 'male, pale and stale'. *The Daily Mail*, 20 July. https://www.dailymail.co.uk/news/article-9804397/Only-23-adults-support-decolonising-university-courses.html

Mitchell, P. (2020). The National Trust is under attack because it cares about history, not fantasy. *The Guardian*, 12 November. https://www.theguardian.com/commentisfree/2020/nov/12/national-trust-history-slavery

Ratcliffe, R. (2012). Why should I study at a Russell Group university? *The Guardian*, 19 December. https://www.theguardian.com/education/2012/dec/19/should-i-go-to-a-russell-group-university

Sian, K. (2019). Racism in UK universities is blocking BAME academics from the top. *The Guardian*, 20 July. https://www.theguardian.com/education/2019/jul/10/racism-in-uk-universities-is-blocking-bame-academics-from-the-top

Smith, N. (2023). 90,000 students to sue their universities over Covid disruption. *ITV News*, 16 February. https://www.itv.com/news/2023-02-16/90000 -students-to-sue-their-universities-over-covid-disruption

White, N. (2022). Just 1% of UK professors are black, new figures reveal. *The Independent*, 1 February. www.independent.co.uk/news/uk/home-news/uk -professors-black-government-figures-b2004891.html

Wilson, J. (2020). Academia looks like a pint of Guinness to me – diverse below, but not at the top. *The Guardian*, 28 January. https://www.theguardian.com /education/2020/jan/28/academia-looks-like-a-pint-of-guinness-to-me -diverse-below-but-not-at-the-top

CHAPTER 7

Universities and the Colonial Production of Knowledge About Students of Colour

Patricia Tuitt

> Demanding more data about subjects that we already know much about is, in my estimation, a perversion of knowledge.
>
> (Ruha Benjamin)

Introduction

The era of European colonisation is one which produced the most sustained perversion of knowledge about the histories, cultures and social and economic lives of the many peoples across the globe who were subjected to colonial rule. For this reason, one of the tasks which postcolonial theory and criticism has undertaken is to expose how the colonial project was advanced, and its concomitant European identity affirmed through, among other things, the publication of fiction and non-fiction texts which, in various ways, depict the abilities of formerly colonised people as weak and inchoate when contrasted with the much-lauded achievements of the colonisers.

This chapter aims to contribute to this body of criticism by revealing how government-supported investigations into the experiences and, above all, the

---

How to cite this book chapter:
Tuitt, P. 2024. Universities and the Colonial Production of Knowledge About Students of Colour. In: Whyte, A., Tuitt, P. and Bourne, J. (eds.) *The Long Walk to Equality: Perspectives on Racial Inequality, Injustice and the Law.* Pp. 141–153. London: University of Westminster Press. DOI: https://doi.org/10.16997/book63.g. License: CC-BY-NC-ND 4.0

academic achievements within British universities of students of colour have reproduced earlier colonial methods for acquiring, documenting and disseminating 'knowledge' about individuals and communities that were the subjects of colonial rule. In the context of the investigations examined, the chapter argues that the methods for collating and interpreting data deployed by government agencies has led to a distorted presentation of students of colour as being inherently resistant to higher learning. Crucially, it argues that the colonising methods underlying the investigations explored are entirely compatible with government-led discourses and strategies aimed at increasing the number of persons of colour present in the full range of public and private institutions, and ensuring that, once recruited to these institutions, they can effectively participate at all levels of their operations. Indeed, 'diversity' and 'inclusion' – as these twin objectives are often referred to in shorthand – are the ostensible goals behind many of the recent forms of government intervention into the management of British universities.

Working from the well-known premise that postcolonial theory and criticism exists precisely to call attention to the fact that colonialism did not end at the conclusion of the formal processes by which previously colonised countries gained independence, the chapter argues that the relation between students of colour and their universities – as represented in the policies that management personnel promote – is structured along colonial lines. Arguably, the most cogent evidence of this fact is to be found in what Aparna and Kramsch refer to as the 'accelerated corporatisation of the European university landscape' (2018: 96) – in which students of colour, 'over-represented in university student populations vis-a-vis their percentage of the general UK population' (Shilliam 2018: 59), have become a 'new source of revenue that can be freely tapped' (Andrews 2018: 134) by British universities.

The argument in the chapter is developed against a framework for understanding how – against the backdrop of initiatives aimed at encouraging and supporting racial diversity and inclusion – British universities use the data which they collect about those within their environs – especially their student populations. In particular, it assesses the impact these data collecting exercises have on the academic achievements of students of colour.

The Quality Assurance Agency (QAA), the Higher Education Statistics Agency (HESA) and Universities UK (UUK) play a pivotal role in the collation and dissemination of data about students of colour in British universities, and it is important to understand that this data provides the basis on which the 'soft law' (policy and guidance) of universities is developed and implemented. A useful framework for analysing such data collecting exercises is provided by Ruha Benjamin in her 2019 book, titled: *Race After Technology: Abolitionist Tools for the 'New Jim Code'*. I use the model of analysis that Benjamin offers to scrutinise three reports/investigations produced by or involving UUK – the organisation that represents British universities. What Benjamin helps me to show is that even when data is collected for ostensibly emancipatory purposes – such as promoting racial diversity and inclusion among university students and academics – their use inevitably brings into being 'soft laws' which 'reflect and reproduce existing inequalities that are promoted and perceived as more objective or progressive than the discriminatory systems of a previous era' (Benjamin 2019: 5–6). To put the matter in terms of postcolonial theory, the question that underlines the chapter is whether data about the colonised is ever safe in the hands of the coloniser.

The chapter is arranged in five parts. The first three parts explore investigations relevant to the question of the academic progress in universities of students of colour in which one or other of the agencies referred to above have been involved. Not surprisingly given its role in representing British universities, UUK was involved in all three reports. Taking the reports in reverse chronological order, the first part addresses a report titled *Black, Asian and Minority Ethnic Student Attainment at UK Universities: Closing the Gap*, which was produced in May 2019 by UUK and the National Union of Students (NUS). The report examined various strategies for tackling disparities in learning outcomes between students of colour and their white university student counterparts. Part two focuses on a report titled *Degree Classification: Transparent, Consistent and Fair Academic Standards*, which was published in November 2018 by UUK, GuildHE and the QAA. The subject of their report was the perceived problem of degree grade inflation. Part three pertains to a report published in 2017 titled *Understanding Degree Algorithms*. Jointly authored by UUK and GuildHE, it consists of a survey of 120 universities and other higher education providers on the policies and guidance (soft laws) against which degree classification decisions are arrived at.

It is to be noted that only the first of the three reports mentioned explicitly focuses on students of colour. However, the principal measure of student attainment at university is the student's degree outcome, which makes it impossible to ignore the effect of findings and recommendations relating to degree grade inflation and degree algorithms on the academic progress and successes of these students. Regrettably, however, few commentators on the academic progress and achievements – specifically on the attainment gap between students of colour and white students – have married these three reports together. As this chapter's more holistic reading aims to show, any positive messages of intent which might be read in the UUK/NUS 2019 report and recommendations are entirely undermined by the two earlier reports, which together lend credence to a degree classification system that cannot but sustain (if not actually widen) the present attainment gap. After briefly outlining the content of these three official investigations, Part Four draws upon Ruha Benjamin's *Race After Technology* in order to advance the argument that despite their ostensible objective of equalising the experiences and outcomes of students of colour to their white counterparts, the reports form part of a larger colonial archive of purportedly objective knowledge about black, Asian and other racialised people.

The concluding part contrasts the three government-led reports with a report of a non-governmental organisation – the Equality and Human Rights Commission (EHRC) – into racial harassment in British universities. The point of the contrast is to demonstrate that what the chapter refers to as colonising narratives about students of colour are not *inevitable*. By resolutely placing the responsibility for improving the conditions of existence of students of colour at universities on university management, the EHRC report rejects the tendency found in other reports to search for solutions *from* students of colour.

Part One: The UUK/NUS Investigation into the Attainment Gap

The UUK and NUS report seeks to 'close the gap' between the attainment of students of colour[1] and their white counterparts by examining the underlying causes behind the disparities in the overall experience of university between 'white UK domiciled students and Black, Asian and minority ethnic UK dom-iciled students' (2019: 5). Differences in experiences found to exist between international and UK students fell outside the scope of the report.

In many ways the report is a classic illustration of Ruha Benjamin's asser-tion that (to refer to the quotation with which this chapter commenced) data is repeatedly demanded about subjects in relation to matters about which enough is already known. For example, in acknowledging that when it comes to determining in which institutions students of colour will study, 'disparities and inequalities continue to exist' (2019: 23), the report adds little to what earlier data gathering exercises have exposed. For example, as early as 2014, HESA data revealed that students of colour are 'under-represented in the Russell Group of twenty-four leading UK universities' (Rathi & Ware 2014).

The tendency to document what has been repeatedly documented is evi-dent throughout the UUK/NUS report. The report acknowledges the absence in universities of 'racially diverse, inclusive environments' (2019: 4 & 12), and recognises that students of colour 'repeatedly cited feelings of discom-fort, isolation and a sense of not belonging' (2019: 23). Ostensibly, the report seeks to bring about a climate which will enable those students to confidently address their concerns with their universities, in contrast to the current environmental context which has seen students of colour 'internalising the inequalities they face' (2019: 7). However, what the report singularly fails to do is to examine whether strategies targeted at university attainment, although not focused specifically on students of colour, 'promote a deficit understanding of those students by considering them to be lacking skills, aspirations or motivations' (2019: 23).

---

[1]   Referred in the report as Black, Asian and Minority Ethnic (BAME).

Part Two: The UUK/GuildHE and QAA Investigation
into Degree Grade Inflation

As a consequence of concerns over the increasing percentage of first and upper-second class honours degrees awarded at British universities, the UK Standing Committee for Quality Assessment (UKSCOA) commissioned UUK, GuildHE and the QAA to produce a report which was to form the basis of a consultation process with universities in an effort to identify the causes and solutions to the problem of degree grade inflation. This report was supplemented by another which, in turn, was commissioned by UKK (on behalf of UKSCOA), titled *The Drivers of Degree Classifications* (Bachan 2018).

The consultation reports covered a ten-year period (academic sessions 2007/8–2016/17), during which it was found that 'pre-1992 universities awarded the highest proportion of upper degrees' (Bachan 2018: 10). Such a finding would initially suggest that the problem of degree grade inflation lay with the more 'elite' universities which, as other researchers have found, have a record of awarding first class and upper-second degree awards to a high percentage of their students. One often-cited example is Imperial College London, which, in terms of the 'upward trend' (UUK et al. 2018: 3) in degree classifications, 'tops the list at 45 per cent of their students being awarded a First' (Richmond 2018: 5). However, readers of these reports were very swiftly made aware that it is not the universities that award higher degrees *per se* which threaten public confidence in the 'usefulness of the honours degree classification system for grading and differentiating student attainment' (UUK et al. 2018: 3), but those universities (predominantly those which attained university status post-1992, post-2003 and post-2012) which are seen to carry the greater 'share of "unexplained" grades' (Bachan 2018: 21). According to this logic, a degree classification grade fails to be considered as a potentially inflated one when it 'cannot be explained by student quality and/ or characteristics, or university expenditure on student and staff facilities and academic services' (Bachan 2018: 6).

Although it is made clear that the number of 'unexplained' degree grades has increased across all universities (Bachan 2018: 20), the general consensus was that 'in general, pre-1992 universities exhibit the lowest level of unexplained increases and newer universities the highest' (ibid.).[2] To put the matter succinctly, the newer universities, where the majority of students of colour gain their degrees (Andrews 2018: 130; Holmwood 2018: 47), award proportionality *fewer* higher degrees than their pre-1992 counterparts, but, on the basis of the criteria agreed by the various report authors – student quality and expenditure on student and staff etc. – the higher degrees that these newer universities

---

[2] See also UUK et al. (2018) where these findings are expressed in similar terms on page 14 of their report.

have awarded are much more liable to be assessed as falling within the category of degree inflating awards.

Part Three: The UUK/GuildHE Report on Degree Algorithms

In 2017, UUK and GuildHE produced a report based on a survey of 120 universities and other higher education institutions on the policies and guidance which provide the framework against which degree classification decisions are arrived at. Relevant to this chapter is the finding in the report to the effect that the expert judgment of academics plays a limited (often non-existent) role in degree classification decisions. Such was not always the case. The judgment of expert examiners used to be decisive in cases where a student performance was on the 'borderline' of two possible degree results. In such instances now it is 'expected that the number of institutions using an automatic algorithm to decide on borderline cases will increase (UUK/GuildHE 2017: 39). According to the UUK/Guild HE report, 65 out of the 120 higher education institutions surveyed dealt with borderline cases by 'automatically' applying the degree algorithm, or by simply not considering borderline cases (2017: 38). Even those institutions which were found to submit borderline cases to the judgment of members of an academic board more often than not constrained that judgment by way of inflexible rules pertaining to when and how that judgment is exercised. For example, another study on the operation of degree algorithms noted that a common practice across the sector in borderline instances is to limit academic judgment to cases where a student is 'within 1% or 2% of the next band' and only 'on the basis of specific criteria such as requiring in excess of 50% of the final year marks to be in the upper band, or specific modules to be included in the final calculation' (Sinclair et al. 2020: 1).

I have argued elsewhere that a degree classification process which does not permit the exercise of academic judgment in 'borderline' cases is incompatible with administrative law (Tuitt 2018). However, I am concerned here with the potential negative impact the removal of academic judgment might have in correcting factors throughout the academic journey of a student of colour which might lead to a lower degree attainment result than that student's grades at entry to university and academic performance throughout university might otherwise dictate. A strong underlying theme of the UUK/GuildHE report is that academic judgement is inimical to 'fair' and 'transparent' decisions (2017: 4), but there are other indications that degree algorithmic design itself produces inequities in terms of student outcomes. For example, in a report that attracted the attention of the mainstream media, David Allen argued that there is a 'real risk that different algorithms could result in different classifications given on a student's mark profile' (2017: 7). As illustration, Allen stated that 'in the case of the individual set of marks, the degree outcome ranges from an upper second (66.69%) to a 1st' (70.72%) (2017: 1).

Although Allen's report sees potential inequities in the current degree classification system, it does not attend to the question of whether those potential inequities – as well as other perceived problems, such as 'degree inflation' and disproportionately low attainments of students of colour – might be helped if expert examiners were given greater scope to exercise their expert judgments in particular cases – especially in those borderline cases where the appropriate degree grade is not obvious. Nor is there much evidence that UKK/GuildHE were alert to the full potential implications of their investigation and conclusions on the attainment gap between students of colour and white students. At best, we find a very oblique reference contained in the 2018 report on degree grade inflation, which merely notes that 'any change to degree algorithm practice must ensure that specific groups, especially those from widening participation backgrounds, are not disadvantaged' (UUK et al. 2018: 33).

Part Four: Universities and 'Race After Technology'

In *Race After Technology*, Ruha Benjamin sets out to expose and analyse the 'symbiotic relationship between technology and society' (2019: 41). In so doing, she explores how data is used and collected in a number of spheres. Although the main focus of the book is on the criminal justice arena, Benjamin's account covers other contexts, including education, health and finance. The fundamental message behind the work is that the way in which data is managed by those authorised to collect, store, analyse and disseminate it produces what the author terms 'coded inequity'. At its most exact, 'coded inequity' is 'the practice of codifying existing social prejudices into a technical system' (2019: 96). According to Benjamin, such processes of reproduction occur even when the purposes behind the data collection exercise appear benign, or, as in the case of the UUK/NUS student attainment gap report, avowedly transformative. Her findings are consistent with the underlying argument of this chapter, which is that current diversity and inclusion initiatives can be wholly compatible with the colonial structures and ideologies that British universities are supposed to be in the process of dismantling.

This 'coded inequity', or the 'datafication of injustice' as the author alternatively names the phenomenon, is particularly revealing when the data collecting exercises directly or indirectly relate to subjects and matters about which much is already known. In such instances, Benjamin argues that 'the hunt for more and more data is a barrier to acting on what we already know' (2019: 116).

Benjamin's book is of particular interest because it speaks to an increasing tendency of universities to want to gather data about those within its environs. Data collecting exercises of the type outlined above are facilitated by increasingly sophisticated technical systems, and the double meaning of the main title to Benjamin's book encourages her readers to reflect on the way the *race after technology* in pursuit of the 'quick fixes' which technological use promises has negatively impacted upon people experiencing marginalisation due to many forms of social construct, such as disability, sexual orientation and gender, as well as race. Crucially, however, Benjamin's examination and critique of the 'social dimensions of technology' (2019: 11) makes clear that in all of these different but interlocking arenas, the lived experiences of people of colour is key. Referencing specifically persons of African and Caribbean descent, Benjamin states that '[t]the plight of Black people has consistently been a harbinger of wider processes ... which then get rolled out on an even wider scale' (2019: 32). It is in this sense that Benjamin opines 'in many ways Black people already live in the future' (ibid.). In the context of British universities and their relation with students of colour, about which this chapter is concerned, Benjamin's work comes as a timely warning that the ostensibly benign – diversity driven – attempt to discover and record evidence about the experiences and academic attainments of students of colour could produce 'coded inquiry', or, to put it in the terms of this chapter, these data collecting exercises form part of a longer colonial archive of knowledge about black, Asian and other racialised people.

As previously stated, postcolonial theory and criticism has long set its sights on various textual depictions of those subject to colonial rule. Such texts take the form of travel guides, novels, histories, legal doctrines, scientific treatises and government inquiries, among others. A common theme in such texts is one of the accomplishments of white individuals and groups above those of individuals and communities of colour. It is a theme that is strongly evidenced in the various reports explored in this chapter. Thus, Benjamin's notion of 'coded inequity' is a very productive way in which past explicitly oppressive colonial projects can be connected with current ostensibly benign and progressive ones of the kind which apparently drive the data collecting exercises that universities are currently engaged in. Casting a critical eye on these developments is important not least because such data forms the basis of the 'soft laws' which make up the fabric of the university. Needless to say, Benjamin's text is perfectly alive to the fact that social biases are frequently embedded in 'legal codes'.[3] The UUK/GuildHE and QAA consultation report on degree grade inflation is a case in point. Here the report authors call for 'changes in regulations, conventions and behaviours' (2018: 21) when assessing the key 'area for further examination' (2018: 21) into the causes of degree inflation. Such changes will

---

[3] The example which Benjamin gives is not of direct relevance to the concerns of this chapter. A major instance of social biases being embedded in an elaborate legal code which offers ostensible protection to individuals against the invasive/abusive use of data and technology is the European Union's General Data Protection Regulation (GDPR). Benjamin argues that such codes invariably contain provisions which allow 'a wide latitude for government officials to revoke data rights in an instant ... [w]hat looks like an expansion of data rights for individuals rests on the ability of governments to revoke those rights from anyone deemed a public threat' (Benjamin 2019: 188).

almost certainly proceed on the assumption that 'academic practice and student study behaviours' (2018: 12) of those academics and students of colour who inhabit post-1992 universities in higher numbers are 'major determinants in the increasing proportion of upper degrees' (ibid.). In turn, such a perception could very well result in academics and students of colour being made to bear the burden of inflationary degree award practices which are happening in those institutions which in fact award the *greater* share of higher degrees, but whose 'explanations' behind the higher awards fit the framework of rationality which the relevant audit agencies have constructed. If post-1992/2003/2012 institutions are pressured to adjust – with a view to correcting perceived degree inflationary results – the degree classifications processes which *already* produce proportionately *fewer* higher awards for their students than the numbers produced by pre-1992 universities, the outcome would almost certainly be a sharp and sudden increase in the attainment gap of students of colour in comparison to their white counterparts. Ultimately the soft law developments which the UUK/GuildHE/QAA consultation report calls for will embed the idea that actions and decisions made within the spaces that are disproportionately inhabited by academics and students of colour are inexplicable and, thus, highly suspect.[4]

Part Five: Concluding Thoughts

Hans Lindahl argues that while the 'distinction between foreign and domestic spaces is contingent; the distinction between own and strange places is constitutive' (2013: 4). To borrow from Lindahl, It is undoubtedly the case that through a constantly iterative process, the places in which UK universities are located have become 'familiar' places for some of their students and 'strange' places for others. Those for whom the UK university setting has been made 'strange' are disproportionately students of colour.

There are many ways in which students of colour are made to feel 'strange' within their universities, and, despite their ostensible objective, the reports analysed in this chapter serve to exacerbate the distance between students of colour and their universities by constantly highlighting—in different and sometimes subtle ways—the 'deficits' in their learning experiences and journeys. However, the most obvious and disquieting way in which students can be estranged from places of learning is through their exposure to actual incidents of racial harassment. It is to be noted that the number of reported incidents

---

[4] These arguments are fleshed out in Tuitt, P. (2019a). Inflating the BAME attainment gap: A response to the consultation report of degree grade inflation, *patriciatuitt .com*. https://www.patriciatuitt.com/single-post/2019/01/28/Inflating-the-BAME -Attainment-Gap-A-Response-to-the-Consultation-Report-on-Degree-Grade -Inflation.

of racial harassment have been sufficiently high to justify investigation by the EHRC. Its report, which was published in 2019, is titled *Tackling Racial Harassment: Universities Challenged.* When setting up the investigation, the EHRC noted that '[r]acial harassment can make people feel that they don't belong.'[5]

This chapter concludes with reference to the EHRC investigation because it is an example of textual presentation of the experiences of students of colour at universities which resolutely problematises the university culture and management and not the students themselves.

According to the EHRC's findings '13% of all current students in British universities ... have suffered from racial harassment, most of whom are 'Black ... and Asian' (2019: 12). Underlying the EHRC's findings and conclusions is a strong warning to universities that they will be held to account for incidents of racial harassment which are seen to be caused or exacerbated by a university which has not provided sufficient evidence that it has paid 'due regard' to the need to eliminate racial 'discrimination, harassment, victimisation' or conduct of a similarly injurious nature; and which, consequently, has not complied with a legal obligation – known as the Public Sector Equality Duty (PSED) – imposed by section 149 of the Equality Act 2010.

The EHRC is the body responsible for the monitoring and enforcement of Equality Act obligations. Among other means at its disposal, it has the power to take action in the courts against public bodies, such as universities, to enforce compliance. Evidence that it will, in appropriate circumstances, take enforcement action against universities is littered throughout the EHRC's report of its investigation. For example, the EHRC made clear that it will no longer tolerate a situation where '[a]lmost half of the students ... who did not report their experiences said this was because they had no confidence that incidents would be addressed by their universities ... [t]his was the single most important reason for a quarter ... of these students' (2019: 59); nor will it tolerate a continued display of ignorance of the Equality Act 2010 definition of harassment (2019: 63); for universities 'must comply with the PSED, and will be legally responsible for harassment committed by their staff and agents unless they have taken all reasonable steps to prevent it, such as having appropriate policies, procedures and training in place' (ibid.). More pointedly, the report's executive summary records that:

> Universities have an incomplete picture of the scale of racial harassment because of underreporting and informal complaints not being recorded routinely. This calls into question the extent to which universities are meeting their PSED obligations which include having regard to the need to eliminate harassment and to foster good relations. To meet

---

[5] See the ECHR's call for evidence from university staff and students. https://www .equalityhumanrights.com/en/inquiries-and-investigations/racial-harassment -higher-education-our-inquiry.

these obligations, universities must have reliable evidence when developing and reviewing their policies and procedures. If a university has a poor understanding of the scale of the problem, this can lead to their priority setting, resource deployment and activities being inadequate to tackle the issues. (2019: 10)

Of particular relevance to the argument that colonising narratives are not inevitable is the fact that the EHRC report does not shy away from warning universities that although the PSED cannot be used to compel them to take specific measures to tackle racial harassment, it could be utilised in cases where governing bodies, through their senior management teams, are found to have prioritised the university's 'reputation above the safeguarding and welfare of their students and staff' (2019: 12). The way in which the PSED will displace the current management priorities that are inconsistent with the duties of care they owe to students of colour in the not too distant future is highlighted in several areas of the report. For example, it is a theme which drives the report's recommendations relating to much-needed changes in university culture (2019: 13–14).

The role of bodies like the EHRC becomes even more important when one reflects on the limited successes students of colour have had when taking complaints of discriminatory teaching, assessment and supervision beyond their universities to the Office of Independent Adjudicator (OIA), and then to the Administrative Court through an application for judicial review.

The role of the courts in relation to student complaints has become increasingly important since the enactment of the Higher Education Act 2014, which established the OIA to act as an independent body for investigating complaints against universities and other higher education institutions. It has long been established that the OIA is amenable to judicial review in respect of its decisions. However, a decision by the Court of Appeal in R (Rafique-Aldawery & Another) v St George's University & Another [2018] is indicative of a desire on the part of the courts to discourage use of the judicial review process as a means of resolving complaints against universities. It will, thus, come as no surprise that few of the claims brought by students of colour, at considerable financial and emotional stress, have been successful. The legal system, dependent as it is on the willingness of an individual to expose their losses and traumas to an adversarial system of adjudication, is unlikely to leave students of colour feeling less exposed to blame for what are often deeply embedded exclusionary practices of their universities.

Supported in large measure by government agencies and courts, universities have, to date, been able to control how they respond to various demands to decolonise their structures, curricula and, above all, their relations with and treatment of students of colour. Through a strategic use of soft law policies and guidance, British universities have been able to claim that experiences at university and the academic attainment of students of colour are due to wider environmental and social factors outside of their control. However, interventions like that brought about by the EHRC have the potential to bring an end to these strategies of disavowal.[6]

References

Allen, D. (2017). Degree algorithms, grade inflation and equity: The UK higher education sector. *Economics Working Paper Series 1801.* https://www2
.uwe.ac.uk/faculties/BBS/BUS/Research/General/Economics-papers
-2018/1801.pdf

Andrews, K. (2018). The challenge for black studies in the neoliberal university. In: Bhambra, G. K., Gebrial, D. and Nişancıoğlu, K. (eds.) *Decolonising the university.* London: Pluto Press, pp. 129–143.

Aparna, K. and Kramsch, O. (2018). Asylum university: Re-situating knowledge-exchange along cross-border positionalities. In: Bhambra, G. K., Gebrial, D. and Nişancıoğlu, K. (eds.) *Decolonising the university.* London: Pluto Press, pp. 93–107.

Bachan, R. (2018). *The drivers of degree classifications.* Universities UK (on behalf of the UK Standing Committee for Quality Assurance), November. https://www.universitiesuk.ac.uk/policy-and-analysis/reports/Documents
/2018/drivers-of-degree-classifications.pdf

Benjamin, R. (2019). *Race after technology: Abolitionist tools for the New Jim Code.* Cambridge: Polity Press.

Equality and Human Rights Commission (EHRC). (2019). *Tackling racial harassment: Universities challenged.* https://docs.google.com/document/d/1h1
0rnrfoYN4K4p2F1yHB95RWJ85HFtODrb-yDOKQaMs/edit

Holmwood, J. (2018). Race and the neoliberal university: Lessons from the public university. In: Bhambra, G. K., Gebrial, D. and Nişancıoğlu, K. (eds.) *Decolonising the university.* London: Pluto Press, pp. 37–53.

Lindahl, H. (2013). *Fault lines of globalisation: Legal order and the politics of a-legality.* Oxford: Oxford University Press.

R (Rafique-Aldawery & Another) v St George's University & Another [2018] EWCA Civ 2520.

Rathi, A. and Ware, G. (2014). Race and academia: Diversity among UK university students and leaders. *The Conversation,* 9 April. https://theconver
sation.com/race-and-academia-diversity-among-uk-university-students
-and-leaders-24988

---

[6] An extended version of this analysis of the EHRC report can be found in Tuitt, P. (2019b). An end to the 'management' of racism in British universities? patriciatuitt
.com. https://www.patriciatuitt.com/single-post/2019/11/08/An-End-to-the-%E2
%80%9CManagement%E2%80%9D-of-Racism-in-British-Universities.

Richmond, T. (2018). A degree of uncertainty: An investigation into grade inflation in universities. *Reform*. https://reform.uk/the-reformer/degree-uncertainty-investigation-grade-inflation-universities

Shilliam, R. (2018). Black academia. In: Bhambra, G. K., Gebrial, D. and Nişancıoğlu, K. (eds.) *Decolonising the university*. London: Pluto Press, pp. 53–63.

Sinclair, N., Wright, C., Edwards, G. and Keane, P. (2017) *Degree classification: Does the calculation model affect the award?* London South Bank University. https://openresearch.lsbu.ac.uk/item/86z1w

Tuitt, P. (2018). Academic judgment and the force of law. patriciatuitt.com. https://b3c06d8a-7cc7-40a2-8161-0b2dbfb92c20.filesusr.com/ugd/433c70_18738f6aa14143f4bad99aefcc3ae235.pdf

Tuitt, P. (2019). Inflating the BAME attainment gap: A response to the consultation report of degree grade inflation. patriciatuitt.com. https://www.patriciatuitt.com/single-post/2019/01/28/Inflating-the-BAME-Attainment-Gap-A-Response-to-the-Consultation-Report-on-Degree-Grade-Inflation.

Tuitt, P. (2019). An end to the 'management' of racism in British universities? patriciatuitt.com. https://www.patriciatuitt.com/single-post/2019/11/08/An-End-to-the-%E2%80%9CManagement%E2%80%9D-of-Racism-in-British-Universities

Universities UK and National Union of Students. (2019). *Black, Asian and Minority Ethnic student attainment at UK universities: Closing the gap.* https://www.universitiesuk.ac.uk/policy-and-analysis/reports/Documents/2019/bame-student-attainment-uk-universities-closing-the-gap.pdf

Universities UK/GuildHE. (2017). Understanding degree algorithms. https://www.universitiesuk.ac.uk/policy-and-analysis/reports/Documents/2017/understanding-degree-algorithms.pdf

Universities UK, GuildHE and Quality Assurance Agency for Higher Education. (2018). *Degree classification: Transparent, consistent and fair academic standards.* https://www.universitiesuk.ac.uk/policy-and-analysis/reports/Documents/2018/degree-classification-academic-standards.pdf

CHAPTER 8

Stop and Search: Past Problems, Current Concerns

Seema Kandelia

Introduction

Powers to stop and search remain one of the most contentious of all police powers. Statistics repeatedly show that people from black and other minority ethnic communities[1] are disproportionately represented in the figures raising questions on its use – in particular, whether stop and search is used unfairly and discriminately. This criticism is not new. One of the contributing factors to the Brixton Riots in 1981 was the misuse of stop and search powers on black people (Scarman 1981). Almost two decades later, the inquiry into the murder of Stephen Lawrence found that the disparities in stop and search were a result of racist stereotyping by individual police officers (Macpherson 1999). The 2011 riots across England further highlighted the difficulties in the relationship between the police and ethnic minorities with stop and search identified as one of the key reasons behind the discontent (Riots Communities

---

[1] There are problems in using the terms 'ethnic minority communities' or 'ethnic minority people', which assume that the experience of all ethnic minority people is the same. However, as there is no consensus on the appropriate terminology, these terms are used with caution in this chapter.

How to cite this book chapter:
Kandelia, S. 2024. Stop and Search: Past Problems, Current Concerns. In: Whyte, A., Tuitt, P. and Bourne, J. (eds.) *The Long Walk to Equality: Perspectives on Racial Inequality, Injustice and the Law*. Pp. 155–176. London: University of Westminster Press. DOI: https://doi.org/10.16997/book63.h. License: CC-BY-NC-ND 4.0

and Victims Panel 2012). A 2017 review into race and the criminal justice system also found that the disproportionate use of stop and search 'continues to drain [the] trust' of ethnic minorities in the entire criminal justice system (Lammy 2017: 20). Recently, a number of high-profile incidents, for example the vehicle stop of MP Dawn Butler and the stop and search of athletes Bianca Williams and Ricardo dos Santos have once again pushed the issue to the centre of public debate. Both cases were viewed by those involved as being triggered by racial profiling (Her Majesty's Inspectorate of Constabulary and Fire & Rescue Services (HMICFRS) 2021).

The power to stop and search is recognised as a useful tool in policing, specifically in the prevention and detection of crime. Its purpose is to allow police officers to 'allay or confirm their suspicions about individuals without exercising their power of arrest' (Home Office 2014: para. 1.4). These powers broadly fall into two types: powers to stop and search where there are reasonable grounds of suspicion for the search, and powers to stop and search without reasonable grounds of suspicion. The latter requires pre-authorisation of a senior officer. Despite their importance, these powers give rise to tensions between the need to provide police officers with the tools to do their jobs and the impact the powers have on people subjected to the intrusions. The persistent disproportionality in the use of stop and search causes considerable and long-lasting damage. It can draw ethnic minority people into the criminal justice system unnecessarily, thereby disrupting lives. It can spark distrust and alienation amongst ethnic minority people, sometimes leading to public disorder. It can also lead to a perception that crime is more prevalent amongst certain groups of people, thus fuelling prejudices. These consequences harm police–community relations and raise questions on the legitimacy of the police.

There have been several reforms to stop and search powers over the years; however, these reforms have failed to address the actual or perceived racial bias surrounding their use. A recent review by HMICFRS (2021) on the disproportionate use of stop and search also found worrying evidence of the police not following the guidelines set out in the law. This chapter will examine the racial disparities behind the use of stop and search, focusing on the current legal provisions and police practice. Although disproportionate use does not necessarily mean discriminatory use, there is evidence to suggest that two are linked. Much of the debate in this area has focused on the police decision making process and the impact this has on the disproportionality rate. The findings suggest that police practice is at odds with the legal provisions.

Stop and Search Powers: A Brief History

The police have a range of legislative stop and search powers available to them. Early stop and search laws contained in the Vagrancy Act 1894 gave wide-ranging powers enabling the police to arrest anyone they suspected of frequenting or loitering in a public place with the intent to commit an arrestable offence (section 4).[2] These powers, known as the 'sus laws', were highly controversial. Historically, they were used in London and other large cities that had a high number of ethnic minority populations, particularly immigrants from the West Indies (Bowling & Phillips 2002; Bridges 2015). Allegations that the laws were being implemented in a disproportionate and discriminate manner were commonplace, particularly in the 1960s and 1970s. According to Yesufu (2013: 281), this 'was an era most Black people would prefer not to talk about because of the oppressive encounters they experienced with the police'. Although the 'sus laws' were eventually abolished by the Criminal Attempts Act 1981, tensions between the police and the black population remained high. Shortly before the Criminal Attempts Act came into force, in April 1981, large-scale riots erupted on the streets on Brixton. The riots were triggered by a heavy-handed approach to policing in the area (Bowling & Phillips 2002). In an operation called Swamp 81, more than 120 officers were deployed to patrol the area with an instruction to stop and search anyone that looked suspicious. Over four days, 943 people were stopped and 118 were arrested, more than half of whom were black. A total of 75 people were charged (ibid.). In the Scarman Report (1981: para. 3.110) that followed, it was acknowledged that the disturbances were 'essentially an outburst of anger and resentment by young black people against the police' and that the mass stop searches were a contributory factor to this. However, the Metropolitan Police Force was not deemed to be institutionally racist, although the report did acknowledge that some police officers, particularly those at the lower level of policing, were guilty of racial prejudice.

Although the Scarman Report did not propose any changes to stop and search powers, continued public concern and the work of campaigning groups led to the acknowledgement that use of these (and other) police powers lacked accountability, and therefore regulation was necessary (Bowling & Phillips 2002; Bridges 2015). In 1984, the Police and Criminal Evidence Act (PACE) was passed to provide a balance between the powers of the police, including stop and search, and the rights of the public. The new legislation, however, did little to calm the tension surrounding the use of stop and search. Statistics continued to show that black people were still being stopped and searched at a disproportionate rate, suggesting that the regulation was ineffective at curbing potential abuses of power (Miller 2010).

Almost two decades after the Scarman Report, the use of stop and search was once again the subject of scrutiny. In 1997, an inquiry was ordered to examine the Metropolitan Police's handling of the murder investigation of Stephen Lawrence, a black teenager who was stabbed to death in 1993. The Macpherson Report (1999: para. 4.61) concluded that the murder investigation had been 'marred by a combination of professional incompetence, institutional

---

[2] In additional to the Vagrancy Act 1894, other national and local laws also gave the police powers to stop and search. See Delsol & Shiner, 2016.

racism and a failure of leadership'. Institutional racism was not limited to the Metropolitan Police Force but extended to all police forces. Institutional racism was defied as:

> The collective failure of an organisation to provide an appropriate and professional service to people because of their colour, culture, or ethnic origin. It can be seen or detected in processes, attitudes and behaviour which amount to discrimination through unwitting prejudice, ignorance, thoughtlessness and racist stereotyping which disadvantage minority ethnic people. (ibid.: para. 6.34)

The Macpherson Report identified the use of stop and search as a prime example of institutional racism in policing. Interestingly, this was attributed to racist stereotyping by individual police officers, rather than the unintentional factors included in the definition of institutional racism. Despite this acknowledgement, the report supported the use of stop and search as a necessary tool in preventing and detecting crime. However, it was suggested that procedures should be in place that would record and monitor stop and search practices as a way of holding individual police officers to account (recommendations 60–63).

Notwithstanding the reforms, the controversy surrounding stop and search persists. The use of stop and search was identified as one of the contributing factors that led to the 2011 riots which took place following the shooting of Mark Duggan by Metropolitan police officers in August 2011. Two days after his death, a peaceful protest against the police turned into widespread disorder. Over five days, thousands of people rioted across towns in England, engaging in acts of violence, looting and arson. Five people lost their lives, and many more lost their businesses. An investigation into the riots noted that the use of stop and search powers was a key factor in the strained relationship between ethnic minority people and the police (Riots Communities and Victims Panel 2012). Following the riots, an examination of the use of stop and search was undertaken by Her Majesty's Inspectorate of Constabulary (HMIC) (now the HMICFRS). It found worrying evidence of non-compliance with the statutory requirements set out in PACE and its associated Codes of Practice (HMIC 2013).

Stop and Search: Reasonable Suspicion

PACE is the most significant piece of legislation which codifies and regulates police powers. Section 1 gives police officers a general power to stop and search any person or vehicle where they have a reasonable suspicion that stolen or prohibited articles, such as offensive weapons, will be found. Other stop and search powers based on reasonable suspicion exist for possession of drugs (section 23, Misuse of Drugs Act 1971) or firearms (section 47, Firearms Act 1968) and persons suspected of terrorist activities (section 43, Terrorism Act 2000).[3] Police can also stop vehicles without reasonable suspicion under section 163 of the Road Traffic Act 1988, although any search must be justified under one of the established stop and search powers.[4]

The accompanying Code of Practice to PACE, Code A (Home Office 2014) provides additional guidance on the exercise of stop and search under the most common powers.[5] It has undergone several revisions since it was first drafted, partly in response to concerns that these powers were continuing to be used disproportionally against minority groups (Bridges 2015; Welsh, Skinns & Sanders 2021). The Code sets out the legal test for reasonable suspicion which first states that the police officer must have a *genuine suspicion* that the stolen or prohibited object will be found, and second, that the suspicion must be *reasonable*. This means that there must be an *objective* basis for the search which is founded on facts, information and/or intelligence, or on the specific behaviour of the person concerned (Code A, paras. 2.2 and 2.6).

Recognising the risk that stop and search powers could be misused, Code A states that these powers must operate fairly and without discrimination. The Code further instructs that personal factors such as age, race, religion or sex (and any of the other relevant protected characteristics set out in the Equality Act 2010) should not form the basis of reasonable suspicion, nor should there be generalisations or stereotypical images about certain groups or people's involvement in criminal activity (para. 2.2B). Welsh, Skinns & Sanders (2021: 66) have noted that 'it is remarkable that a legislative code of practice directs, in effect, that people should not be stopped just because they are black or Muslim, and is a rare example of the law attempting to take into account the social reality of policing on the streets'.

Despite the attempt to root out racial and other discrimination, in practice, applying the concept of reasonable suspicion is problematic. Even though the number of stop and searches have decreased over the last 10 years for every ethnic group, overall, people from ethnic minority communities continue to be disproportionately subjected to these powers. Between April 2019 and March 2020, there were six stop and searches for every 1,000 white people, 54 for every 1,000 black people, 15 for every 1,000 Asian people, 16 for every 1,000 mixed ethnicity and 18 for every 1,000 'other' (Home Office 2021). This means that people from ethnic minority groups are four times more likely to stopped and searched compared to white people, and black people specifically are nine times more likely (HMICFRS 2021). Most stop and searches are conducted to

---

[3] This is not an exhaustive list of police stop and search powers. For a more comprehensive list, see Annex A of Code A, Home Office, 2014.

[4] For an analysis of the link between vehicle stop checks and stop search powers, see Pearson & Rowe 2023.

[5] A separate code exists for those people stopped and searched under the terrorism legislation. See Home Office 2012.

find drugs. The HMICFRS (2001) reports that drug searches contribute significantly to the ethnic disproportionality rate even though there is no evidence of a link between ethnicity and drug use. The grounds of suspicion for searching black people for drugs were also weaker than comparable searches on white people, and fewer drugs were found during searches on black people. This not only questions the effectiveness of the use of stop and search, but such practices also risk alienating black people and damaging police-community relations.

Although Code A states that that the most effective searches are those that are based on accurate and current intelligence or information, the HMICFRS (2021) review shows that most searches are self-generated by the police based on what they have heard or seen (55%), rather than on third party information (37%) or intelligence (9%). Moreover, black and Asian people are subjected to police-generated stop and searches more than white people. The review also notes that from the cases that were analysed, 14% had recorded no reasonable grounds of suspicion, 33% had weak grounds of suspicion, 42% had moderate grounds of suspicion and 21% had strong grounds of suspicion. Weaker grounds of suspicion are linked to lower find rates, which shows that these powers are more effective when the basis of the stop and search is lawful and fair (ibid.).

Focusing solely on the figures, however, only provides a partial picture. Statistics inform us of the number of people that have been stopped and searched according to their ethnicity, but they do not give us any insight into the decisions behind the use of these powers and whether they are in fact being used discriminately. Searches initiated by the police, whether rightly or wrongly, affect public trust and confidence in the police. It is therefore important to explore the extent to which police officer decision making contributes to the disproportionality rate and whether the process is shaped by racial prejudices.

Disproportionality and Police Decision Making

As noted, while racial disparities in stop and search practices do not necessarily mean that there is discrimination, without explanations for the differences, these powers will continue to be perceived as operating unfairly and unlawfully. Even in the absence of any concrete evidence of discrimination, disproportionality is still a problem not least because it can bring people into unnecessary and invasive contact with the police which in turn affects the legitimacy of the police (Quinton 2015). Advocates for stop and search would, however, argue that it is a vital tool in preventing and detecting crime and keeping the public safe, which outweighs any intrusions on the liberty of the person (see Bradford & Matteo 2019).

Disproportionality can only be understood in the wider context in which the police function. Street level policing involves a high level of discretion. For example, police officers must decide the areas they patrol and what incidents they become involved with. These decisions are often based on subjective generalisations which are defined as 'broad understandings that officers have about people, places, or situations that are more likely to be associated with offending' (Quinton, Bland & Miller 2010: 35). Although such generalisations are necessary for effective police work, this can cause tension with the requirement for stop and search to be based on objective criteria as outlined in Code A.

Psychological research on unconscious or implicit bias[6] offers further insight into the police decision making process and the disproportionality in stop and search. Unconscious or implicit bias refers to the beliefs that we hold that sit outside our conscious awareness, over which we have no control, but which influence our attitudes and behaviour (James 2018). It is a process where our brains automatically make 'quick judgments and assessments of people and situations, influenced by our background, cultural environment and personal experiences' (Equality Challenge Unit 2013: 1). Whether we recognise these biases or not, these judgments are difficult to detect and control because they are entrenched deep in our thinking. These biases or beliefs, however, could 'unintentionally favour or disadvantage people who are seen to belong to particular social groups' (Quinton & Packham 2016: 14). Research shows that there are various types of implicit racial biases prevalent in society which can influence people's actions (Holroyd 2015).

The occupational culture of the police, sometimes referred to as cop culture or canteen culture, is also relevant to understanding the police decision making process. Occupational culture is not a static term and different understandings exist (see Westmarland 2008; Loftus 2010; and Holdaway 2013). Reiner (2000: 87) defines it as 'the values, norms, perspectives and craft rules that inform police conduct'. These informal rules, often passed down from experienced colleagues, shape the way police officers make decisions and carry out their everyday role. In this way, practices that are wrong can become normalised or systematic across police teams or entire forces, resulting in some people receiving different treatment to others. One of the core characteristics of occupational culture identified by Reiner (2000) is racial prejudice. The Macpherson Report (1999) also identified racism as a systematic problem in the police force, although this was mostly attributed to unwitting institutional behaviour rather than deliberate behaviour. Disproportionate stop and searches, however, were singled out as being a result of racist stereotyping by individual police officers. Even though the reforms that were proposed in the Scarman (1982) and Macpherson (1999) Reports were aimed at reducing prejudice in the police force, the impact that these reforms have had is questionable.

---

[6] Although unconscious or implicit bias are broadly similar terms and are often used interchangeably, for some, implicit bias questions the extent to which these biases are unconscious, particularly in a world where we are now more aware of discrimination and prejudices. See Equality Challenge Unit 2013.

The culture within the police force has come under fresh scrutiny recently, particularly following the high-profile abduction, rape and murder of Sarah Everard in March 2021 by a serving Metropolitan Police Office, Wayne Couzens, under the pretence of a lawful arrest (Fulford LJ 2021). The investigation into the circumstances of her death revealed that Couzens had exchanged racist and misogynistic messages with fellow officers which were grossly offensive. There had also been allegations of sexual misconduct against Couzens which had not been investigated or adequately dealt with (Dodd, Topping & Haroon 2021). The case has sparked a wider debate about the attitudes and conduct of police officers, with recognition that behavioural problems in the police force are not just a case of a few bad apples (Syal 2022). In February 2022, an investigation by the Independent Office for Police Conduct (IOPC) found evidence of bullying, misogyny and racism amongst a number of police officers predominately based at Charing Cross police station (IOPC 2022). Following this, in March 2023, Baroness Casey's review into the standards of behaviour and internal culture of the Metropolitan Police Service found the largest police force in the country to be institutionally racist, misogynist and homophobic (Casey 2023). In relation to stop and search, the report found that black Londoners 'are more likely to be stopped and searched, handcuffed, batoned and tasered, are overrepresented in many serious crimes' (ibid.: 17) and that 'enough evidence and analysis exists to confidently label stop and search as a racialised tool' (ibid.: 317).

Researching the extent to which racial bias plays a part in police decisions to stop and search is difficult because of its implicit nature and the awareness amongst police officers of allegations of discrimination, particularly in the aftermath of the Macpherson Report. There is evidence to suggest that overt racism, such as the direct use of racist language, is not as prevalent or accepted as it once was (Quinton 2011, 2015; Pearson & Rowe 2020). However, indirect discrimination could help explain the disproportionality rate. Quinton's (2011) research into the formation of suspicions found that police officers take a variety of factors into account when deciding who to stop. Factors could include being known to the police, staring, avoiding eye contact, walking around aimlessly, wearing sports clothing, driving too fast or too slowly, or hanging around a certain area. Police officers often struggled to express why they were suspicious, but indicated it was down to hunches and just knowing (ibid.).

These hunches could be linked to implicit racial biases or occupational practices which see people from certain groups as more hostile than others. For example, research on racial biases shows that black people are more likely to be associated with committing a crime, carrying a weapon or being bad (Glaser, Spencer & Charbonneau 2014). This view may help explain why force is 5.7 times more likely to be used on black people than on white people (HMICFRS 2021). Black people are also nine times more likely to have Tasers drawn on them and eight times more likely be handcuffed when being compliant than white people (ibid).

Loftus' (2009: 144) research on police culture also found that the 'stereo-typing of black and minority ethnic men as inherently criminal was evident' on occasions, although the response of the police to these biases varied. In some circumstances, proactive encounters with ethnic minority people were avoided out of the police's fear of accusations of racism. On other occasions, discriminatory stereotyping could result in more stop and searches on ethnic minority people. Similarly, Quinton (2015) found that police officers continue to negatively stereotype people from ethnic minority groups and that forming suspicions based on stereotypes was a likely cause of disproportionality in stop and searches.

There have been several high-profile cases recently which suggest that racial profiling continues to be an influencing factor in decisions to stop and search. In July 2020, Bianca Williams, a British athlete and her partner, Ricardo dos Santos, a Portuguese sprinter, were stopped by the police whilst travelling in a Mercedes car with their three-month old baby. They were handcuffed and searched for drugs and weapons, and their baby's details were added to the MERLIN database (IOPC 2020b).[7] Following the incident, an investigation was opened by the IOPC to investigate whether the stop and search was appro-priate and proportionate, and whether racial profiling or discrimination played a part in the decision to stop their car (IOPC 2020a). The investigation con-cluded in February 2022 with a recommendation that the five officers involved in the incident should face gross misconduct proceedings (IOPC 2022a).

As well as adults, children can be also stereotyped as criminal. In Decem-ber 2020, a 15-year-old black girl (Child Q) was strip searched at school by two female police officers who knew she was menstruating. The search took place after teachers wrongly suspected that she was carrying cannabis and called the police. During the search, there was no appropriate adult present, and the child's parents were not notified. Furthermore, no authorisation for the search had been sought (Gamble & McCallen 2022). This is in clear breach of the regulations.

Strip searches are part of the police's stop and search powers. Under Code A, there are two types of searches that could take place: a 'more thorough search' where a police officer requires an individual to remove more than their outer clothing, for example, a t-shirt (para. 3.6) and 'searches involving exposure of parts of the body' where a person is required to remove all or most of their clothing (para. 3.7). Under PACE Code C (Home Office 2019), a person can also be required to stand with their legs apart and bend down (Annex A, para. 11 (e)). Child Q was subjected to the latter type of search.

---

[7] The MERLIN database is the safeguarding tool used by the Metropolitan Police Force to store details of any child aged 17 and under who has become known to the police (IOPC 2020b).

Given the intrusive nature of a strip search, under Code A, a strip search must be reasonable and necessary and conducted in private (paras. 3.6 and 3.7). It is questionable whether the search on Child Q was reasonable and necessary given that nothing of significance was found in a search of her clothing or bag (Gamble & McCallen 2022). Code C further states that a search should be authorised by a supervising officer and that in cases where the person is under 18, an appropriate adult should be present (Annex A, para. 11(c)). As noted, these safeguards were not adhered to.

Allegations from Child Q's family that she was racially profiled were upheld by a safeguarding review into the case which found that racism and 'adultification bias' was likely to be a factor in the decision to carry out a strip search (Gamble & McCallen 2022: 34). The concept of adultification is:

> a form of bias where children from Black, Asian and minoritised ethnic communities are perceived as being more 'streetwise', more 'grown up', less innocent and less vulnerable than other children. This particularly affects black children, who might be viewed primarily as a threat rather than as a child who needs support. (NSPCC 2022)

As can be seen in the case of Child Q, a criminal justice response was deemed by those in power to be more appropriate than a safeguarding approach. This indicates that there are problems of racism not just within the police force, but perhaps in other sectors too (Davis & Marsh 2020).

National statistics on the use of strip searches were released for the first time in March 2023 (Children's Commissioner 2023). The figures show that Child Q's case was not an isolated incident. Between 2018 and mid-2022, there were 2,847 strip searches of children aged between 8 and 17 years old in England and Wales. Approximately a quarter of these searches (24%) were on children between 10 and 15 years old. Fifty-one per cent of the total number of searches required no further action, which raises questions as to whether the use of the power was justified. One of the key safeguards requiring an appropriate adult to be present was not met in 52% of the cases. Moreover, of all the boys that were strip searched, 38% were black. This means that black children are six times more likely to be strip searched, while white children are around half as likely to be searched (ibid.: 9). In some police force areas, the figures are much higher. For example, of the 650 strip searches of children that took place in the Metropolitan Police area between 2018 and 2020, on average, 58% were black, as identified by the police officer (Children's Commissioner 2022). In 2018, the figure was as high as 75%. The impact of a strip search on children is of significant concern. Being strip searched is a humiliating experience that can cause long-lasting trauma and serious harm to the child, particularly in cases where the safeguards in Codes A and C have not been followed (Nickolls & Allen 2022).

In recent years, the push for more intelligence-based policing has led some forces to create surveillance tools to identify and risk-assess potential offenders. For example, the Metropolitan Police Force has set up a gang violence matrix, a database which contains the personal details of people associated with gangs (Metropolitan Police n.d.). There has been strong criticism that such surveillance tools racially profile people, particularly black boys and men. An Amnesty International report (2018) found that in July 2016, 87% of people on the matrix were from an ethnic minority background; 78% were black. This has led commentators to conclude that the 'gang label is disproportionately attributed to BAME people' (Williams & Clarke 2016: 10). The gang violence matrix is used by police to inform stop and search practices, including what areas to patrol and who to stop. This means that people who are on the gang violence database could be stopped and searched more frequently (Williams 2018).

In response to concerns about discriminatory stop and search practices, the police often explain the racial disparities in ways that do not focus on police practice, for example, by reference to high rates of offending by ethnic minorities or because of their availability in the population (Shiner 2010). Such defences are questionable though, as research shows that stop and searches in areas where there is a large number of ethnic minority people is not justified by the levels of crime in these places (Quinton 2015; Vomfell & Stewart 2021). Regarding the available population, this is shaped by societal factors such as housing policy, unemployment levels and school exclusions which result in certain groups being present on the streets during the day (Bowling & Phillips 2007); however, police discretion is still important. The available population is influenced by both organisational decisions and individual officers' decisions on where to patrol or what calls to respond to (Shiner et al. 2018; Pearson & Rowe 2020). Vomfell and Stewart's (2021) research found that deployment decisions contribute to the over-searching of black and Asian people and this, combined with individual officer bias, has an additional negative effect on black people. A report by the IOPC (2022b) also noted that the grounds for stop and search are often weak and influenced by assumptions about a person based on their ethnicity and age, rather than information and/or intelligence, or on the specific behaviour of the person concerned, as required by Code A.

These findings cast doubt on the ability of law to effectively regulate the use of stop and search. Although Code A states that reasonable suspicion should be based on objective criteria, this is problematic because, in practice, police officers need a certain level of discretion to enable them to do their job, and subjectivity is a part of this. According to Ellis (2010: 2010), it is racist police officers that need to be tackled not subjectivity. He notes:

What appears to have occurred through the introduction of the concept of 'reasonable suspicion' into the stop and search context is a shift of focus from rooting out racism to rooting out subjectivity. This is both impossible, as decision-making processes cannot be divorced from subjectivity, and simply futile, as subjectivity (for example the development of personalised policing expertise) is at the heart of much good policing work.

Moreover, Quinton (2011) found that the law only had a limited impact on the police decision making process. When initiating stop and searches, police officers worked within their own understanding of reasonable suspicion and officer practice varied considerably. However, the requirement to have reasonable suspicion provided some level of constraint to unlawful practices. If this is the case for stop and search powers that require reasonable suspicion, then stop and search powers that do not require reasonable suspicion have much weaker levels of control on police discretion and discriminatory practices.

Stop and Search: No Reasonable Suspicion

Under certain circumstances, the police have the power to stop and search persons or vehicles where there are no grounds for reasonable suspicion of criminal activity. The most notable power of this type is found in section 60 of the Criminal Justice and Public Order Act 1994 which permits a senior police officer, at the rank of inspector or higher, to authorise the use of stop and search powers in specified locations where there is reason to believe that serious violence may occur or that persons are carrying offensive weapons or dangerous instruments. Authorisations are usually set for a duration of 24 hours which can be extended up to 48 hours by a superintendent. The power should, however, operate for the shortest period necessary. It should not be used to stop and search people for reasons unconnected to the authorisation or to discriminate against anyone unlawfully (Code A, para. 214A). Those in favour of section 60 view it as an essential tool in responding to violent crime (House of Commons 2020). Those against it point to its ineffectiveness, the possibility of abuse and the harm it could do to police-community relations (Brown 2020).

The power to stop and search without individualised reasonable suspicion is highly controversial. When the authorisation is in effect, any police officer can stop and search any individual or vehicle for offensive weapons or dangerous instruments without any reasonable suspicion. Section 60 was originally aimed at tackling violence at specific events, for example, hooliganism at football matches. It is now frequently used to combat knife crime, gang violence, gun crime and low-level disorder where there is no other relevant power. In the year ending March 2020, 18,081 people were stopped and searched under this power, which represents an increase of 35% from the previous year and the third consecutive annual increase (Home Office 2020). However, arrest rates remain low. In the year ending March 2020, it was just 4% (ibid.). Even though the power should be used for the shortest period necessary, in practice, certain areas are often subjected to section 60 powers continuously (Bridges 2015; Welsh, Skinns & Sanders 2021). Moreover, these powers are being used disproportionately on members from ethnic minority groups, more so than stop and searches where reasonable suspicion is required. HMICFRS (2021) reports that black people were 18 times more likely to be searched than white people under section 60 powers. Despite the problems with section 60 powers, the government has rolled back some of the limits on the use of section 60 powers (Nickolls & Allen 2022), making it easier to authorise area-wide stop and searches that do not require reasonable suspicion.

Prior to 2011, sections 44 to 47 of the Terrorism Act 2000 contained similar provisions to section 60. Under these provisions, a person could be stopped and searched without any reasonable grounds of suspicion that the person was involved in terrorist related activity. Like stop and search under section 60, authorisation by a senior police officer was required and could be given only if it was expedient for the prevention of acts of terrorism. These provisions were repealed following the European Court of Human Right's (ECtHR) decision in *Gillian and Quinton v the United Kingdom* (2010) in which the court held that sections 44 and 45 stop and searches violated the right to privacy under Article 8 of the European Convention on Human Rights 1950. In its reasoning, the court noted that despite the 28-day limit for authorisations, the Metropolitan Police District had been operating under a continuous rolling programme of authorisation since the powers came into force (para. 81). It further acknowledged the risk of arbitrariness and discrimination in granting police officers a wide discretion to authorise and carry out stop and searches on those suspected of engaging in terrorist activities (paras. 83–85). The Court therefore concluded that the powers of authorisation and confirmation were 'neither sufficiently circumscribed nor subject to adequate legal safeguards against abuse' (para. 87). As a result of the judgment in *Gillian*, section 44 stop and searches were suspended and subsequently replaced by Section 47A in 2012. Although section 47A did not put in place the usual requirement for there to be a reasonable suspicion of an individual, the authorising officer must reasonably suspect that an act of terrorism will take place and that the powers are necessary to prevent such an act.

Replacing section 44 stop and searches has called into question the legality of section 60 stop and searches (Bridges 2015).[8] Section 44 was better regulated, as the giver of the authorisation had to inform the Secretary of State as soon as

---

[8] Similar provisions that permit 'suspicionless' stop and searches are contained in Schedule 7 of the Terrorism Act 2000. Choudhury and Fenwick (2011: 175, 167) note that this power is having the 'single most negative impact' on British Muslim communities and 'silently eroding Muslim communities' trust and confidence in policing'.

it was reasonably practicable. This was deemed by the ECtHR as an inadequate check on the misuse of stop and search. Section 60 contains no such provision. The authorisation need only be given by a senior police officer; there is no requirement for confirmation by the Secretary of State or any higher authority. The ECtHR also expressed concern at the continuous rolling nature of stop and search under section 44. As mentioned, this is also a concern with the section 60 powers. Finally, the ECtHR acknowledged the risk of discriminatory use of stop and search against people from ethnic minority communities. It was noted that the guiding Code of Practice was insufficient in reducing this risk (Bridges 2015).

In contrast to the approach of the ECtHR, the legislative and statutory guidance covering the operation of section 60 has been held to be a sufficient safeguard against the potential abuse of 'suspicionless' stop and searches. In the case of *R (on the application of Roberts) v Commissioner of Police of the Metropolis and another* (2015), the UK Supreme Court was required to assess whether these powers were compatible with the right to privacy under Article 8 of the European Convention on Human Rights. Noting the various safeguards in the legislation, the Code of Practice and other guidance documents, and the existence of accountability mechanisms, the Court held that section 60 powers were not in violation of Article 8. Ip (2017: 538) notes that the Court's discussion of the safeguards 'does little more than note their formal existence'. For example, although there is reference to the work of the HMIC, there is no acknowledgement of the HMIC's 2013 report which found a lack of compliance with the Code of Practice, a lack of training for both authorising and junior police officers in the use of section 60, limited overall supervision of stop and search activity, and problems with record keeping. HMICFRS (2021) follow-up report notes that while there have been some improvements in these areas, there are still significant gaps and more needs to be done. This calls into question the safeguards in the legislation and statutory codes.

The Court in *Roberts* further noted that although there was a risk that these powers could operate in an arbitrary and discriminatory way, this risk was outweighed by the great benefit to the public, specifically a reduction in serious violence often involving offensive weapons and gangs. Interestingly, the Court went on to justify the use of section 60 by noting that gangs were largely made up of young people from black and other ethnic minority groups, and therefore it was these individuals who would benefit the most from a reduction in serious violence (para. 41). It is questionable whether people from ethnic minority groups, especially those who are frequently exposed to stop and search, would see it this way.

Despite the problems with stop and search powers that do not require reasonable suspicion, an additional 'suspicionless' stop and search power was enacted via the Police, Crime, Sentencing and Courts Act 2022. The power allows police officers to stop and search people who are under a Serious Violence Reduction

Order[9] without a need to have any reasonable grounds of suspicion or authorisation from a senior police officer. The new power is being piloted before a
decision on a national roll-out is made.

Recording Requirements

To act as a safeguard against unauthorised searches, Code A includes a
requirement to keep records of each stop and search. This was one of the key
amendments to stop and search recommended in the Macpherson Report. The
data should include the date, time and place of the search, the object of
the search, the power authorising the search, the identity of the officer carrying
out the search and, importantly, the ethnicity of the person searched (para. 4.3).
It used to be the case that the name and address of the person searched also had
to be recorded, as well as other information, but this requirement was dropped
partly to ease the 'needless' bureaucracy especially as stop and search activity
had increased (Shiner 2010). As Shiner (2015: 154) notes, dropping the names
and addresses of individuals makes it 'more difficult to monitor repeat searches,
measure effectiveness and hold officers to account'. Moreover, the HMICFRS
(2021) has found that there is a failure to record ethnicity data which hides the
real disproportionality rate. This affects the police and the public's understanding of how stop and search powers are used and the impact they could have on
people from ethnic minority groups.

Police were also previously required to record all stop and accounts, but this
too has been dropped. Stop and account is a non-legislative power (Home
Office 2013; Pearson & Rowe 2023) which allows police officers to stop any
member of the public and ask them to account for their presence, their actions
or what they are carrying in a public place. No search is conducted. As there
is no national requirement to record these stops anymore, any information
regarding disproportionality in its use is unknown, although some data suggests that black people are more likely than white people to be stopped and
asked to account for their presence (StopWatch 2022).

Thus, the requirement to record stop and searches (and the lack of a requirement to record stop and account) is inadequate to effectively monitor police
practice and hold police officers to account. In fact, as Reiner (2015: xii) notes,
'[t]he list of unacceptable criteria for reasonable suspicion (ethnicity, age, style
of dress, etc.) could be cynically interpreted as advice on how to complete
acceptable records rather than guidance on what did constitute objectively reasonable grounds'. This view is supported by Quinton (2011) and Ellis (2010)

---

[9] This order is issued to people convicted of offences involving knives or offensive
weapons (chapter 1A Sentencing Act 2020, as amended by s.165, Police, Crime, Sentencing and Courts Act 2022).

who both found that police officers creatively constructed records that fit with the law, downplaying the real factors that influenced their decision to initiate a stop and search.

Accountability Measures

Although the Codes of Practice accompanying PACE are statutory codes, failure to comply with them will not necessarily render a police officer liable to criminal or civil proceedings (PACE, section 67). Any breach of the provisions could, however, result in a disciplinary hearing for police officers, and the evidence gathered from an unauthorised stop and search could render that evidence inadmissible in court (PACE, section 67 and Code A, para. 5.6). The responsibility to monitor stop and search activity falls on the supervising police officer. This could be through direct supervision, examining stop and search records, asking officers to account for their conduct and record keeping, or through complaints made against the police officer (Code A, para. 5.5). Body worn cameras can also be viewed to establish the circumstances surrounding a stop and search, although recent reviews by the HMICFRS (2021) and IOPC (2022b) indicate that the use of such cameras and the monitoring of the footage needs to be improved. The disciplinary measures taken against police officer will depend on the nature of the conduct but could involve warnings or performance reviews through to gross misconduct hearings (College of Policing 2014).

The possibility of disciplinary action, like the requirement to keep records, are internal mechanisms that rely on police supervisors having the will to hold junior policers officers to account. The lack of any statutory penalties allows police discretion to operate relatively unchecked, thus limiting the power of the law to protect people against unlawful stop and searches. As Bowling and Phillips (2007) note, a person who refuses to comply with an officer's request to stop and search commits a criminal offence, but a police officer who conducts an unlawful search is not criminally penalised. Unlawful stops may, however, be challenged through civil proceedings, but Shiner (2015: 165) emphasises that 'litigation only ever deals with a minority of cases and is costly, uncertain and slow'.

Other accountability measures include the work of bodies such as the IOPC and the HMICFRS which, through their reviews of police practice and individual cases, provide an additional layer of scrutiny of police powers. The latest HMICFRS (2021) review of the disproportionate use of stop and search has been referred to throughout this chapter and highlights numerous shortcomings in police activity. The IOPC's (2022b) recent national stop and search learning report also identifies problems with the use of stop and search, particularly involving ethnic minority people, and makes proposals for improvement in police practice. The work of these bodies is valuable in keeping the issue of racial discrimination at the forefront of the debate.

Conclusion

Although practices vary across different police forces and not all officers hold the same views, this chapter has shown that racial biases can and do influence police practice on stop and search which contributes to the disproportionality rate. Moreover, intelligence-based policing, bringing with it concerns about racial profiling, could exacerbate rather than ameliorate the problems (see Keane 2023). Through the introduction of legislation and the Codes of Practice, the law has attempted to curb any misuse of these powers mainly by prohibiting decisions based on generalisations and stereotypes and introducing better monitoring practices. However, the police decision making process is complex and involves a high level of discretion and some level of unconscious bias, both of which are difficult to regulate in practice. Despite the legal reforms, every year, the statistics tell the same story: people from ethnic minority groups are overrepresented in the figures. This shows that existing regulations are ineffective in curtailing the disproportionate use of stop and search. Despite the difficulty in regulating stop and search, there needs to be a continued effort at rooting out discriminatory practices in policing, many of which only come to light after official investigations have been initiated or after accounts of questionable stop and searches appear in the media. Although training programmes on the law, on racial biases and on the damage caused by unfair and unlawful stop and searches are crucial, these on their own are not enough. There are other barriers to reform that need to be addressed, such as changes to the organisational culture and internal police resistance (see Shiner 2015; and Miller et al. 2020).

Recent events such as the killing of George Floyd by a police officer in the USA in May 2020 and the Black Lives Matter protests that followed demonstrate the negative impact that the use of police powers can have on individuals, communities and the police themselves. This could be a turning point in our understanding of discriminatory police practices; however, we have been here before, for example, with the flawed investigation into the murder of Stephen Lawrence. It appears that we are still facing the same challenges in rooting out discrimination in stop and search: racial biases, poor monitoring practices and a lack of an effective enforcement mechanism. Unless change actually means change, it is difficult to continue justifying the use of stop and search as it currently operates.

References

Amnesty International. (2018). *Trapped in the matrix. Secrecy, stigma, and bias in the Met's Gangs Database.* https://www.amnesty.org.uk/files/2018-05/Inside%20the%20matrix.pdf?VersionId=VtHJ.NawP4favLWa0mjswpaSStRrPneB

Bowling, B. and Phillips, C. (2002). *Racism, crime and justice.* Harlow: Pearson Longman.

Bradford, B. and Tiratelli, M. (2019). Does stop and search reduce crime? *UK Justice Policy Review* FOCUS 4: 1–14.

Bridges, L. (2015). The legal powers and the limits. In: Delsol, R. and Shiner, M. (eds.) *Stop and search: The anatomy of a police power.* Basingstoke: Palgrave Macmillan. pp. 9–30.

Brown, J. (2020). *Police powers: Stop and search.* London: House of Commons Library.

Casey, L. (2023). *An independent review into the standards of behaviour and internal culture of the Metropolitan Police Service. Final Report.* https://www.met.police.uk/SysSiteAssets/media/downloads/met/about-us/baroness-casey-review/update-march-2023/baroness-casey-review-march-2023.pdf

Children's Commissioner. (2022). *Strip search of children by the Metropolitan Police Service – new analysis by the Children's Commissioner for England.* London: Children's Commissioner.

Children's Commissioner. (2023). *Strip search of children in England and Wales – analysis by the Children's Commissioner for England.* London: Children's Commissioner.

Choudhury, T. and Fenwick, H. (2011). The impact of counter-terrorism measures on Muslim communities. *International Review of Law, Computers & Technology,* 25(3): 151–181.

College of Policing. (2014). *Code of ethics. A code of practice for the principles and standards of professional behaviour for the policing profession of England and Wales.* London: College of Policing.

Criminal Justice and Public Order Act 1994.

Davis, J. and Marsh, N. (2020). Boys to men: The cost of 'adultification' in safeguarding responses to Black boys. *Critical and Radical Social Work,* 8(2): 255–259.

Delsol, R. and Shiner, M. (2006). Regulating stop and search: A challenge for police and community relations in England and Wales. *Critical Criminology,* 14: 241–263.

Dodd, V., Topping, A. and Siddique, H. (2021). Sarah Everard's killer might have been identified as threat sooner, police admit. *The Guardian,* 30 September. https://www.theguardian.com/uk-news/2021/sep/30/sarah-everards-killer-might-have-been-identified-as-threat-sooner-police-admit

Ellis, D. (2010). Stop and search: Disproportionality, discretion and generalisations. *The Police Journal,* 83: 199–216.

Equality Act 2010.

Equality Challenge Unit. (2013). *Unconscious bias and higher education.* London: ECU.

Fulford L. J. (2021). *Sentencing remarks.* 30 September. https://www.judiciary.uk/wp-content/uploads/2021/09/Wayne-Couzens-Sentencing-Remarks.pdf

Firearms Act 1968.

Gamble, J and McCallen, R. (2022). *Local child safeguarding practice review. Child Q.* 14 March. https://chscp.org.uk/wp-content/uploads/2022/03/Child -Q-PUBLISHED-14-March-22.pdf

Gillian and Quinton v the United Kingdom Application no. 4158/05 (2010) ECHR 28, (2010) 50 EHRR 45.

Glaser, J., Spencer, K. and Charbonneau, A. (2014). Racial bias and public policy. *Policy Insights from the Behavioral and Brain Sciences*, 1(1): 88–94.

Her Majesty's Inspectorate of Constabulary (HMIC). (2013). *Stop and search powers: Are the police using them effectively and fairly?* London: HMIC.

Her Majesty's Inspectorate of Constabulary and Fire & Rescue Services (HMIC-FRS). (2021). *Disproportionate use of police powers. A spotlight on stop and search and the use of force.* London: HMICFRS.

Holdaway, S. (2013). Police race relations in the Big Society: Continuity and change. *Criminology & Criminal Justice*, 13(2): 215–230.

Holroyd, J. (2015). Implicit racial bias and the anatomy of institutional racism. *Criminal Justice Matters.* 101(1): 30–32.

Home Office. (2012). *Code of practice for the exercise of stop and search powers under Sections 43 And 43a of The Terrorism Act 2000, and the Authorisation and Exercise of stop and search powers relating to Section 47a of, and Schedule 6b to the Terrorism Act 2000.* London: Home Office.

Home Office. (2013). *Stop and search.* https://webarchive.nationalarchives.gov .uk/ukgwa/20130125094331/http://www.homeoffice.gov.uk/police/powers /stop-and-search/

Home Office. (2014). *Revised code of practice for the exercise by: Police Officers of Statutory Powers of stop and search. Police officers and police staff of requirements to record public encounters. Police and Criminal Evidence Act 1984 (PACE) – Code A.* London: Home Office.

Home Office. (2019). *Revised code of practice for the detention, treatment and questioning of persons by Police Officers. Police and Criminal Evidence Act 1984 (PACE) – Code C.* London: Home Office.

Home Office. (2020). *Police powers and procedures, England and Wales, year ending 31 March 2020 – 2nd edition.* London: Home Office.

Home Office. (2021). *Stop and search.* 27 May. https://www.ethnicity-facts -figures.service.gov.uk/crime-justice-and-the-law/policing/stop-and -search/latest

House of Commons. (2020). *Home Affairs Committee oral evidence: The Macpherson Report: twenty-one years.* https://committees.parliament.uk /oralevidence/572/default/

Independent Office for Police Conduct (IOPC) (2020a). *IOPC launches independent investigation into stop and search in Maida Vale, London.* 7 July. https://www.policeconduct.gov.uk/news/iopc-launches-independent -investigation-stop-and-search-maida-vale-london

Independent Office for Police Conduct. (2020b). *IOPC investigating five Met police officers for misconduct following Maida Vale stop and search.* 8 October.

https://www.policeconduct.gov.uk/news/iopc-investigating-five-met
-police-officers-misconduct-following-maida-vale-stop-and-search

Independent Office for Police Conduct. (2022a). *Operation Hotton: Learning report.* https://www.policeconduct.gov.uk/sites/default/files/Operation%20 Hotton%20Learning%20report%20-%20January%202022.pdf

Independent Office for Police Conduct. (2022b). *National stop and search: Learning report.* https://www.policeconduct.gov.uk/national-stop-and-search-learning -report-april-2022

Ip, J. (2017). The legality of 'suspicionless' stop and search powers under the European Convention on Human Rights. *Human Rights Law Review*, 17(3): 523–544.

James, L. (2018). The stability of implicit racial bias in police officers. *Police Quarterly*, 21(1): 30–52.

Keane, D. (2024). Assessing the contribution of the International Convention on the Elimination of Racial Discrimination to global racial equality. In: Whyte, A., Tuitt, P. and Bourne, J. (eds.) *The long walk to equality: Perspectives on racial inequality, injustice and the law.* London: University of Westminster Press, pp. 13–32.

Loftus, B. (2009). *Police culture in a changing world.* Oxford: Oxford University Press.

Loftus, B. (2010). Police occupational culture: Classic themes, altered times. *Policing and Society*, 20(1): 1–20.

Lammy, D. (2017). *The Lammy Review. An independent review into the treatment of, and outcomes for, Black, Asian and Minority Ethnic individuals in the criminal justice system.* 8 September. https://assets.publishing.service.gov .uk/government/uploads/system/uploads/attachment_data/file/643001 /lammy-review-final-report.pdf

Macpherson, W. (1999). *The Stephen Lawrence Inquiry. Cm 4262-I.* London: The Stationery Office.

Metropolitan Police. (n.d.). *Gangs violence matrix.* https://www.met.police.uk /police-forces/metropolitan-police/areas/about-us/about-the-met/gangs -violence-matrix/

Miller, J. (2010). Stop and search in England. A reformed tactic or business as usual? *British Journal of Criminology*, 50: 954–974.

Miller, J., Quinton, P., Alexandrou, B. and Packham, D. (2020). Can police training reduce ethnic/racial disparities in stop and search? Evidence from a multisite UK trial. *Criminology & Public Policy*, 19: 1259–1287.

Misuse of Drugs Act 1971.

Nickolls, L. and Allen, G. (2022). *Police powers: Stop and search.* London: House of Commons Library.

NSPCC. (2022). *Safeguarding children who come from Black, Asian and minoritised ethnic communities.* 25 April. https://learning.nspcc.org.uk /safeguarding-child-protection/children-from-black-asian-minoritised -ethnic-communities#skip-to-content

Pearson, G. and Rowe, M. (2020). *Police street powers and criminal justice: Regulation and discretion in a time of change*. London: Hart Publishing.

Pearson, G. and Rowe, M. (2023). Gone fishing: The operation of police vehicle stops in England and Wales. *Criminology & Criminal Justice*. https://doi.org/10.1177/17488958231155275

Police and Criminal Evidence Act 1984.

Quinton, P. (2011). The formation of suspicions: Police stop and search practices in England and Wales. *Policing and Society*, 21(4): 357–368.

Quinton, P. (2015). Race disproportionality and officer decision-making. In: Delsol, R. and Shiner, M. (eds) *Stop and search: The anatomy of a police power*. Basingstoke: Palgrave Macmillan, pp. 57–78.

Quinton, P., Bland, N. and Miller, J. (2010). *Police stops, decision-making and practice*. London: Home Office.

Quinton, P. and Packham, D. (2016). *College of Policing stop and search training experiment. An overview*. London: College of Policing.

R (on the application of Roberts) v Commissioner of Police of the Metropolis and another [2015] UKSC 79.

Riots Communities and Victims Panel. (2012). *After the riots. The final report of the Riots Communities and Victims Panel*. London: Riots Communities and Victims Panel.

Reiner, R. (2000). *The politics of the police*. Oxford: Oxford University Press.

Reiner, R. (2015). Foreword. In: Delsol, R. and Shiner, M. (eds.) *Stop and search: The anatomy of a police power*. Basingstoke: Palgrave Macmillan, pp. x–xiv.

Scarman, L. G. (1981). *Scarman Report: The Brixton disorders, 10–12 April 2001*. London: HMSO.

Shiner, M. (2010). Post-Lawrence policing in England and Wales: Guilt, innocence and the defence of organizational ego. *British Journal of Criminology*, 50: 935–953.

Shiner, M. (2015). Regulation and Reform. In: Delsol, R. and Shiner, M. (eds.) *Stop and search: The anatomy of a police power*. Basingstoke: Palgrave Macmillan, pp. 146–169.

Shiner, M., Carre, Z., Delsol, R. and Eastwood, N. (2018). *The colour of injustice: 'Race', drugs and law enforcement in England and Wales*. London: StopWatch, Release and the London School of Economic and Political Science.

StopWatch. (2022). *Stop and account factsheet*. 14 September. https://www.stop-watch.org/what-we-do/research/stop-and-account-factsheet/

Syal, R. (2022). Met police culture problems 'not just a few bad apples', says acting head. *The Guardian*, 20 April. https://www.theguardian.com/uk-news/2022/apr/20/met-police-culture-problems-not-just-a-few-bad-apples-says-acting-head

Terrorism Act 2000.

Vagrancy Act 1894.

Vomfell, L. and Stewart, N. (2021). Officer bias, over-patrolling and ethnic disparities in stop and search. *Nature Human Behaviour*, 5: 566–575.

Welsh, L., Skinns, L. and Sanders, A. (2021). *Sanders and Youngs's criminal justice*. Oxford: Oxford University Press.

Westmarland, L. (2008). Police cultures. In: Newburn, T. (ed.) *Handbook of policing*. Cullompton: Willan Publishing, pp. 253–280.

Williams, P. (2018). *Being matrixed: The (over)policing of gang suspects in London*. London: StopWatch.

Williams, P. and Clarke, B. (2016). *Dangerous associations: Joint enterprise, gangs and racism. An analysis of the processes of criminalisation of black, Asian and minority ethnic individuals*. London: Centre for Crime and Justice Studies.

Yesufu, S. (2013). Discriminatory use of police stop and search powers in London, UK. *International Journal of Police Science and Management*, 15(4): 281–293.

CHAPTER 9

Race, Populism, and Immigration: The Transactional Partiality Problem

Rebecca H. Smith

From this day forward, a new vision will govern our land. From this moment on, it's going to be America First. Every decision on trade, on taxes, on immigration, on foreign affairs, will be made to benefit American workers and American families .... We will seek friendship and goodwill with the nations of the world – but we do so with the understanding that it is the right of all nations to put their own interests first. (Donald Trump, Inaugural Address, 20 January 2017)

The aim is to create, here in Britain, a really hostile environment for illegal immigrants. (Theresa May, Hostile Environment Policy Speech, 2012)

Introduction

Within the dominant liberal-egalitarian political philosophy of the West we find two competing ideologies. Firstly, with roots as deep as Kant,[1] the ideal of

---

[1] Kant's supreme principle of the doctrine of virtue enjoins us to act in accordance with a maxim of ends that it can be a universal law for everyone to have: Kant, I.

How to cite this book chapter:
Smith, R. H. 2024. Race, Populism, and Immigration: The Transactional Partiality Problem. In: Whyte, A., Tuitt, P. and Bourne, J. (eds.) *The Long Walk to Equality: Perspectives on Racial Inequality, Injustice and the Law*. Pp. 177–199. London: University of Westminster Press. DOI: https://doi.org/10.16997/book63.i. License: CC-BY-NC-ND 4.0

impartiality requires us to recognise that every individual and their competing personal viewpoints matters equally, and that we should therefore treat others in a way which respects that moral equality. By contrast, theories of partiality defend the idea that people may permissibly favour the satisfaction of their own concerns, desires, and interests over those of others.[2] This includes both the individual self-interest we are naturally disposed to, and the special preferences we often hold for the success of the lives of our family, friends, and loved ones over the lives of others. The central question which has motivated philosophical investigations of partiality theory over the years is not what do we all *desire* for the flourishing of our own lives, but rather what is *justifiable* for us to demand in pursuance of our own flourishing, given that everyone possesses an equal moral claim to flourish? On what moral grounds are people justified in showing special care and attention towards the success of their own lives over the lives of others if, in truth, we all matter equally?

This old philosophical debate is being tested anew in contemporary immigration policy in both the US and the UK. The inexorable pull of self-interest is clearly on display in one of ex-President Trump's most controversial immigration policies—the notorious Proclamation No. 9645;[3] and again in the implementation and broadening of the 'Hostile Environment' and 'No Recourse to Public Funds' (NRPF)[4] immigration policies under Theresa May's reign as UK Home Secretary (2010–2016) and subsequent Prime Ministership (2016–2019) respectively. Trump's Executive Order effectively instituted a travel ban against several Muslim-majority countries by barring immigrants from Iran,

---

(1996 [1797]). *The metaphysics of morals.* Edited by M. Gregor. Cambridge: Cambridge University Press. pp. 395–396.

[2] For debates on the moral permissibility of partial concern for the self, see Cottingham, J. (1991). The ethics of self-concern. *Ethics,* 101(4): 798–817; Scheffler, S. (2010). Morality and reasonable partiality. In: Feltham, B. and Cottingham, J. (eds.) *Partiality and impartiality: Morality, special relationships, and the wider world,* Oxford: Oxford University Press. pp. 98–130; and Nagel, T. (1991). *Equality and partiality.* Oxford: Oxford University Press.

[3] https://travel.state.gov/content/travel/en/us-visas/visa-information-resources/presidential-proclamation-archive/presidential-proclamation9645.html. It should be noted that this Proclamation has now been rescinded under President Biden in Proclamation 10141 'Ending Discriminatory Bans on Entry to the United States', 20 January 2021.

[4] Section 115 of the Immigration and Asylum Act 1999 states that a person will have 'no recourse to public funds' if they are 'subject to immigration control'. This means they have no legal entitlement to the majority of welfare benefits, including income support, housing benefits, and a range of other allowances and tax credits. This legal status includes those lawfully seeking asylum, and persists until they have obtained permanent settled status either by being granted Indefinite Leave to Remain or by becoming naturalised citizens. The Citizens Advice Bureau currently estimates that 1.4 million individuals are affected by this legal status, leaving them at risk and vulnerable within many different poverty indicators.

Libya, Syria, Somalia, and Yemen without individually granted Executive exception, while the UK's 'Hostile Environment' immigration policy portfolio, implemented largely via the Immigration Acts of 2014[5] and 2016,[6] aimed to make life so untenable for any immigrant without paperwork evidence of their Indefinite Right To Remain that they would voluntarily choose to leave. This included enacting measures blocking such immigrants from using vital NHS services, working, or renting property.[7]

These policies have not remained unchallenged by the law in either jurisdiction. In the 2018 case of *Trump v Hawaii and the Muslim Association of Hawaii* (*Trump v Hawaii and the Muslin Association of Hawaii* 585 US 2018) Hawaii's judicial challenge to Proclamation 9645 lost to a 5-4 majority in the US Supreme Court on the basis that the policy passed the 'rational review' basis for Constitutionality (*Trump v Hawaii* 32). In other words, the predominantly Muslim travel ban was upheld as Constitutional by the highest court in the US jurisdiction on the basis that it was 'plausibly related' to a legitimate government interest in protecting national security under the Immigration and Nationality Act (8 U.S.C. §1182 *Inadmissible Aliens*). Specifically, the US Supreme Court found that the travel ban was a lawful exercise of the broad discretion granted to the Presidency under S1182(f) of the United States Code to 'suspend the entry of aliens into the United States on the grounds of national security' (*Trump v Hawaii* 33–38). Nor did the Proclamation violate Section 1152(a)(1)(A) U.S.C., which bars discrimination based on nationality in the issuance of visas. The Court held that while that section prohibits discrimination, it did not limit a President's authority to block the entry of nationals of certain countries (*Trump v Hawaii* 21). Furthermore, the Supreme Court Justices observed that 'while that word "suspend" often connotes only a temporary deferral of normal immigration status, the President was not bound to prescribe in advance a fixed end date for his entry restriction' (*Trump v Hawaii* 13).

This decision was far from unanimous or uncontroversial. Justice Sonia Sotomayor filed a dissenting opinion in which Justice Ruth Bader Ginsburg joined, criticising the majority for 'ignoring the facts, misconstruing our legal precedent, and turning a blind eye to the pain and suffering the Proclamation inflicts upon countless families and individuals, many of whom are United States citizens' (*Trump v Hawaii*, Sotomayor, J Dissenting, 1). Justice Sotomayor found that the majority had incorrectly chosen to apply the rational basis standard of scrutiny and that, in fact, a higher level of scrutiny

---

[5] Immigration Act 2014, 14 July 2014.
[6] Immigration Act 2016, 12 May 2016.
[7] Joint Council for the Welfare of Immigrants. (2020). The hostile environment explained. www.jcwi.org.uk/the-hostile-environment-explained; Kirkup, J. and Winnett, R. (2012). Theresa May interview: We're going to give illegal migrants a really hostile reception. *The Telegraph*, 25 May. https://www.telegraph.co.uk/news/0/theresa-may-interview-going-give-illegal-migrants-really-hostile/

was required in this case (ibid.: 15). She further noted that even if the rational basis test had been appropriately applied here, the Proclamation should still have failed on the grounds that, in the President's own words, it was originally and continues to be 'a total and complete shutdown of Muslims entering the United States' (ibid.: 4). Nonetheless, in the wake of this decision, on 31 January 2020, the then President Trump doubled down on his immigration restrictions with Proclamation No. 9983, which added to the existing travel restrictions under Proclamation 9645 by further limiting the issuance of Immigrant Visas, including Diversity Visas, to nationals of Myanmar (Burma), Eritrea, Iran, Kyrgyzstan, Libya, Nigeria, North Korea, Somalia, Sudan, Syria, Tanzania, Venezuela, Yemen, and Sudan.[8]

What makes the US Supreme Court's decision in *Trump v Hawaii* especially remarkable is the extent to which the legal interpretation of the highest court in the US jurisdiction departed from both academic and popular opinion on the fundamental question of what constitutes discrimination. As a spokes-man from the Urban Justice Centre in New York said of Proclamation 9645, 'the borders are closing and they're closing fastest on people of color and the Muslim religion' (Siddiqui 2018), while the director of the American Civil Liberties Union immigrants' rights project gave a statement saying, 'this ruling will go down in history as one of the Supreme Court's great failures … [they] are not upholding this country's most basic principles of freedom and equality' (McCarthy & Siddiqui 2018). Indeed, wider academic opinion seemed not merely strongly opposed to Proclamation 9645, but genuinely horrified by the failure of US Constitutional law to redress this seemingly straightforward violation of its own 14th Amendment non-discrimination guarantee. So where in truth does the fault, if any, lie? Did US constitutional law fundamentally fail to guarantee equal protection for some of the most vulnerable racial and religious minorities in the world? Or is the President's latitude to restrict immigration in the interests of national security under S1182(f) USC a reasonable exercise of political partiality at the national level, towards American citizens?

Returning to the UK immigration context, in May 2018 the UN Special Rapporteur on Contemporary Forms of Racism, Racial Discrimination, Xenophobia and Related Intolerance, Professor E. Tendayi Achiume, found that the 'Hostile Environment' affected not just 'irregular' or illegal immigrants, or those simply without the correct documentation, but was in fact significantly overbroad, also catching 'racial and ethnic minority individuals with regular immigration status' including many who are 'British citizens and have been

---

[8] https://travel.state.gov/content/travel/en/us-visas/visa-information-resources /presidential-proclamation-archive/presidential-proclamation9645.html ?wcmmode=disabled. It should be noted that both Proclamations 9645 and 9983 have now been rescinded under President Biden's Proclamation 10141. See https://www .whitehouse.gov/briefing-room/presidential-actions/2021/01/20/proclamation -ending-discriminatory-bans-on-entry-to-the-united-states/

entitled to this citizenship as far back as the colonial era' (Achiume 2018: paras. 33–34, 37). She concluded that the policies were 'destroying the lives and livelihoods' of ethnic minority communities, including people with rightful citizenship status, and those who had been long-term settled residents in the country: 'where a strategy for immigration enforcement is so overbroad, and foreseeably results in the exclusion, discrimination, and subordination of groups and individuals on the basis of their race, ethnicity or related status', she wrote, it 'violates international human rights law' (ibid.).[9]

Further to this, the UK's 'Hostile Environment' directly resulted in the national shame of the Windrush scandal, in which Caribbean migrants arriving in the UK between 1948 and 1973 as Commonwealth citizens with full rights to settle, live, and work in the UK without restriction, and with a statutory guarantee of a permanent right of abode in the UK enshrined in the Immigration Act 1971,[10] were denied these rights due to the lack of paperwork explicitly recognising these entitlements. As the 'Hostile Environment' really began to bite between 2012 and 2018, many of these original Windrush generation (named after the ship HMT Empire Windrush which docked in June 1948, bringing workers from Jamaica, Trinidad and Tobago, and other islands, to help fill post-war UK labour shortages)[11] found they lacked now-essential paperwork after the Home Office had destroyed thousands of their landing cards and other vital records of their arrival.[12] By 2018, many of the original Windrush generation, now aged 60 and over, were told they must 'prove they had lived in the UK since before 1973, and must show at least one official document from every year they had lived here'[13] – an impossible task, which then resulted in hundreds of distressing wrongful detentions, deportations and the irreparable disruptions of lives. The crisis eventually became the subject of an independent report published in March 2020, the 'Windrush Lessons Learned Review', which, although it shied away from declaring a full finding of institutional racism on the part of the Home Office, did conclude that 'these failings demonstrate an institutional ignorance and thoughtlessness towards the issue of race and the history of the Windrush generation' (Williams 2020).

Thus, parallel questions arise in both the US and UK contemporary immigration context: to what extent is it justifiable, or merely morally permissible

---

[9] See also Luh, Shu Shin. (2018). We will continue to challenge the 'hostile environment' policy, whatever name the government gives it. *Legal Action Group.* https://www.lag.org.uk/article/205494/we-will-continue-to-challenge-the--lsquo-hostile-environment-rsquo--policy--whatever-name-the-government-gives-it

[10] Immigration Act 1971, 28 October 1971.

[11] BBC. (2021). What is Windrush and who are the Windrush generation? 27 July. https://www.bbc.co.uk/news/uk-43782241

[12] https://www.jcwi.org.uk/the-hostile-environment-explained

[13] Joint Council for the Welfare of Immigrants. (2020). The hostile environment explained. www.jcwi.org.uk/the-hostile-environment-explained

perhaps, for nation States to grossly restrict immigration entitlements in pursuit of their own national self-interest before the moral duties we owe to others from outside our own political community? In this chapter, I will argue that while there are good reasons for recognising the moral legitimacy of partial reasons for action at the individual level, this does not necessarily endorse, nor logically imply, that the same is true of strongly self-preferencing, partial behaviour at the political level. The moral account of partiality at the individual level does not extend to justify nationally protectionist policies at the political level, nor does it legitimise a State in abdicating its moral responsibilities towards vulnerable non-citizens, for example lawful asylum seekers and refugees, in preference for protecting its own national interests first. As such, this leads to significant conclusions about the moral justifiability of a State acting to prioritise their citizens' interests above those of non-citizens. This is both a useful refinement of earlier work on the justifiability of partiality in general, and a clarifying moment regarding the many legal and moral objections to the rise of nationalistic and protectionist immigration policies in contemporary US and UK foreign policy.

The Kantian Nature of Partial Value

In previous work I have argued for a Kantian account of the moral legitimacy of a certain degree of partial reasons for action at the individual level (Smith 2014). It may be helpful to repeat the basics of this argument here. Kant writes of the supreme principle of the doctrine of virtue:

> A human being is an end for himself as well as for others, and it is not enough that he is not authorized to use either himself or others merely as means … it is in itself his duty to make the human being as such his end … Humanity in one's person is the object of respect which he can demand from every other man, but which he must also not forfeit. Hence he can and should value himself … And this self-esteem is a duty of man to himself. (Kant 1797, 6:395–396)

On this grounding, I support a particular conception of partiality theory which justifies individuals acting in self-preferencing ways on the grounds that taking seriously the equal objective importance of all lives (as the doctrine of impartiality requires us to do) also therefore requires us to recognise the objective importance of our *own* lives. As such, we have an ethical responsibility to live well for ourselves (see also Dworkin 2011: 202–210). Our ability to form, revise, and pursue our own individual conceptions of the good life is an intrinsic part of what it means to take seriously the impartial ideal that every individual life is of objective equal moral worth, because our own subjectivity is an irreducible part of that objectivity. I suggest that once this is recognised, the philosophical issue is no longer *whether* the moral legitimacy of partiality can be justified within an egalitarian moral theory which respects the equal moral worth of all, but rather to recognise that it is actually *required* by it. The next question in this line of inquiry, which this chapter seeks to engage with, is to what extent might it be permissible to show the kind of national self-interest US Proclamations 9645/9983 or the UK's 'Hostile Environment' endorse at the political or State level? Could this Kantian account of the moral legitimacy of partiality at the individual level also ground and justify a State's right to favour its own citizens by excluding others through immigration restrictions?

Such a suggestion faces immediate issues, for it is far from self-evident that a theory of partiality at the individual level could simply be scaled up to the national or State level for a number of reasons, not least the heightened moral imperative on political governance to display a good faith interpretation of impartiality towards the governed at the public level. A further problem is that, without additional qualifications, this Kantian vision of the moral value in individual partiality could become a rather unwieldy tool, and especially so at the political level. Johann Frick has argued recently that it is generally accepted in the political realm that States, 'as the primary organs of our collective self-governance, frequently pursue policies that strongly favour the interests of citizens over those of foreigners, including restricting immigration on grounds of legitimate partiality towards the national self-interest' (Frick 2020: 1). Indeed, he says, this is often viewed not merely as morally permissible behaviour but, in fact, as morally *required* of States to give some measure of priority to the interests of citizens over non-citizens (ibid.: 1–2). However, interestingly, Frick goes on to suggest that while it may be morally permissible for a State to show a degree of priority towards its own citizens over foreigners in the same way that one might give priority towards one's friends and family under a Dworkinian conception of associative obligations (Dworkin 1986), it is not permissible if that very partiality towards the national 'in-group' is practised under conditions where eligibility for membership of that in-group is unjustly restricted in the first place. He writes:

> If we illicitly exclude a person from the in-group then we cannot licitly appeal to the fact of that exclusion, and that they do not stand in associative relationships with us, to justify giving their interests less priority in a way which disadvantages them. (Frick 2020: 9)

This would seem to suggest certain moral limitations on a State's right to enact restrictive immigration policies in furtherance of their own citizen's interests— but just what are these moral constraints that should operate on the interplay of self-preferencing reasons for action when issues of foreign and immigration policy are at stake? Are there any particular moral limitations on the value of partiality that would prevent, for example, the kind of national or political self-interest of the US Immigration Proclamations 9645/9983 or the UK's 'Hostile

Environment', and if so what are they? Or does the Kantian account of individual partiality actually pave the way for the abdication of our moral responsibilities towards others, particularly those immigrants who are most vulnerable and excluded from full citizenship and even mainstream society, that these kinds of policies seem to endorse?

Utilitarian theory and the heightened justificatory burden for political policies

The Kantian account of individual partiality outlined above is a characteristically anti-utilitarian one. Utilitarianism, as a moral theory of the right, advocates for a flat equalitarian landscape in which nothing and no one has a stronger moral claim over one's reasons for action unless and until it directly speaks to the issue of maximising utility overall. So, for example, utilitarian principles of justice would indict you for saving your last £5 to buy your own child the best nutritious meal possible instead of using that money to buy a quick and cheap warm meal for a homeless person in the street. Clearly, by utilitarian calculations, the Pareto-efficiencies in utility gained by giving the homeless person their only hot meal of the day significantly outweigh those of feeding your own child again when they have already been eating like royalty at nursery all day. Against that view, the Kantian account of individual partiality constructs a moral recognition of the fact that while we do indeed have strong impartial moral duties to aid the homeless person with a hot meal, the utilitarian theory nevertheless makes a fundamental moral mistake by failing to recognise the special moral character of the parent-child relationship. Part of this argument includes recognition of the fact that it is natural to us as humans to favour feeding our own children before we feed others; but that naturalism by itself is not, and cannot be, the whole story. Rather, it is that nourishing and cherishing special partial relationships, for example with our children, should be recognised as part of what makes human life valuable— and not just for the particular individual involved.

This argument, like other partialist theories before it,[14] suggests that that caring more for oneself and one's loved ones is not necessarily or automatically morally illegitimate, as utilitarianism leads us to conclude. On the contrary, it is part of what leading a human life not only often does but indeed *should* involve, as a matter of ideal. Partial and self-preferencing reasons for action add value to a human life; nourishing a child is part of what gives life meaning, purpose, and value, through that special relationship. These kinds of self-interested ends do therefore have a degree of moral legitimacy at the individual level. Significantly, however, this can only be so provided that our self-preferencing

---

[14] See Cottingham 1991; Scheffler 2010; and Nagel 1991.

reasons for action are developed and interpreted in accordance with our objective moral duties towards others first, as lexical priority.[15] So to subscribe to wholly impartialist moral theories like utilitarianism, which deny the moral permissibility of engaging in partial relationships or pursuing partial ends in one's life, is to miss (or rather to mistake) the larger part of what moral theory is supposed to achieve: a blueprint for how real human beings, as opposed to selfless, utilitarian automatons, ought best live their lives (Cottingham 1991: 801).

Regarding the theoretical possibility of justifiable partiality at the national, State, or political level, the methodological shortcomings of utilitarian theory are again instructive. In *A Theory of Justice* Rawls (1971) argues that utilitarianism is a teleological theory which prioritises maximising utility due to a unique feature: a methodological extension from the manner of rational choice appropriate for an individual to that of a theory of social choice. In other words, utilitarian principles of justice hold that since it is rational for an individual to seek to maximise her overall utility by trading off alternative options and opting for the best overall net gain, it must therefore also be rational for society to trade off individual interests and concerns against each other at the public level as well. Rawls writes:

> The most natural way of arriving at utilitarianism is to adopt for society as a whole the principle of rational choice for one man ... the [utilitarian] impartial spectator is the perfectly rational individual who identifies with and experiences the desires of others as if these desires were his own. In this way he ascertains the intensity of these desires and assigns them their appropriate weight in the one system of desire the satisfaction of which the ideal legislator then tries to maximize by adjusting the rules of the social system ... The correct decision is essentially a question of efficient administration. This view of social cooperation is the consequence of extending to society the principle of choice for one man, and then, to make this extension work, conflating all persons into one through the imaginative acts of the impartial spectator. (Rawls 1971: 26–27)

The most important part of Rawls's analysis to draw out here is what I call his 'extension critique'. This is the claim that because utilitarian theory extends the method of rational choice from the individual to the social, by subjecting discrete individuals' interests to a social aggregate in pursuit of maximising utility overall, it therefore fails to take adequate moral account of the due plurality and distinctness of individuals and their separate moral identities. In other words, the utilitarian extension of the methodology of rational choice from that of an individual to the social *illegitimately* distributes utility gains and losses: while utility trade-offs might be acceptable if rationalised and borne within

---

[15] This is a significant qualification of the general partialist thesis.

one individual life, they become illegitimate when distributed across different individual lives. This is why Rawls concludes as he does: that 'utilitarianism does not take seriously the [moral] distinction between persons' (ibid.: 27).

Thus, we have learned a more detailed lesson about the moral permissibility or otherwise of self-preferencing immigration policies at the State level: while it may be understandable that an individual might go about making purely self-regarding decisions by seeking to maximise their net utility gain overall, it is a mistake of rational practical deliberation to replicate that social aggregating, utility-maximising methodology at the public level. This is because by doing so we ascribe utility losses across different individual lives *without full justification*. In other words, to borrow Scanlon's (1998) famous phase: we 'owe each other' an independent justification for public decisions which is accessible to all who must live with the consequences of that decision, especially when it affects the success or failure of different individuals' morally discrete and equal claims. Utilitarianism cannot provide this kind of independent justification to those individuals who stand to lose the satisfaction of their claims as a result of the decisions it endorses, because its very methodology views discrete individual interests as commensurable—and, therefore, ultimately overridable. It preserves no methodology for ensuring each morally discrete individual claim is rightfully treated with equal moral respect. So, when judging a particular political decision, we should look first for the reasons we can offer those who must live with that decision in order to justify it. Or, to put it another way, we should first ask ourselves: what reasons there are that undermine its justifiability to all those who stand to be affected by it? In what ways might a particular political policy be unjustifiable to those who must live with the consequences of it?

Along these contractualist lines, Nagel (1991) argues that the ideal of political legitimacy requires that political principles are those no one could reasonably reject. 'If such a hypothetical unanimity were discoverable,' Nagel writes, 'it would explain the rightness of the answer' (ibid.: 34–36). This would mean that political decisions ought to be justified in ways the individuals who are expected to comply with them could not reasonably reject. If an individual might reasonably reject a particular political policy it would, in Nagel's view, demonstrate a lack of political legitimacy. On this account of political morality, political decisions which simply reflect a commensurate aggregate of individual interests alone do not, and indeed cannot, provide that kind of legitimacy. This is because we can only arrive at legitimate political decisions if, and when, we take seriously our heightened explanatory and justificatory burdens towards those who will have to live under the decisions we make, and who stand to lose out if that decision fails to pay due regard to the equal moral claims of all. Crucially, when we do fail in this way to offer fully justified political decisions, and when States do fail to treat those subject to their decisions with a good faith account of moral equality regarding their personal interests, they not only lose political legitimacy but, significantly, to borrow Dworkin's phraseology, they also fail to generate the kind of associative obligations within that political community that are necessary in order to justifiably require citizens to obey the laws they put out (Dworkin 1986: 188).

This study of utilitarianism's moral failings is able to demonstrate two important conclusions regarding the value of partiality at both the individual and the political level. Firstly, that it is a mistake of individual moral theory to rule out permissible partiality at the individual level because doing so forces an unnatural, inhuman, and virtue-less flat moral landscape upon us, which misses the special value partial ends and relationships have for human lives. Secondly, it would be a mistake of social and political theory to think we can simply reflect and replicate an aggregate sum of discrete individual partial interests at the general or State level, because doing so ignores the heightened burden on political governance to explain and justify political decisions to all those who stand to lose out under them. Returning to the context of the US and UK immigration policy examples discussed above, this theoretical grounding suggests an identical problem of practical deliberation. While it might be cognitively understandable that individual citizens concerned with protecting national jobs, economic development, or national security may personally favour restricting immigration in order to increase *their* chances of interest satisfaction, in fact, to simply replicate and aggregate those subjective partial interests at the political level by enacting restrictive immigration policies, without further effort at independent justification of those policies to those who stand to lose the right to enter, or to claim the international legal right to asylum, makes the very extension mistake Rawls warned us of.[16] It does not take individual moral claims to equal respect seriously, and fails to establish the requisite independent justification necessary to command political legitimacy.

Transactional Partiality Theory

The philosophical issues of partiality at the political level may be described as a problem of transactional partiality which, I suggest, paints a particular account of the democratic voting process which problematises the suggestion that individual voters may rightfully cast their ballots in predominantly self-interested ways. The hypothesis that individuals do, in fact, vote in self-interested ways is not new, and has been criticised on a number of grounds in prior work (Shabman & Stephenson 1994). Nonetheless, it is generally true that individual endorsement of particular political policies is frequently inextricable from individual self-interest. For example, someone with a personal investment in a particular conception of national sovereignty might justify their vote for Brexit on

---

[16] This argument identifies a similar need for independent justification of immigration restrictions as Frick (2020) argued for on the basis of illicit discrimination in granting 'in-group' membership.

these grounds; a CEO of an international company is more likely to favour voting for a candidate promising vast corporate tax cuts; and someone who lacks
comprehensive medical insurance because of pre-existing medical conditions
might foreseeably be inclined to vote for legislative reform promising a regulated private medical insurance market. Indeed, some theorists have claimed
that self-interest and 'external preferences' about the success or failure of others' interests are inevitably inextricably linked, since no voting methodology
is able to separate out preferences regarding the assignment of social goods,
opportunities, and resources to others from preferences regarding one's own
allocation of these goods.[17]

My suggested theory of transactional partiality proposes that when particular demographic groups vote for strongly nationalistic or protectionist political
candidates on the basis of their own strongly held partial interests, for example
in protecting jobs, domestic economic development, or national security, they
then become willing to engage in a political transaction. In return for political
policies which replicate their subjective partial concerns, they become willing to
countenance (or perhaps overlook as necessary 'collateral damage') serious discriminatory practices and racial injustices which result from those nationalist
and protectionist political policies—including those they might not otherwise
have condoned were it not for the fact that their own deeply held partial interests are felt to be at stake. For example, according to the Gallup Polls, political
supporters of the Trump presidency since his successful election campaign in
2016 appear to fall into several main categories of subjective partial interest-
holders: tax-cut advocates; social conservatives; anti-immigrationists; religious
evangelicals; supporters of an absolutist interpretation of Second Amendment
rights for unrestricted gun ownership; and libertarian advocates of State dereg-
ulation of business and economic interests (Newport 2018).[18] According to
data gathered by the Voter Support Group in June 2017, 'voters who held views
of immigrants, Muslims, minorities, and feminist women as the undeserving
"other" were particularly susceptible to Trump's appeal in both the Primaries
and the 2016 General Election' (Griffin & Teixeira 2017). Furthermore, the
Views of the Electorate Research (VOTER) survey found that Trump did very
well among white individuals without a four-year college degree, who tended
to be dependent on low-skilled jobs, and were particularly vulnerable to structural economic change and relatively poor physical health and high mortality

---

[17] For a theoretical exploration of the inextricable relationship between self-interest
and other-regarding preferences about distributive justice in social goods, see
Dworkin 1977: 234.

[18] There is obviously the possibility of a substantial degree of overlap amongst these
groups, as well as some outliers who are harder, if not impossible, to categorise in
any general way. Extensively evaluating empirical data on this is not within the primary scope of this chapter, and so these categories here should be taken as speculative only, for the purposes of exploring the main theoretical arguments.

(ibid.). By contrast, white voters with four years or more of college level education were a relative point of weakness for Trump (ibid.). Even more interestingly, Trump supporters stood out in the survey for displaying a preference for making immigration harder: 52% compared to 38% among supporters of other candidates in the Republican Primaries, and 51% compared to 32% among Clinton voters in the 2016 General Election (ibid.). Trump Primary supporters also registered the highest level of agreement that rising diversity would put too many demands on government services. The survey also included questions regarding perceptions of short-term economic pessimism: one asked respondents whether they and their family were better off, worse off or about the same financially as they were a year previously; the other asked them whether they thought the economy was getting better or worse. On both these measures, Trump supporters were notably pessimistic (ibid.). Long-term pessimism was also widespread among Trump supporters, with two thirds of Trump primary supporters agreeing that 'life today for people like them is worse than it was 50 years ago', compared to about half of other candidates' supporters (ibid.).

Overall, the study concluded that 'the broad picture that emerges from these data is that Trump supporters were distinctively hostile to Muslims, opposed to immigration, critical of modern feminism, worried about rising diversity, and unenthusiastic about free trade agreements' (ibid.). This is true of Trump supporters across both the Republican Primaries and the General Election. Furthermore, it concluded that 'this descriptive portrait of political support for Trump is consistent with an influential explanation for Trump's appeal particularly among white working-class voters in communities that have seen better days ... Such a toxic interaction between economic frustration and cultural reaction would be consistent with the historical record on the rise of right populisms' (ibid.). Thus, against this background of latent racial and cultural resentment in the US electorate, my theory of transactional partiality suggests that, for example, in order to secure the satisfaction of their partial interests in having stronger border controls, voters from the anti-immigration demographic become increasingly willing to overlook or tolerate the enforcement of hard-line 'zero-tolerance' immigration policies, regardless of the discriminatory effect on vulnerable racial minorities that such policies have or, indeed, the destruction of the traditional 'family unit' that social conservatives frequently vaunt (Monico et al. 2019).

One such zero-tolerance immigration policy was announced by the US Department of Justice on 7 May 2018. According to this policy, all migrants who crossed the US-Mexico border without permission, including those seeking asylum, were detained and criminally charged. Prior to the Trump 2016 administration, it was common practice to parole families together, as a unit, to await their immigration cases (Southern Poverty Law Center 2022). However, the Southern Poverty Law Center reports that no exceptions were made to this new policy for parents crossing the US border with young children (ibid.). Undocumented asylum seekers were imprisoned and any accompanying children under the age of 18 were handed over to the Department of Health and Human Services, which held them either in Office of Refugee Resettlement shelters or other care arrangements across the country (ibid.). Hundreds of these children, including infants and toddlers, were under the age of five (ibid.).

Tragically, parents have since been unable to track or reunite with their children because the US government failed to create a formal tracking system coordinated among the agencies involved. As a result, reliable figures for the number of children separated under the policy are, at the time of writing, unknown. However, by 11 October 2018 Amnesty International had published a report citing US Customs and Border Patrol data indicating that 6,022 'family units' had been separated between 19 April 2018 and 15 August 2018 (Amnesty International 2018). By 18 January 2020 the *Los Angeles Times* was reporting that the official government count of children separated from their parents or guardians under the policy had reached 4,368 (Davis 2020). Reports also emerged of cases of paternal suicide in jail, after suffering a nervous breakdown upon being separated from family at the border (Southern Poverty Law Center 2022), and that children were being kept in a series of cages made of metal fencing (ibid.). The *Associated Press* reported that overhead lighting in the detention centres stayed on 24 hours a day, that children were sleeping under 'large foil sheets', older children were forced to change younger children's diapers, and that children had no books or toys (Merchant 2018). On 22 August 2019 *The New York Times* reported that detained migrant children held in a Texas facility had not been able to bathe since crossing the border, that their clothes were soiled, and they lacked access to soap, toothbrushes, or toothpaste (Dickerson 2019). Even more shocking, on 27 February 2019 came reports that the Federal Government had received more than 4,500 complaints of sexual abuse of immigrant children held in detention between October 2014 and July 2018. Of the 1,303 cases considered to be the gravest, 178 included accusations of sexual assault by adult staff, including rape, fondling, kissing and watching children shower (Haag 2019).

While the policy has now thankfully come to an official end, after ex-President Trump signed an Executive Order declaring that it was now the policy of his Administration 'to maintain family unity, including by detaining alien families together where appropriate',[19] the period during its operation marks the darkest stain on the US humanitarian record. As lawyers from the NYU Reiss Center on Law and Security have argued, the criminalisation of those seeking asylum is not only deeply unethical but actually unlawful under the UN Convention and Protocol Relating to the Status of Refugees (UNCSR 51)— even if those seeking asylum enter the country illegally (Satterthwaite & Riddell

---

[19] Executive Order, affording Congress an opportunity to address family separation, 20 June 2018, https://www.whitehouse.gov/presidential-actions/affording-congress -opportunity-address-family-separation, although reports allege that it was still in unofficial practice for a lot longer.

2018). Furthermore, the separation of children from their families may cause such mental and emotional trauma as to amount to torture (ibid.), contravening US obligations under the UN Convention Against Torture and Other Cruel, Inhuman, or Degrading Treatment or Punishment (UNCAT 1984).

It speaks to the depth of anti-immigration feeling in the voting electorate that such extreme policies as this were even countenanced, let alone put into practice and tolerated for so long; and yet it appears to be the result of a political bargain struck between individual voters and their elected representatives. As long as the Trump Administration could guarantee its demographic supporters the satisfaction of their core partial interests through strongly protectionist immigration policies, their political allegiance remained with him. Evidence from the Gallup Polls seems to corroborate this theory of transactional partiality, showing that if the Trump Administration had failed to secure his voters' partial interests, for example, as it had failed to do regarding his 2016 campaign promise to repeal the previous Administration's Patient Protection and Affordable Care Act 2010 ('Obamacare') which overhauled national medical insurance coverage, those demographic voter groups who cast their ballots on the grounds of that particular partial interest basis are far more likely than others to become swing voters in retaliation—highlighting the highly transactional and partial nature of voting preferences in practice.

Objections

It may be objected here that perhaps there is nothing particularly wrong with the idea of transactional partiality. After all, is it not the point of the democratic process to vote for what we individually think best, and to find the 'best fit' political candidate to take action in response to our concerns? What exactly is the flaw in a political transaction between individual partial interest holders and their elected representatives who promise to act on behalf of those interests? To this objection it may be responded that the problem identified by the transactional partiality theory appears at two levels: at the public and at the individual level. Firstly, at the public level, and as previously noted, simply replicating an aggregate of individual partial, self-interested views in a political policy, without subjecting it to the heightened explanatory and justificatory burden that political decisions need to meet in order to command legitimacy, is to make the mistake of practical deliberation that Rawls highlighted in his extension critique of utilitarianism. The democratic political process must find a way of justifying the political decisions it puts out to the individuals who are expected to comply with them. It must go further, and do more work, than merely reflect a simple commensurate aggregate of individual interests alone. While individual citizens who may be concerned with protecting national security might favour restricting immigration in the way hard-line, zero-tolerance policies do, simply to replicate and reflect their subjective partial interest at the political level, without independent justification of it to those who lost their legal right to claim asylum, or to those who are still unable to find their separated children, makes the very extension mistake of practical deliberation Rawls warned us of.

The second flaw in any objection against my theory of transactional partiality on the grounds that this is simply how voters are entitled to cast their ballots, identified at the individual level, is that this kind of objection misses the crucial civic responsibility we hold when we exercise our democratic right to cast our ballots. While there are many different theories of voting ethics, it is a common thread amongst them that part of our civic duty is to identify relevant political issues, gather political information, and to deliberate responsibly about that information towards a decision point when we exercise our right to vote (Brennan 2016a). Democratic theory positions individual citizens as partial authors of the laws their elected representatives put out. Accordingly, every citizen has a duty to vote in 'publicly-spirited ways' (ibid.). It has been argued that: 'To cast a … ballot is to *identify oneself* in a morally significant way with the … policies that the organization espouses' (ibid.). This, it is suggested, is grounds for holding voters to a form of associative moral liability for the moral failings of their chosen political representative, regardless of whether that representative ever actually succeeds to political office, or whether the particular voting individual's exercise of their ballot had any appreciable material effect on the overall election result (Brennan & Lomasky 1993: 186).

It has been suggested that this account of individual voter's civic responsibility is analogous to that of a doctor's responsibility to their patients, or a parent's responsibility towards their children (Brennan 2016b). In much the same way that doctors and parents have a responsibility to promote their patient's or children's interests, and to do so in a sufficiently informed and rational way, it may be said that voters owe similar duties of care to the governed. Voters should certainly vote for what they perceive individually to be the best alternative, but they should also make their political decisions in a reasonably informed and rational way (ibid.). Altruism should therefore also play a vital part in this decision-making process. The choices voters make have a significant impact on political outcomes, and can help determine matters of peace and war, life and death, prosperity and poverty (ibid.). For this reason, voting can be said to be a 'morally charged activity', bringing with it a degree of moral responsibility for the effect one's voting choices have on others under the jurisdiction of those elected (Brennan 2011). As Professor Jason Brennan argues, 'to the extent it is wrong for me to express sincere support for illiberal, reckless, or bad ideas, it would also be wrong for me to vote for candidates who support those ideas' (Brennan 2016a). As such, it does therefore make the kind of morally flawed bargain my theory of transactional partiality highlights when individuals exercise their democratic right to vote in pursuance of strongly self-interested grounds without further serious effort to recognise that by taking part in the democratic process, and by actively participating as co-authors of the law, they are choosing a political distribution of social and public goods not just for themselves but for everyone, including dissenting minorities, children, non-voters, resident aliens, and non-resident individuals coming from other countries who stand to be affected by their decisions (ibid.). To take one's civic responsibility in voting seriously is to cast one's ballot in a way that communicates a reasoned choice about how best the State should work for all, not just for oneself.

A second potential objection might mistake my position with that of cosmopolitanism. To deal with this objection immediately, it should be noted here that my argument so far does not adopt a fully blown cosmopolitanist position, nor does it deny that there is a legitimate space for States to act in their citizens' best interests, or that States owe their own citizens a special duty of care. Cosmopolitanism, in brief, is derived from the Greek word *kosmopolitēs* (meaning 'citizen of the world'), and broadly encompasses the idea that all human beings should be considered citizens of a single world community, and as such are entitled to equal consideration and respect regardless of their physical location or political jurisdiction. In its more stringent forms, cosmopolitanism might be interpreted as calling for the denial of the existence of special obligations within national or local political organisations (Kleingeld & Brown 2019). My theory of transactional partiality does not endorse such a position, and fully allows that States, as leaders of political communities, may be said to owe their own citizens a species of special obligation to promote their interests. This special obligation comes with certain moral parameters, however, to moderate State protectionism with due regard for the ideals of impartiality and moral equality. Thus, while this chapter should not be taken as a call for full cosmopolitanism, it does put forward an argument for better understanding the nature and extent of permissible national partiality in a world with vast inequalities and growing global injustices. There is a significant difference between populist political policies adopting a utilitarian methodology to maximising their voters' individual preference-satisfaction, and true majoritarian democracy which operates above a baseline of fundamental protections and guarantees for universal individual rights. Populist political policies, which aim to appease the most interests of 'ordinary voters' without subjecting the expression of those interests to the heightened justificatory burden, cannot be said to have met this basic requirement of political morality.

A third potential objection to my theory of transactional partiality might proceed along the lines that the Trump Administration has indeed met the heightened justificatory burden for immigration Proclamations 9645/9983. National security, it might be said, is an entirely justifiable reason for restricting immigration from certain States, perhaps even those 'pre-identified as deficient in information-sharing practices' by the Department of Homeland Security, and on that basis already known to present a national security concern (*Trump v Hawaii* 4). Indeed, the rationality of such measures forms the key part of the judicial Constitutionality review of the Supreme Court, which found that the immigration Proclamation was indeed 'plausibly related' to a legitimate government interest in protecting national security under the Immigration and Nationality Act (*Trump v Hawaii* 32). One's view on the success of this objection will necessarily depend on one's prior view of conflicts of rights, a full investigation of which is beyond the current scope of this chapter. However, in brief, it can be observed that there is a putative conflict here between one legal entity's right to restrict immigration and to protect national security and several other legal entities' rights to find safe refuge from violence and persecution; to non-discrimination in the administration of immigration and asylum status; to access to family members within the immigration system; and to the timely legal reviewability of Executive decisions to limit immigration. In essence, one legal entity appears to have a right to dictate that others can no longer enter the country, while other legal entities appear to have a right that entitles them to claim an assortment of entry rights, and both entitlements appear to be in fatal conflict with one another. One could argue that prioritising national security in the way ex-President Trump did, without a legal right of review, is a violation of legal proportionality requirements. Or one might suggest that legislating to keep certain ethnic, religious, or national demographic groups out of the country wholesale is ultimately indefensible, given State legal obligations of equal protection before the law and the international legal right to claim asylum and have one's family life respected. Ultimately, one's answer to these questions will inevitably depend not just on the legal interpretation of US and international immigration law, human rights guarantees, and the correct degree of Constitutional oversight of the exercise of Executive discretion, but also a prior theory of the conflicts of rights—and unfortunately it is not within the scope of this chapter to posit a fully legalised analysis of Proclamations 9645/9983. Rather, the purpose of this chapter's argument is to use the Supreme Court litigation over their Constitutionality to highlight the crucial and important extra work that is being done by the heightened justificatory burden for the legitimacy of political policies.

If it really was necessary to restrict immigration in the way Proclamations 9645/9983 did in order to protect US national security, then our heightened explanatory and justificatory burden will have been successfully met. But the precise benefit of the heightened justification burden to explain and defend this kind of policy fully to those who stand to lose under it, is that it requires more from our legal system than the US Supreme Court's rational review test provided. It requires more than just a declaration from the Executive that a Muslim travel ban policy furthers a legitimate State interest in national security, or that a particular State has been blacklisted for substandard information sharing. Rather, the full heightened justificatory burden proposed here requires proof not only that national security is a 'genuine' interest legitimately at stake here, and that restricting immigration is rationally and proportionately linked to it, but further that such measures can be fully justified to those who stand to lose the fundamental human right to claim asylum under it. What measures have been taken to mitigate or compensate for the loss of the invaluable and universal fundamental legal right to claim asylum to those imprisoned and separated from their families at the border? Such mitigation and compensation measures might entail, for example, some inquiry into the veracity and effectiveness of the Executive's national security claims; perhaps a mandatory end date to the travel suspension, rendering it truly temporary rather than indefinite; perhaps a full right to timely legal review and appeal of Executive refusals to make exceptions to the suspension in individual immigration cases; perhaps even a proportionality assessment, which would take into account more than just the originating nation State as the decisive factor in refusing immigration status; or perhaps the decriminalisation of those seeking asylum, even where they have crossed the border unlawfully; and the preservance of the international legal right to seek asylum as a family unit. Any number of further measures like these might go some way towards mitigating the effect of hard-line immigration policies like Proclamations 9645/9983, and thereby make a better case that such political measures have met their heightened justificatory burden and do indeed command the political legitimacy they claim.

Conclusion

This chapter has argued for a Kantian account of individual partiality, on the grounds that human beings are ends for themselves as well as for others, and as such we owe ourselves a particular ethical duty of self-respect which permits us to act in certain self-interested ways. The study of the moral failings of utilitarian theory was then used to show that not only is it a mistake to rule out the idea of permissible partiality at the individual level, but further that we cannot simply aggregate and reflect a sum of individual partial preferences at the political level. This theoretical grounding was used to identify what I have called a 'heightened justificatory burden' on political governance to justify political policies to all who stand to be affected by them. The ability to provide justifying reasons for a particular political policy which render it reasonable and unrejectable by those who stand to lose out under it, is a function of basic political legitimacy. Populist political policies, which commit to a sort of political transaction with subjective individual voters by seeking to maximise their partial, self-interested concerns in return for their committed political support, makes a fundamental mistake of practical moral deliberation. It wrongly extends the utilitarian methodology of rational choice from the individual level to the public, and by doing so illegitimately, and ultimately unjustifiably, ascribes utility losses across individual lives, thereby failing to generate fully justified political decisions. Lacking this degree of political legitimacy, populist laws and policies fail to generate political obligations on the part of citizens to obey them.

This chapter has also argued that just because partiality may be justified as having a certain degree of moral legitimacy at the individual level, as a matter of personal moral theory, the same is not necessarily true for States and political institutions. This is because the latter have no parallel reasons to individual moral agents regarding the special value in self-respect, or the ethical responsibility to live well by forming, revising, and pursuing individual conceptions of the good. By contrast, their value is political legitimacy, and their standing obligation is to improve and build upon that legitimacy. Thus, while the moral legitimacy in partiality at the individual level still stands, it requires careful further nuancing before it becomes too unwieldy a tool at the public level. Specifically, it is imperative that we recognise that the value in individual partiality does not necessarily or logically imply, endorse, or tolerate political populism at the national level.

This argument is not a call for cosmopolitanism, and it does not deny that there is a legitimate space for States to act in their citizens' best interests, nor does it deny that States owe their citizens a special duty of care. This remit to promote the interests of a State's own citizens does, however, come with distinct moral parameters to moderate national protectionism with due regard for the ideal of impartiality, equal moral respect, and global justice. Thus, while on the one hand it may indeed be not merely permissible but, in fact, morally required of individuals to entertain their own partial reasons for action, on the other hand it is far from straightforward for States or political institutions to do the same at the public level. The salient difference is of the requisite moral parameters for practical deliberation at the personal as opposed to the political level, and that is a lesson we should have learned from Rawls nearly 40 years ago.

References

Literature

Brennan, G. and Lomasky, L. (1993). *Democracy and decision: The pure theory of electoral preference.* New York: Cambridge University Press.
Brennan, J. (2011). *The ethics of voting.* Princeton: Princeton University Press.
Brennan, J. (2016a). The ethics and rationality of voting. In: Zalta, E. N. (ed.) *The Stanford encyclopaedia of philosophy.* https://plato.stanford.edu/archives/win2016/entries/voting/
Brennan, J. (2016b). The ethics and rationality of voting, S3.2: The epistemic ethics of voting. In: Zalta, E. N. (ed.) *The Stanford encyclopaedia of philosophy.* https://plato.stanford.edu/entries/voting/
Cottingham, J. (1991). The ethics of self-concern. *Ethics*, 101(4): 798–817.
Dworkin, R. (1977). *Taking rights seriously.* London: Duckworth.
Dworkin, R. (1986). *Law's empire.* Cambridge, MA: Harvard University Press.
Dworkin, R. (2011). *Justice for hedgehogs.* Cambridge, MA: Harvard University Press.
Frick, J. (2020). National partiality, immigration, and the problem of double-jeopardy. In: Sobel, D., Vallentyne, P. and Wall, S. (eds.) *Oxford studies in political philosophy, volume 6.* Oxford: Oxford University Press.
Kant, I. (1797 [1996]). *The metaphysics of morals.* Edited by M. Gregor. Cambridge: Cambridge University Press.

Kleingeld, P. and Brown, E. (2019). Cosmopolitanism. In: Zalta, E. N. (ed.) *The Stanford encyclopaedia of philosophy*. https://plato.stanford.edu/archives/win2019/entries/cosmopolitanism/

Monico, C., Rotabi, K., Vissing, Y. and Lee, J. (2019). Forced child-family separations in the southwestern US border under the 'Zero-Tolerance' policy: The adverse impact on well-being of migrant children (Part 2). *Journal of Human Rights and Social Work*, 4: 180–191. https://doi.org/10.1007/s41134-019-00095-z

Nagel, T. (1991). *Equality and partiality*. Oxford: Oxford University Press.

Rawls, J. (1971). *A theory of justice*. Cambridge, MA: Harvard University Press.

Scanlon, T. M. (1998). *What we owe to each other*. Cambridge, MA: Belknap Press, Harvard University Press.

Scheffler, S. (2010). Morality and Reasonable Partiality. In: Feltham, B. and Cottingham, J. (eds.) *Partiality and impartiality: Morality, special relationships, and the wider world*. Oxford: Oxford University Press, pp. 98–130.

Shabman, L. and Stephenson, K. (1994). A critique of the self-interested voter model: The case of a local single issue referendum. *Journal of Economic Issues*, 28(4): 1173–1186.

Smith, R. (2014). Moral equality and rights: A specificationist account of rights in conflict. Thesis (PhD), University College London.

Legislation

US

8 U.S.C. §1182 Inadmissible Aliens
Patient Protection and Affordable Care Act 2010

UK

Immigration Act 1971, 28 October 1971
Immigration and Asylum Act 1999, 11 November 1999
Immigration Act 2014, 14 July 2014
Immigration Act 2016, 12 May 2016

International

UN General Assembly, *Convention Against Torture and Other Cruel, Inhuman or Degrading Treatment or Punishment*, 10 December 1984, United Nations, Treaty Series, vol. 1465, p.85. UN General Assembly, *Convention Relating to the Status of Refugees*, 28 July 1951, United Nations, Treaty Series, vol. 189, p.137.

Cases

US

Trump v Hawaii and the Muslim Association of Hawaii, 585 US (2018)

Web Resources

Achiume, E. T. (2018). *End of mission statement of the special rapporteur on contemporary forms of racism, racial discrimination, xenophobia and related intolerance at the conclusion of her mission to the United Kingdom of Great Britain and Northern Ireland. UN Human Rights Office of the High Commissioner.* https://www.ohchr.org/en/statements/2018/05/end-mission-statement-special-rapporteur-contemporary-forms-racism-racial

Amnesty International. (2018). *Catastrophic immigration policies resulted in more family separations than previously disclosed.* 11 October. https://www.amnestyusa.org/reports/usa-catastrophic-immigration-policies-resulted-in-more-family-separations-than-previously-disclosed/

BBC. (2021). What is Windrush and who are the Windrush generation? 27 July. https://www.bbc.co.uk/news/uk-43782241

Davis, K. (2020). US Officials say they are highly confident to have reached tally on separated children: 4,368. *Los Angeles Times*, 18 January. https://www.latimes.com/world-2018nation/story/2020-01-18/u-s-officials-say-they-are-highly-confident-to-have-reached-tally-on-separated-children-4-368

Dickerson, Caitlin. (2019). There is a stench: Soiled clothes, and no baths for migrant children at a Texas center. *New York Times*, 21 June. https://www.nytimes.com/2019/06/21/us/migrant-children-border-soap.html

Executive Order. (2018). Affording Congress an opportunity to address family separation. 20 June. https://www.whitehouse.gov/presidential-actions/affording-congress-opportunity-address-family-separation

Griffin, R. and Teixeria, R. (2017). The story of Trump's appeal: A story of Trump voters. *Voter Study Group.* https://www.voterstudygroup.org/publication/story-of-trumps-appeal

Haag, M. (2019). Thousands of immigrant children say they were sexually abused in US detention centers, report says. *New York Times*, 27 February. https://www.nytimes.com/2019/02/27/us/immigrant-children-sexual-abuse.html

Joint Council for the Welfare of Immigrants. (2020). *The hostile environment explained.* www.jcwi.org.uk/the-hostile-environment-explained

Kirkup, J. and Winnett, R. (2012). Theresa May interview: We're going to give illegal migrants a really hostile reception. *The Telegraph*, 25 May. https://www.telegraph.co.uk/news/0/theresa-may-interview-going-give-illegal-migrants-really-hostile/

Luh, S. S. (2018). We will continue to challenge the 'hostile environment' policy, whatever name the government gives it. *Legal Action Group*, September. https://www.lag.org.uk/article/205494/we-will-continue-to-challenge -the--lsquo-hostile-environment-rsquo--policy--whatever-name-the -government-gives-it

McCarthy, T. and Siddiqui, S. (2018). Trump hails 'tremendous victory' after Supreme Court upholds travel ban. *The Guardian*, 26 June. https://www .theguardian.com/us-news/2018/jun/26/trump-supreme-court-upholds -travel-ban

Merchant, N. (2018). Hundreds of children wait in border patrol facilities in Texas. *AP News*, 18 June. https://apnews.com/9794de32d39d4c6f89fbef aea3780769

Newport, F. (2018). Evangelicals and Trump. *Gallup*, 31 May. https://www .news.gallup.com/opinion/gallup/232283/evangelicals-trump.aspx

Satterthwaite, M. and Riddell, R. (2018). Zero tolerance and the detention of children: Torture under international law. *Just Security*, 21 June. https:// www.justsecurity.org/58269/zero-tolerance-detention-children-torture -international-law/

Siddiqui, S. (2018). Trump's travel ban: What does the Supreme Court's ruling mean? *The Guardian*, 21 June. https://www.theguardian.com/us-news /2018/jun/26/trump-travel-ban-supreme-court-ruling-explained

Southern Poverty Law Center. (2022). *Family separation: A timeline.* 23 March. https://www.splcenter.org/news/2020/06/17/family-separation-under -trump-administration-timeline

Trump, D. (2017). *Inaugural Address.* 20 January. https://www.politico.com /story/2017/01/full-text-donald-trump-inauguration-speech-transcript -233907

US Department of State, Bureau of Consular Affairs. (2021). Rescission of Presidential Proclamations 9645 and 9983, 10 March. https://travel.state .gov/content/travel/en/News/visas-news/rescission-of-presidential-procla mations-9645-and-9983.html

Williams, W. (2020). Windrush lessons learned review. Gov.UK, 31 March. https://www.gov.uk/government/publications/windrush-lessons-learned -review

Notes on the Editors

Avis Whyte is a Senior Research Fellow, Senior Lecturer and Academic Professional Development Fellow at the University of Westminster, London, UK. She is an experienced researcher with expertise in researching the legal profession. Avis is a member of Westminster Law School's Centre on the Legal Profession and was a member of the University's Diversity Focus Group from 2006 until 2011.

Patricia Tuitt is a legal academic working within the field of postcolonial studies. Formerly Professor and Dean of the School of Law at Birkbeck, University of London, UK, she now curates an online resource (patriciatuitt.com), consisting of academic articles, book reviews and blog posts. Her publications include the monographs *False Images: Law's Construction of the Refugee* (1996) and *Race, Law, Resistance* (2004). She is co-editor of *Critical Beings: Law, Nation and the Global Legal Subject* (2004) and *Crime Fiction and the Law* (2016). Patricia is Vice-Chair of the Executive Board of Liberty and a member of its Policy Council. She is on the Editorial Committee of Feminist Legal Studies and the Board of Global Research Network (GRN).

Judith Bourne is Head of the Department of Law, and Professor of English Law, at the University of Roehampton, UK. She practised as a barrister and has been teaching Land and Equity & Trusts Law for the past 25 years. Her research has centred on feminist perspectives on law, in particular the legal history of the first women lawyers. She is currently researching early diverse members of the Bar.

Notes on the Contributors

Anna Chronopoulou is a Senior Lecturer in Law at the University of Westminster, London, UK. She studied for her PhD on the notion of neo-tribal sociality in the legal profession, at Birkbeck College, University of London, UK. She has extensive working experience in both the public and private sectors of legal education in the UK, Greece and Brazil. She has published widely in the area of the legal profession in England and Wales. Her research focuses on representations of legal professionals in popular culture.

Seema Kandelia is a Senior Lecturer in Law at the University of Westminster, London, UK. Prior to joining Westminster Law School, Seema worked in the human rights field with organisations such as the Human Rights Centre (University of Essex), the Organisation for Security and Cooperation in Europe (OSCE Prague Office), the UN Office of the High Commissioner for Human Rights (Geneva), the Commonwealth Human Rights Initiative (New Delhi) and the Centre for Capital Punishment Studies (University of Westminster). Her main areas of teaching and research are international human rights law and criminal justice, with a particular focus on capital punishment and whole life sentences.

David Keane is an Assistant Professor in Law at Dublin City University, Ireland. He researches in the field of international human rights law with a particular focus on the International Convention on the Elimination of All Forms of Racial Discrimination (ICERD). He has published four books and over thirty journal articles and book chapters on human rights, ICERD, minority rights and related areas.

Rebecca H. Smith is Lecturer in Law, Royal Holloway, University of London, UK. She holds a PhD in Jurisprudence, an LLM in Public International and International Human Rights Law from UCL and an LLB from the University of

Sussex. She has previously been a Teaching Fellow in Jurisprudence at UCL and has also acted as Associate Editor of the UCL Jurisprudence Review. Her doctoral research explored the potential for consonance between contemporary egalitarian rights theory and specificationist methodologies for the resolution of incommensurable value conflicts. Her current research interests lie in normative jurisprudence and analytic moral philosophy, with a particular focus on the philosophical foundations of rights and their conflicts.

Georgia Vasileiadou is a qualified lawyer at the Court of First Instance of Thessaloniki, Greece. She has recently started working as a legal advisor at the Luxembourg Institute of Science and Technology, and was previously a researcher at the Centre of International and European Economic Law, Greece (2018–2022). She holds an LLM in Business Law and Corporate Social Responsibility from Paris-Dauphine University PSL and an LLM in Commercial Arbitration from Democritus University of Thrace.

Index

Milton Keynes UK
Ingram Content Group UK Ltd.
UKHW020751160224
437945UK00009B/37